Cambridge Studies in Early Modern British History

JOHN SKELTON
AND THE POLITICS
OF THE 1520s

Cambridge Studies in Early Modern British History

Series editors

ANTHONY FLETCHER
Professor of Modern History, University of Durham

JOHN GUY
Reader in British History, University of Bristol

and JOHN MORRILL
*Lecturer in History, University of Cambridge, and
Fellow and Tutor of Selwyn College*

This is a new series of monographs and studies covering many aspects of the history of the British Isles between the late fifteenth century and the early eighteenth century. It will include the work of established scholars and pioneering work by a new generation of scholars. It will include both reviews and revisions of major topics and books which open up new historical terrain or which reveal startling new perspectives on familiar subjects. It is envisaged that all the volumes will set detailed research into broader perspectives and the books are intended for the use of students as well as of their teachers.

Titles in the series

JOHN SKELTON
AND THE POLITICS
OF THE 1520s

GREG WALKER

British Academy Postdoctoral Fellow, University of Southampton

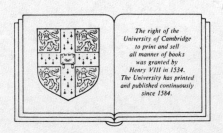

The right of the
University of Cambridge
to print and sell
all manner of books
was granted by
Henry VIII in 1534.
The University has printed
and published continuously
since 1584.

CAMBRIDGE UNIVERSITY PRESS

Cambridge

New York   New Rochelle   Melbourne   Sydney

Published by the Press Syndicate of the University of Cambridge
The Pitt Building, Trumpington Street, Cambridge CB2 1RP
32 East 57th Street, New York, NY 10022, USA
10 Stamford Road, Oakleigh, Melbourne 3166, Australia

First published 1988

Printed in Great Britain by
Redwood Burn Limited, Trowbridge, Wiltshire

British Library cataloguing in publication data
Walker, Greg
John Skelton and the politics of the
1520s. – (Cambridge studies in early
modern British history).
1. Skelton, John, *1460?–1529*
Political and social views
I. Title
821'.2   PR2348

Library of Congress cataloguing in publication data
Walker, Greg.
John Skelton and the politics of the 1520s / Greg Walker.
p.   cm. – (Cambridge studies in early modern British history)
Includes index.
ISBN 0 521 35124 3
1. Skelton, John. 1460?–1529 – Political and social views.
2. Political satire, English – History and criticism.   3. Politics in
literature.   4. Politics and literature – Great Britain
– History – 16th century.   5. Great Britain – Politics and
government – 1509–1547.   I. Title.   II. Series.
PR2348.W35 1988
821'.2—dc 19   87–22687

ISBN 0 521 35124 3

For Sharon
and for my grandfather
Mr Arthur Mapley

CONTENTS

ACKNOWLEDGEMENTS

In any academic study one benefits greatly from the advice and assistance freely offered by colleagues and more experienced scholars in one's chosen field. I am pleased to say that my case was no exception.

My greatest material debt is to the President and Fellows of the British Academy. The awards, first of a Major State Studentship to finance my postgraduate research, and then of a Postdoctoral Research Fellowship have allowed me to complete this study and to continue with further work in related fields. Without their financial help and encouragement my career would not have been possible.

I am also particularly grateful to the History Department of Southampton University, its staff and secretaries, for making my stay there so enjoyable, and to the staff of the Manuscripts Room at the British Library, of Southampton University Library and of the University of Nottingham Library. Thanks are also due to my sub-editor, Ms J. E. Hardy, for her assistance in the completion of this manuscript.

I owe a debt of gratitude to many academics who have kindly given of their time to aid my studies. I must thank the lecturers in Southampton's History Department, Dr J. N. Ball, Mr A. C. Duke and Dr K. M. Sharpe, whose teaching stimulated my interest in the sixteenth and seventeenth centuries. I am also indebted to Dr S. J. Gunn of Merton College, Oxford, for allowing me to read an unpublished paper and discussing his research with me. For their willingness to discuss Skelton with me, whether in person or through exchange of correspondence, I would also like to thank Dr P. Neuss, Professor A. F. Kinney, Professor V. J. Scattergood and Dr J. Bromley (née Robertson), who kindly read an early draft of chapter 5 of this book. I must also thank my friends and contemporaries at Southampton and elsewhere, Mr S. J. Smart, Mr S. Vine and Mr R. P. Mardle for their encouragement and assistance in matters large and small through the years.

Greater still is my debt to Mr P. J. Gwyn, whose painstaking, helpful and always rigorous criticism and advice have greatly assisted the production of this study, much of which he has kindly read in draft form. I am also grateful to him for the chance to read and cite from two chapters of his forthcoming study of Wolsey, and to discuss the Cardinal and his policies on a number of occasions.

That this book has appeared in print is due in great part, not only to the encouragement offered by the editors of this series, for which I am extremely grateful, but also to the advice and assistance given to me by Professor Sir Geoffrey Elton. His kindness in agreeing to read what was a sprawling doctoral thesis and his subsequent continuing guidance have enabled me to produce from it the present somewhat more succinct text. My gratitude to Professor Elton for his invaluable help is matched only by my admiration for his ability to answer the many, often arcane, problems and queries which I posed him, all in faultless fashion and most before breakfast on the day he received them.

Finally, my greatest academic debt is to Dr G. W. Bernard, whose teaching inspired me to undertake this research, and whose advice and guidance whilst it was underway were of incalculable value. His research, teaching and writing have provided an example of what historical scholarship should be. If this study has its good points, the credit must be due in large part to Dr Bernard. If it has not, the fault is entirely mine.

ABBREVIATIONS

Full references are given in the notes.

B.I.H.R.	Bulletin of the Institute of Historical Research
B.L.	British Library
D.N.B.	*Dictionary of National Biography*
Dyce	A. Dyce (ed.), *Poetical Works of Skelton*
Edwards	H. L. R. Edwards, *Skelton, The Life and Times of an Early Tudor Laureate*
E.E.T.S.	Early English Text Society
E.H.R.	*English Historical Review*
E.L.N.	*English Language Notes*
Heiserman	A. R. Heiserman, *Skelton and Satire*
H.L.Q.	*Huntington Library Quarterly*
L.P.	*Letters and Papers, Foreign and Domestic, of the Reign of Henry VIII*
Nelson	W. Nelson, *John Skelton, Laureate*
P.M.L.A.	*Publications of the Modern Language Association of America*
Pollard	A. F. Pollard, *Wolsey*
P.R.O.	Public Record Office
R.Q.	*Renaissance Quarterly*
Scattergood	V. J. Scattergood (ed.), *John Skelton: The Complete English Poems*
Sp. Cal.	*Calendar of State Papers, Spanish*
S.T.C.	*Short-Title Catalogue of Books Printed in England, Scotland, and Ireland . . . 1475–1640*
St. P.	*State Papers of Henry VIII*
Ven. Cal.	*Calendar of State Papers Venetian*
Vergil	P. Vergil, *Anglica Historia*

SELECT GLOSSARY

alcumyn	imitation gold
ammas	clerical overgarment
as ryght as a rammes horne	(proverbial) i.e. crooked
avaunsid	advanced
babyon	baboon
belapped	wrapped
bereth . . . on hand	deceives
bestadde	beset
bordon	burden
botell	bundle
bownte	bounty, largess
byde	abide
bylles	bills (polearms)
cheryston pytte	small pit for child's game involving cherry stones
chorlyshe	churlish, ill-mannered
cond	conned, learned by rote
crake	boast
creaunser	tutor
cronel	wreath or crown
cum gariopholo	with cloves
currys of kynde	curs by nature (i.e. vicious, unthinking)
daucocke, dawpate	fool (from (jack)daw, a foolish bird)
derayne	contest with force
deyntely	daintily
embassades	embassies, ambassadors
enfatuate	infatuated
escrye	condemn
fayctes	acts (facets?)

xii

Fidasso de Cosso	'Have faith in yourself'
fonde	foolish, conceited
gambaudynge	dancing (gambolling)
Gargone	Gorgon
glaymy	slimy
gramatolys	windbags
graundepose	grampus
gresly	grisly
guerdon	reward (comeuppance)
Jacke Breche	a commoner
jacounce	jacinth
knakkes	trivia
kote	coot
lawghyth	laughs
layser	leisure
losel, lorell	rogue
lowre	cower, stoop
Mahound	Mohammed (false idol)
males	wallets, purses
Mantycore	mythical monster compounded of mismatched parts
marciall	martial
mated	checkmated (beaten, killed)
mawme(n)t	false idol (from corruption of Mohammed)
mellis	meddles
mokkyshe	scornfully
Moryshe	Moorish
moyles	mules
Murrioun	Moor
myseracion	mercy
nodypollys	fools
nolle	head
nutshales	nutshells (worthless things)
on and hothyr	one and another
parbrake	vomit
parcele	part, section
paule(s)	a fine cloth
pavys	shield
perdurable	everlasting
'pleris cum musco'	'an electuary with musk'
plucke the crowe	grasp the nettle

plummis	plums
plumnet	lead pencil
pomegarnet	pomegranate (emblem of Catherine of Aragon)
popagay	parrot (popinjay)
porpose	purpose or porpoise
postyll	a gloss (on a text)
prate	speak
primordiall	first, earliest
provynciall	bishop
pyll	peel, strip
pyllyd pate	bald head
quatryvyals	parts of the quadrivium (arithmetic, geometry, astronomy, music)
quayre	book
quyt	quit, repaid
rammysche	foul
rebawde, rybawde:	low-born rogue
recheles	recklessly
reculed	retreated
remorde	criticise
rotchettes	cloaks, mantles
rowme	present office or status
'Save habeler Castylyano'	'can you speak Castillian?'
scryve	write
serpentens	small cannons
seymy	greasy, slimy
silogisari	logical argument
slaundrys obliqui	slanderous abuse
soccoure	succour
sophistice	shrewdly, using learning
stounde	a moment
styckis	sticks
sutys	suits, suitors
termys	expressions or argument (more generally, literary style or scholarship)
trold	rolled up
troughte	truth
tryvyals	parts of the Trivium (grammar, rhetoric, logic)

tummrell	wagon
tryhumfythe	triumphs, exalts
ulula	weep
urcheons	hedgehogs
warkys	works
wonders	wondrous

INTRODUCTION

In 1521, John Skelton, a poet in his sixties, living in a tenement in the precincts of Westminster Abbey, put pen to paper. 'My name ys Parott', he wrote,[1]

> ... a byrd of Paradyse
> By Nature devysed of a wonderowus kynde,
> Deyntely dyeted with dyvers delycate spyce,
> Tyll Eufrates that flodde, dryvythe me into Ynde,
> Where men of that contre, by fortune me fynde,
> And send me to greate ladyes of estate;
> Then Parot moste have an almon or a date. (1–7)

Such was the unlikely beginning of one of the most intriguing campaigns of character assassination ever undertaken. For the parrot, Skelton's mouthpiece, was sent forth to lampoon and revile no less a figure than Thomas, Cardinal Wolsey, Lord Legate *a latere*, Archbishop of York and Lord Chancellor of England, the chief minister of Henry VIII. During the next five months the poem which Skelton had begun, *Speke, Parott*, was followed by five supplementary envoys which ridiculed, in particular, Wolsey's arbitration of the Calais Franco-Imperial conference of 1521[2] and, in general, the very way in which he ruled. Then, in 1522, *Speke Parott* made way for a more explicit satire, *Collyn Clout*, in which the poet, speaking through the persona of Collyn, a simple countryman, launched a barely concealed assault on what he declared to be the dangers inherent in Wolsey's dominance of Church and state, his monopoly of the King's ear and his personal vices. Finally, in the Autumn of 1522, Skelton wrote *Why Come Ye Nat To Courte?*, an open and vicious invective aimed directly at the Cardinal which accused him of every crime from perjury to treason and of every malady from megalomania to the pox. Then, suddenly, the attacks ceased and within months the poet was writing at Wolsey's behest, penning in subsequent poems lines of fulsome praise of his erstwhile target.[3]

---

[1] *Speke, Parott*, lines 1–7. All quotations and line references are from John Scattergood (ed.), *John Skelton: The Complete English Poems* (London, 1983).
[2] See chap. 3, below.
[3] *The Garlande or Chapelet of Laurell* (hereafter *The Garlande*) 1587–93, and *Howe the Douty Duke of Albany* (hereafter *The Douty Duke*) 523–31.

1

As source material for a study of the early 1520s these poems have never undergone serious scrutiny. Partly because of a lack of external evidence concerning the poet and partly, no doubt, owing to a greater interest in other aspects of Skelton's poems, critics and historians alike have largely allowed the poet's political comments to stand unquestioned. For those biographers and literary critics primarily interested in charting the development of the poet's 'art', it has usually been enough to analyse *how* the satires were written: to trace the literary precursors of a device such as a parrot narrator, from classical literature, through Jean Lemaire de Belges' *Epistres de l'amant verd*, to Skelton's use of the convention; to comment on the use of rustic orators in anti-clerical satires, or to speculate on the origins of the 'Skeltonic' verse-form. They have left unanswered the questions concerning exactly what it was that the poet used such vehicles to convey, and whether or not his purpose had any applicability to the political situation which he was satirising. For them it has been enough to assume that Skelton's description of his times, and particularly his apparent conception of Cardinal Wolsey, were accurate and thus required little examination.[4] Alternatively, historians who have used Skelton's testimony in their accounts *have* considered the comments made (although hardly in any depth) but have failed to pursue the underlying implications. For those commentators anxious to further the traditional view of the Cardinal's character and regime, it has usually been enough simply to insert into their argument a brief passage from *Why Come Ye Nat To Courte?* or *Collyn Clout* to the effect that Wolsey was proud, or corrupt, or tyrannical (or whichever other axe was at their grindstone at the time) as if this alone was sufficient confirmation of their theses.[5] Other writers, who have wished in some way to rescue the Cardinal's reputation from the worst calumnies of his critics, have cited the same passages as evidence of the prevalent popular misconceptions concerning the prelate's good works, or of the malicious attacks of an opposing faction.[6] In either case the poet's political position has been assumed as given. To the hostile historian he speaks for the common-sense values of the traditionalist courtiers, the no-

---

[4] S. E. Fish, *John Skelton's Poetry* (Yale, 1965); Nan Cooke Carpenter, *John Skelton* (New York, 1968); Ian A. Gordon, *John Skelton, Poet Laureate* (Melbourne and London, 1943); H. L. R. Edwards, *Skelton: The Life and Times of an Early Tudor Poet* (London, 1949); M. Pollet, *John Skelton, Poet of Tudor England*, trans. from the French by J. Warrington (Lewisberg, 1971). A. H. Heiserman, *Skelton and Satire* (Chicago, 1961), subscribes to a diametrically opposed but equally unhelpful opinion. For him Skelton's satires were entirely literary in their conception and relevance, and thus were hardly stimulated by their immediate political context at all. Indeed, for Heiserman, the historical Wolsey was merely an incidental figure in poems which were designed as general explorations of the satiric convention.

[5] R. Lockyer, *Tudor and Stuart Britain 1471–1714* (London, 1964), p. 41; N. Williams, *Henry VIII and His Court* (London, 1971), p. 52; S. Anglo, *Spectacle, Pageantry, and Early Tudor Policy* (Oxford, 1969), p. 238 and chaps. V–VII generally.

[6] A. F. Pollard, *Wolsey* (London, 1929).

bility and the populace at large, outraged at the disastrous quasi-innovations of the upstart; to the apologist he represents all that was inert and medieval about the Court and the people Wolsey had to overcome. At no point does either group stop to ask how sensible such stereotyping might be, an omission which does a grave disservice to our understanding of Wolsey's role in the politics of the early 1520s.

The purpose of this study is to make good that omission, to attempt to locate Skelton in his contemporary context, both politically and socially, and to offer some suggestions about the motivation behind his critical stance – or rather his series of critical stances, for, as was noted above, there was a series of clear shifts of attitude and approach even within the poet's 'anti-Wolsey' trilogy, shifts which will have to be examined closely if any valid comments are to be made concerning the satires. Simply to know what Skelton said is not enough. The Wolsey poems, beginning with the hostile satires of 1521–2 and continuing into the laudatory commissioned works of 1523, pose several crucial questions to the student concerned with their value as an historical source, whether for an analysis of Wolsey's character or for the political situation during his ascendancy. How accurate a reflection are they of perceptions of Wolsey and his governance? Does Skelton actually believe what he appears to be saying? And, if so, is he expressing a consensus, or simply the grievances or an individual or small group of malcontents? How perceptive are the poet's allegations? Did he enjoy a privileged position at Court from which to observe his target, or was his viewpoint merely that of an external observer of Court affairs? Immediately one approaches such questions more specific problems concerning the poet and his texts present themselves. First, and most obviously, why did Skelton write them? Why produce and circulate what appear to be suicidally dangerous writings? And, having done so, why clearly sign one's own name under each one, as Skelton did? And then, why abruptly cease such writings and begin to praise the former *bête noire* in subsequent poems? Why also did not Wolsey, when confronted with these texts (if indeed he was), act to stifle them as he had done in other cases, either by suppressing the poems or by imprisoning their author? Finally, how popular were the satires? Were they peddled at every street corner and quoted in every alehouse, or were they merely circulated among an intimate group of conspirators? And, in a wider context, does this imply that Wolsey was universally reviled in the 1520s, or that, if he had enemies, they were forced to work in secret, using covert means of expression?

It may well be that many of these questions can never be satisfactorily answered. But, in order to approach as close to an answer as the available evidence will allow, it will be necessary to rewrite some of the assumptions which underpin the accepted Skeltonic biography. In order to see how the

Wolsey satires came to be written, one needs, I should like to suggest, to understand the nature of Skelton's career up to their conception. Unfortunately, in any attempt to reach such an understanding, one is immediately faced with the major barrier to all Skeltonic biographical studies. For the known facts of the poet's life are fewer than those of almost any other major poet since Longland. The figure which history has bequeathed to us is thus skeletal in the extreme. But what contemporary records have failed to provide has been more than compensated for by the more or less fanciful assumptions of subsequent criticism, which has swathed the historical Skelton in layer upon layer of adhesive myth, until the original figure has been all but lost among the mythical accretion.

Maurice Pollet began his study of the poet's life and work with the laudable declaration: 'I considered Skelton's case impossible of solution except by the Cartesian method of systematic doubt, by passing through the sieve of criticism every document we possess.'[7] Despite the occasional stride in that direction however, the dictates of writing a biography for publication seem to have forced him to allow the skeleton to retain some of its mythical shrouds in order that a tolerable narrative might be produced from a small collection of largely mundane and occasionally maddeningly scrappy contemporary records. As the present study is under no such constraint to provide an entertaining narrative it should be possible to close the holes in Pollet's sieve a little further and, by a policy of systematic doubt applied to each aspect of the problem, to produce a more acceptable summary of Skelton's career and of his relationship to the political figures and events which he describes. That is not to say that one needs here to enter into a discussion of all the minutiae of a long biography; to do so would be both tedious and unhelpful to our present concern. The sum of the known facts, and a large amount of the mythical addition, can be found in H. L. R. Edwards' biography of the poet,[8] which, despite its shortcomings, remains the best account available. Our concern here is only with those aspects of the biography which are relevant to the production of the Wolsey poems, and those in which the accounts of the biographers are in need of substantial revision. It may well be that such a demythologising exercise might yield a merely negative net result, in that a few layers of mythical camouflage might be removed without being replaced by any more real clothing. But even this will be valuable in providing a small step towards a clearer picture, not only of Skelton, but also of Cardinal Wolsey, and of the Court and country during his ascendancy.

[7] Pollet, *Poet of Tudor England*, p. xii.   [8] See note 4, above.

1

John Skelton and the Howards: the question of patronage

Once one begins to apply the critical sieve to the Skeltonic biography, it rapidly becomes apparent that even the most cherished and fundamental assumptions about the poet appear in need of radical revision. That Skelton was the factional tool of the Howard family, writing his satires against Wolsey at their behest, has been the basis of all interpretations of his poetry since the first modern biography, that of H. L. R. Edwards, appeared in 1949, and that assumption has long been a commonplace among historians seeking to explain their existence. That these initially baffling texts can be dismissed as simply an outgrowth of the familiar world of factional intrigue has many times come to the rescue of an historian who, without such a ready explanation to hand, would have needed to look far deeper into their provenance and import.[1] Indeed, for the literary critic and historian alike, the 'Howard connection' has been a general answer for all the difficulties within the Skeltonic canon.[2] But how valid is this factional explanation of the satires?

Certainly there is an internal logic to the assertions of the Howard school which gives their case an initial attractiveness. Wolsey, the argument runs, was seen by the Duke of Norfolk, and by the Howard family generally, to have been behind the execution, in May 1521, of Edward Stafford, third duke of Buckingham, the father of Elizabeth Stafford, who had married Thomas Howard, earl of Surrey, Norfolk's son and heir to the dukedom. Their anger at this event, added to their other grievances, born of Wolsey's domination of the Council and of the King's ear, caused them to search for a

---

[1] See, Christopher Haigh, 'Anticlericalism and the English Reformation', *History*, 68 (1983), pp. 391–407, esp. p. 394; J. J. Scarisbrick, *Henry VIII* (London, 1968), p. 229, and 'Cardinal Wolsey and the Common Weal', in E. W. Ives, R. J. Knecht and J. J. Scarisbrick (eds.), *Wealth and Power in Tudor England: Essays Presented to S. T. Bindoff* (London, 1978), pp. 45–67; Pollard, *passim*. For the latest restatement of this case, see A. F. Kinney, *John Skelton: Priest as Poet* (London, 1987).
[2] See, for example, Edwards, p. 149.

measure of revenge and, for want of a better outlet, they vented their spleen upon the Cardinal through 'their poet'.[3]

This argument can, I think, be comprehensively dismantled by the simple application of the critical sieve, even without pointing out the obvious incongruity of a family as powerful as the Howards resting satisfied, if it was revenge they desired, with a few pieces of ribald verse.

The first observation which must be made is that this model of courtly intrigue centres on a notion of Howard/Wolsey rivalry for which no real evidence exists for the period under discussion.[4] Thomas Howard I was, if anything, an ally of Wolsey's rather than his rival. The two worked together on the King's Council in 1513, and shared the same political objectives, both favouring an aggressive policy against the French, and the then Earl of Surrey's victory at Flodden ideally complemented the then Royal Almoner's organisation of the French campaign, thus allowing both to gain material rewards at the completion of a job well done. Howard was restored to his father's dukedom, whilst Wolsey took the first steps up the ladder of preferment which would lead from the sees of Lincoln and Tournai to the Archbishopric of York and the Cardinalate. The two then sat, and apparently co-operated, at the head of the Council throughout the next decade, with Norfolk being described by the Venetian ambassador, Giustiniani, in 1519, as 'very intimate with the Cardinal'.[5] What evidence there is suggests that Howard, happy with the restoration of his family's honours, was a loyal and trusted Crown servant, content to conduct his own affairs in his locality and to support Wolsey's handling of Crown policy. His was a stabilising rather than a fractious influence at Court. When, for example, rumours were circulating about the expulsion of the 'minions' in 1519, and when allegations of a Wolsey-instigated purge of potential rivals for royal favour seem to have reached the ears of Giustiniani, it was Norfolk who attempted to refute them and to defuse the situation by suggesting that the changes had been brought about by the King's own desire to end his riotous lifestyle and to 'lead a new life'.[6] Had he harboured any ill-will toward the Cardinal, it would have been far easier for Norfolk to have allowed such uncomplimentary and possibly damaging rumours to circulate unchallenged.

That the Duke was not associated with any agitation or intrigues against the status quo is further suggested by the fact that when Henry became concerned at the activities of his leading noblemen and instructed Wolsey to 'keep good watch' on them, he named Suffolk and Northumberland, Buck-

[3] *Ibid.*, chaps. 12 and 13.
[4] The only evidence which Scarisbrick cites to illustrate such antagonism to Wolsey on the part of the nobility is, ironically, Skelton's poetry, see Scarisbrick, *Henry VIII*, p. 229.
[5] Rawdon Brown, *Four Years At The Court Of Henry VIII*, 2 vols. (London, 1854), II p. 316 (*L.P.*, III (i) 402).
[6] Rawdon Brown, *Four Years*, II pp. 270–1 (*L.P.*, III (i) 235).

ingham and Derby but omitted Thomas Howard I's name from his list.[7] That Henry had implicit trust in Norfolk is also evidenced by his decision to leave the Duke in England in the role of informal regent whilst the majority of the Court and nobility travelled to Guisnes for the meeting at the Field of Cloth of Gold during 1520. It has been suggested that Norfolk may have resented the fact that he thus could not accompany his sovereign on the journey, but it is a measure of his dependability that he took no steps to convert his possible disappointment into subversive action.

The notion that Thomas Howard II, Norfolk's son and heir, bore a life-long resentment against Wolsey also seems difficult to square with the available evidence. For, if his ramblings from the Tower when under fear of death are discounted as the mixture of confused memories and paranoiac accusations which they seem to have been, it appears that only in 1529, after the Cardinal's fall from absolute royal favour, did he begin to act in the manner one would expect of a political opponent. Additionally, if one takes the Howards to have been at odds with Wolsey during this period, it is extremely difficult to account for the fact that, in 1515 or shortly thereafter, Thomas Howard I's third son, lord Edmund, chose, when in financial straits, to petition for aid, not to the King nor even to his own father, but to Wolsey. 'My duty remembryd', he wrote, 'humbly I benseche youre Grace to be my good lorde, for with owt youre graceus helppe I am uttyrly undone. Syr so yt is that I am so far in danger off the King's lawys by reasone off det that I am in, that I dare not go a brode, nor cum at myne owne howss.'[8] This letter, 'wretyn with the hand of hym that ys assurydly yours', seems hardly to represent the spirit of animosity between the Howards and Wolsey suggested in some accounts.

Thus the notion of the Howards attacking Wolsey through 'their poet' in revenge for the death of Buckingham does not fit with what evidence there is of the Howards' behaviour and attitudes at the time. More tellingly, the notion does not ring true because Skelton was not in any sense 'the Howard's poet'. The idea of Skelton as a Howard client seems to be a myth

[7] B.L. Additional MS 19398 f.644 (*L.P.*, III (i) 1).

[8] H. Ellis (ed.) *Letters Illistrative of English History*, 3 vols. (London, 1824, 1827, 1846), third series, I p. 160. For Thomas Howard's accusations from the Tower, see B. L. Cotton MS, Titus B I 99–101 (*L.P*, XXI (ii) 554). Equally unconvincing as evidence of a feud is the suggestion that Howard was 'exiled' in Ireland by Wolsey in 1520–2 as a means to keep him from the court (D. Hay (ed. and trans.), *The Anglica Historia of Polydor Vergil*, Camden Society, 84, (London, 1950), p. 265; *L.P.*, IV (iii) 5750). Surrey left for Ireland not as an unwilling victim of Wolsey's malice but as the recipient of conspicuous honours and signs of royal favour. He took with him one hundred of Henry's own bodyguard and the superior title of Lieutenant of Ireland, unused since 1460. Far from being consigned to oblivion he was entrusted with the execution of Henry's new 'politique' policy for the subjugation of Ireland, a policy about which King, Cardinal and Lieutenant maintained a running debate throughout Howard's period of office. As a result the latter, rather than being exiled, obtained a place in the political limelight greater than that which he left.

created at the beginning of this century, although based on earlier misunder-standings, and perpetuated by subsequent biographers and historians as a convenient explanation for a complex puzzle.

Where then does this 'Howard myth' originate and where might those bio-graphers who, without fail, refer to it as if it needed no supporting evidence have found it?[9] Contemporary sources are notably silent on the matter. There is no mention of a Howard link in the *Merie Tales, Newly Imprinted and Made by Master Skelton Poet Laureate*,[10] a largely apocryphal collec-tion of ribald stories and *gestes* published in 1567. Similarly the earliest bio-graphers do not refer to such a noble connection. There is no such reference in John Bale's *Scriptorum* for example.[11] What in fact seems to constitute the 'Howard connection' is a series of biographical coincidences and oblique references in the poems themselves, some more noteworthy than others.

The only concrete reference to a direct link between Skelton and a member of the Howard family comes in his aureate allegory *The Garlande or Chapel-et of Laurell*, printed by Richard Faukes on 3 October 1523,[12] in which the poet meets with 'the noble Cowntes of Surrey'. Referring to him as 'my clerke', she bestows on him a garland of laurel leaves woven by her gentle-women, and he, in return, offers each of the ladies a dedicatory lyric.[13] The poem, as proponents of the Howard school are not slow to point out, was 'studyously dyvysed at Sheryfhotten Castell, in the foreste of Galtres', which, as a favoured residence of the Lords Lieutenant in the North, was the home of the Howards on several occasions in the period 1490–1523, when both the first and second Thomas Howards conducted campaigns and tours of duty along the northern borders. The poem, the Howard school alleges, is thus clear evidence of a direct patron–client relationship between the Thomas Howards and Skelton, as the poet was clearly living in the Howard household and writing to order for the family, only months after the com-pletion of the last and most vicious satire, *Why Come Ye Nat?*. The date of *The Garlande*'s publication, 3 October 1523, surrounded by the other less obvious allusions to the Howards in earlier texts, is thus taken as the un-shakeable cornerstone of the patronage argument. As we shall see, it begs a number of questions and makes a number of mistaken assumptions. The date of the poem's publication, for example, need not indicate that 1523 was also

---

[9] Ian A. Gordon, *John Skelton, Poet Laureate*, (Melbourne and London, 1943) pp. 30—3 and *passim*; Heiserman, pp. 2, 3; M. Pollet, *John Skelton, Poet of Tudor England*, trans. from the French by J. Warrington (Lewisburg, 1971), pp. 119, 147; Nan Cooke Carpenter, *John Skelton* (New York, 1968) pp. 11, 34, 88, 103 and *passim*.

[10] *S.T.C.* 22618 (1567).

[11] J. Bale, *Scriptorum Illustrium Maioris Brytannie, quam nunc Angliam ad Scotiam Vocant: Catalogus* (Basle, 1557–9) (hereafter *Scriptorum*). The relevant portion is reprinted in Edwards, p. 306.

[12] *S.T.C.* 22610; Scattergood, pp. 312–57.

[13] *The Garlande*, lines 766–1085.

the year of composition. However, if we are to make any sense of the inter-dependent web of supposed allusions to Howard patrons in the texts, each must be examined individually so that their merit, or lack of merit, can be judged.

The first and earliest passage in the canon which has been taken to refer to a Howard connection occurs in the Court-satire *The Bowge of Courte*, in which, after a highly conventional astrological introduction, the poet mentions the physical location in which he will dream the allegorical vision which will be the poem.

> At Harwyche Porte, slumbrynge as I laye,
> In myne hostes house called Powers Keye (34–5)

It has been suggested that one can identify Skelton's resting place with a real building in Harwich, owned by John Howard, first duke of Norfolk (d.1485).[14] In Payne Collier's *Household Books of John, Duke of Norfolk* one can find the following reference,[15]

Power / The XIV Day of September (1481), my lord
[Howard] at my lordes Howse at the Key / xiijs iijd

This, it is suggested, reveals that 'John Howard owned a house, or a public house, as Power's Key is identified by some writers, on the quay or wharf, and that a man named Power (later identified as one "Breton, called John Power of Croysy in Garrande") had charge of it'. This in turn, it has been argued, implies that Skelton was living at John Howard's expense in Harwich when he wrote the poem, which M. J. Tucker dates from the astrological references within it as completed in 1480 and not, as usually accepted, in 1498, when John Howard was, of course, dead, and his son and heir Thomas I was in residence, not in Norfolk but in Sheriff Hutton castle.[16]

Does one have here then, the first clear evidence of a long career of Howard service? Tucker's identification of the building is certainly suggestive (although the syntax of the passages concerned means that it is no more than that). But suggestive of what? One must note at the outset that the assumption that 'Powers Keye' and 'my lordes Howse at the Key' are identical is far from certain. If one examines the *Household Books* closely one can find many references to John Power. These largely involve the provision of victuals and maritime building materials, such as the 'three barels hereng' for which lord John paid 16s 8d, or the ship's timbers and sail cloth which

---

[14] M. J. Tucker, 'Setting for Skelton's *Bowge of Courte*: a speculation', *E.L.N.*, vii (1970), pp. 168–75.

[15] J. P. Collier (ed.), *Household Books of John, Duke of Norfolk, and Thomas, Earl of Surrey, 1481–90* (Roxburghe Club, 1844), (hereafter *Household Books*) p. 110; cited in Tucker, 'Setting' p. 173.

[16] Tucker, 'Setting', p. 173.

Power provided.[17] Clearly the relationship between Power and the Howards was of long standing, and the former certainly seems to have provided a great deal of merchandise for both lords John and Thomas I. However there is no hint that the latter's patronage went any further than such commercial transactions. Power is never listed amongst those men obliged to provide troops or service for Howard's levies (such as those raised for his Scottish expedition of 1481), and no payments to him are recorded except those for clearly defined goods and services. At no time does his name appear on the household wages bill, and no monies are listed as being received from Power in the form of rent, as one might expect if, as Tucker suggests, Power was 'taken on' as a tenant in a Howard house. On the contrary there are strong hints within the account books that Power was an independent innkeeper and provisioner.[18] That Howard 'toke Power' at the former's house at the quay, then, need not mean that Power was taken onto the Howard payroll or into his livery. The word 'toke' litters the *Household Books*, and seems to have meant no more than 'gave payment'. Power was 'toke' elsewhere, for example for 'reparacions' for which he was paid 13*s* 4*d*, whilst 'the players of Kokesale' were taken, for providing a Christmas play, and given 3*s* 4*d*.[19] All that one can thus say with any certainty is that John Power, who had many commercial dealings with the Howards, ran an inn of some kind, probably called 'Power's Keye', in Harwich, and that lord John Howard also owned a house on the same quay. To assume that the two houses were one and the same involves a degree of speculation.

Let us, however, pursue this speculation a little further. If it were the case that 'Power's Keye' and Howard's house were synonymous, what would that tell us about Skelton and his relationship with the Howards? The entire case clearly rests on the accuracy of the controversial dating of the poem as a work of 1480. For if that is correct it is possible that the poet's residence in a house with Howard connections might suggest a link between Skelton and John Howard. If the more commonly accepted dating of 1499 is correct then no such link need exist, for the nobleman was long-dead and, even if his family continued to control the inn, any kind of patronage implied by Skelton's temporary residence there, some three hundred miles from the current family residence at Sheriff Hutton, could only have been of the most indirect kind. On this crucial question of dating, the pro-Howard case is far from certain, being based exclusively on an interpretation of the astrological evidence provided by the introduction to the text:

> In autumpne, whan the sonne in Vyrgyne
> By radyante hete enryped hath our corne;
> When Luna, full of mutabylyte,

[17] *Household Books*, p. 148.   [18] See, for example, *ibid.*, p. 201.   [19] *Ibid.*, pp. 118 and 145.

As emperes the dyademe hath worne
Of our pole artyke, smylynge halfe in scorne
At our foly and our unstedfastnesse;
The tyme when Mars to werre hym dyd dres;
I, callynge to mynde the great auctoryte
Of poetes olde, whyche, full craftely,
Under as coverte termes as coude be,
Can touche a troughte and cloke it subtylly . . .
. . . was sore moved to aforce the same (1–11, 17)

Such a passage deserves far longer discussion than is possible here. The use of astrological data to assign a date to the text is initially persuasive but ought not to pass unquestioned.[20] The allegorical use which the poet makes of the astrological data, for example, suggests that he is doing rather more here than simply informing us of the time and place of the text's composition. The passage acts as a proem to the mood and theme of the poem to follow. The season, autumn, as well as being in dream-lore the time most conducive to *insomnia*, the 'wild dreams of pursuit' prompted by anxiety that Skelton/Drede will describe,[21] is also the time of nature's decline into infertility after the richness of summer. It is a time of great bounty, as the sun (significantly 'in Vyrgyne' in her innocence and mercy) has ripened the corn, yet it is also the end of that richness, when the crop will have to be harvested, by those who can do so, for the lean months to follow. As in nature, so in the Court of the poem to follow. For there it is also a time of great wealth, for the vessel conveying the *Bowge*, or rewards, of Court, is in harbour. Yet the setting there too is, by implication, autumnal. For the innocent Courtly Ideal, which, like the sun, has created the wealth, is everywhere in decline; it has been overrun by the vicious and grasping courtiers, anxious to reap their own individual harvests whilst the ship remains in port, for fear of the consequences of being left on the quay when it departs. Hence, in the text, the innocent, bountiful sun is replaced by the shifting faces of the new regent, Luna (who, significantly, appears 'As emperes', and is not the thing itself), who, in her 'mutabylyte', represents the dominance of Fortune over the fallen Court, as she smiles 'halfe in scorne' at the rapacity and intrigues of her unstable courtiers. Unlike the sun, she is fickle, barren and merciless, promising only a harsh winter for those who have elevated her, as the courtiers have elevated Fortune or *Bone aventure*, to the status of a false goddess (hence the false crown, or diadem, she wears, which is simply an effect of the 'pole artyke' or Corona Borealis.[22]) Finally, the poet refers to Mars preparing for war, which both suggests the impending violence of the new Court (the

---

[20] Tucker, 'Setting', pp. 169–73.
[21] Heiserman, p. 21; S. E. Fish, *John Skelton's Poetry* (Yale, 1965) pp. 71–2.
[22] Scattergood, p. 395, nn. 2–6.

poet–dreamer Drede, one must note, is forced into suicide by the violent plots of his new-found enemies), and prefigures the poet's own stance as he 'declares war' with his pen on the prevailing courtly vices which he describes.

Even so brief a précis of the most obvious allegorical themes of the passage makes it clear that it would be naive to see it as simply a dating device. In addition, one has to be aware of the purely conventional elements within the passage. Perhaps Skelton, in following an extremely common literary formula, was as much concerned to include in the passage those elements which convention dictated and his plot required as to provide any more specific contemporary details. One might note that the poet follows another convention – the evocation of authoritative guidance, by calling for help, not to the muses, but to 'the great auctoryte / Of poetes olde' (lines 8–9), a clear indication that he was consciously harking back to tradition in the text thus far.

It was, of course, not beyond a poet and scholar of Skelton's skill and learning to produce an introduction to his text which both allowed him to manipulate the conventional *topoi* for allegorical effect and accurately to date the poem, but with so intricately woven a pattern of images and formulae as is evident here one is well advised to tread carefully before deciding the precise import of a figure or phrase. It is vital to provide external evidence to support the case, yet there is only the reference to 'Powers Keye', which need not be conclusive. While it is possible to show that there may well have been a house called 'Powers Keye' in existence in 1480–1, it cannot be demonstrated that the same house, or inn, was not still run by the same proprietor, or still bore his name, eighteen years later when the poem was printed. Indeed, the pro-Howard case is made even less convincing by the admission of its leading advocate that the astrological evidence in fact fits, not simply one date, but two: 1480 is one possible date, but the other is 1499, the very year in which the text was published from the presses of Wynkyn de Worde.

Thus, evidence for assigning the poem to 1480 rather than 1499 could equally well be evidence supporting the later date. All that can be argued in defence of the earlier possibility is that the 1499 date cannot be correct as it is 'rather close' to the date of publication.[23] But such a suggestion implies an extremely naive view of the poet's technique of composition. Need he have started writing the prologue in the autumn of 1499, in Harwich, and then continued systematically to compose the verses in the order in which they were to be published, before hastily penning the conclusion and racing back to Westminster to allow de Worde to set up the presses before the year closed? Under such circumstances the proximity of the date apparently alluded to in the prologue to the date of publication might militate against the 1499 dating. Is it not more reasonable, however, to assume that the text was,

[23] Tucker 'Setting', p. 170.

as most compositions are, composed in various drafts over an extended period of time, whether all in Harwich or all or part in Westminster or the royal household, and that the prologue, which summarises in allegorical form the main themes of the poem, was added later, *after* the main body of the satire had been composed, to prepare the work for publication? Then, if indeed the astrological configurations referred to within it do carry a serious dating function, it would not stretch credulity too far to imagine the poet adding the current date to the prologue to denote the completion of the final draft.

Indeed, all logic seems to point towards 1499 as the more acceptable date for the poem's composition. Is it likely, for example, that the poet would have composed the piece in 1480 yet waited until 1499 to publish it? It is true that he was to hold on to texts in later life and resurrect them for use, or re-use, later, but those cases do not bear comparison with *The Bowge*. When, for example, he represented old copies of the *Speculum Principis* and the *Chronique de Rains* to Henry VIII after his coronation, these seem to have been primarily 'panic' measures, indicative of the need to find a text, any text, to dedicate to the King in order to grasp a favourable moment to seek advancement at Court, whilst when the poet had *The Garlande* published in 1523, some twenty-five years after its original composition, the text showed extensive signs of reworking and frequent revision.[24] No such signs are evident in *The Bowge*, nor does it bear any dedication to a patron.

What implications do these conclusions have for the reference to 'Powers Keye' and for Skelton's clientage? It seems that the problem of the Howard connection is little further towards a solution; the same questions concerning the inn remain. As has been suggested, much could have happened to the building between 1480 and 1499 which has gone unrecorded. Even if the Howards did control it in 1480, and that is an assumption which the available evidence does not permit us to make, they could have lost it subsequently, whether by sale or through confiscation after their ill-fated support for Richard III at Bosworth. Thus the reference need not signify patronage. Indeed, perhaps Skelton did not visit the inn at all and the reference to it and to Harwich were made simply for their effect on the rhythm and rhyme-scheme of the verse rather than for their literal accuracy. The poet, after all, needed to set the poem at a port, as the satire concerned a trading ship, so perhaps he simply inserted the name of a sea-port and of a well-known inn to add maritime colour to the narrative. But, if the assertion of residence *is* to be taken literally, what is to be made of the phrase 'myne hostes house'? Clearly, for the reasons outlined above, this need not be taken as a reference to Lord John Howard. More likely it refers to the innkeeper, whether the eponymous Power or some anonymous successor (one might

[24] See p. 21, below.

note that throughout *The Canterbury Tales* Harry Bailey, the innkeeper at 'The Tabard', is referred to as 'our hoste'). Indeed this possibility makes the seemingly tautological syntax of 'myne hostes house called Powers Keye' seem less peculiar. One might perhaps have expected the poet to state that he was staying 'with myne hoste', or 'at Power's house', not at mine host's house called 'Powers Keye'. But, if, nineteen years after the entries in the *Household Books*, an anonymous successor to Power was now the resident patron of 'Powers Keye', and thus 'myne hoste' and Power were not one and the same, the distinction would be a necessary one.

Thus when Skelton refers to 'myne hoste' he need not be referring to the hospitality of the Howards. But if one, for a moment, assumes that he was; if the pro-Howard thesis is given the benefit of the most generous doubt, what does that tell us about the poet's connections with the noble family? Clearly even this stretching of the evidence does not come near to providing the basis for the definite patronage link which the Howard school would wish us to accept. If the poet was in Harwich in or around 1498 as a guest of the Howards, it must surely have been by way of a very indirect invitation. For, if it was a case of the family treating 'their poet' to some hospitality, surely, as has been suggested above, it would have been at Sheriff Hutton, where Thomas Howard I and his wife were in residence, that he would have been fêted, and not in Harwich. And what is the poet supposed to have offered in return for this many-times-removed hospitality? Not, it seems, anything over-generous by way of poetic gratitude. Indeed if this is a patron–client relationship, then one needs to revise radically what one normally accepts that phrase to imply. For, if the passage under consideration was included in *The Bowge* as a compliment to or flaunting of a sponsor, might one not reasonably expect to find something a little more direct than this reference to an inn or house in Harwich? If the patron–client link was as strong as those critics who favour the Howard school suggest, it is surprising that the literary thanks for services rendered were not more definite. Who would have been capable of understanding such an allusion? Probably only the patron and the poet themselves, and the former could hardly have been flattered by so fleeting a comment, particularly so if he realised that what Skelton was in fact saying was that, at an inn (possibly) associated with the courtier–nobleman Thomas Howard, he was visited by a vision which revealed the vice-ridden nature of the Court and the treacherous designs of its courtiers.

It follows that this reference in *The Bowge* does not point to any significant connection between Skelton and the Howards. It seems that those critics who use such supposed hints to make grand claims for the poet's patronage, and thus for the motivation behind his political writings, are constructing an essentially circular and self-reflexive argument. The reference, they argue, is significant because it points to the Howards, and the Howards were Skelton's patrons. Why do they say that the Howards were Skelton's patrons? Essentially because a significant reference such as this tells them so. That the reference is only significant if one begins with the assumption that it must be is soon forgotten, and a mythology begins to develop around a couplet which is intrinsically far from significant, and may have been prompted by any number of considerations other than a desire to point to Howard patronage.

But, if the 'Powers Keye' reference in *The Bowge* need not imply such sponsorship, what other evidence remains as the basis of the Howard connection? One can perhaps begin by discounting the various, more or less fanciful, observations of his biographers, based on the physical proximity to the various Howard estates in Norfolk of Skelton's rectory at Diss. Despite the suggestion that 'during his residence at Diss he could hardly have escaped riding over to pay his respects at Kenninghall',[25] such a possibility is far from acceptable as evidence and certainly does not indicate that Skelton was a Howard client. As the following chapter will suggest, the choice of the rectory at Diss for Skelton's living seems to have had little or nothing to do with the wishes of the dominant local nobility. It was chosen because it was one of the livings in the gift of lady Margaret, countess of Richmond, the mother of Henry VII, who had the supervision of the royal children's education and thus would have been responsible for Skelton's employment during his period as a royal tutor.[26] Similarly, despite Brie's suggestion that it was the Countess of Surrey, and Edwards' that it was Agnes, duchess of Norfolk, who commissioned Skelton to translate de Geguileville's *Pelerinage de la vie humaine* into English,[27] it is more likely to have been lady Margaret to whom Skelton referred when he wrote in *The Garlande* that

> Of my ladys grace at the contemplacyoun,
> Owt of Frenshe into Englysshe prose,
> Of Mannes Lyfe the Peregrynacioun,
> He did translate, enterprete, and disclose
> (1219–22)

Such oblique references and obscure possibilities cannot stand as the basis for any defensible assertion of a Howard connection for the poet. Yet what of those other occasions on which Skelton speaks directly of a member of the Howard family? Can the evidence of a long career in their service be found here? Certainly the evidence of Skelton's dedications does not recommend such a possibility. For, of the fifty-six extant poems, prose pieces and a single drama which remain of the canon, not one of them bears a formal, or even informal, dedication to either of the Thomas Howards or their house. Of

---

[25] Edwards, p. 207.
[26] *Ibid.*, p. 55.
[27] Friedrich Brie, 'Skelton-Studien', *Englische-Studien*, 37 (1907), pp. 1–86; Edwards, pp. 206–7.

Skelton's works three bear dedications to Cardinal Wolsey, at least as many again carry commendations to the King, one small anthology is dedicated to the former Peterhouse academic William Ruckshaw, another, now lost, commends the Bonnehommes of Ashridge, and there are elegies for Henry VII, lady Margaret and Henry Percy, fourth earl of Northumberland. One cannot but be surprised at the singular lack of formal dedication to the Howards.[28]

This leaves just one overtly commendatory reference to a Howard in the entire canon: those passages complimenting 'the noble Cowntes of Surrey' in *The Garlande*. As was noted above, the introduction to that text declares that it was 'studyously dyvysed at Sheryfhotten Castell, in the foreste of Galtres' in Yorkshire, which was a regular residence of the Lords Lieutenant in the North, an office held by both Thomas Howards on various occasions throughout the period between their political rehabilitation in 1489 and the publication of the poem in 1523. Thus, as many critics have pointed out, it is quite reasonable to infer that Skelton was at Sheriff Hutton as a guest of the Howards.[29] This assertion is given considerable support by what follows in the substance of the text. For the poet–dreamer of the allegory, having been taken by Dame Pallas to the Court of the Queen of Fame, is then escorted by Occupation to 'a postern gate', through which

> She brought me to a goodly chaumber of astate,
> Where the noble Cowntes of Surrey in a chayre
> Sat honorably... (768–70)

The Countess then instructs her gentlewomen to produce

> A cronell of lawrell with verduris light and darke
> [which] I have devysyd for Skelton, my clerke;
> For to his servyce I have suche regarde,
> That of our bownte we wyll hym rewarde
> (776–9)

Here is the most substantial evidence for the Howard connection and the basis of all the theories of the Howard school. For this, quite clearly, is a statement from the poet's own pen which asserts a meeting with the Countess in which she refers to him as 'my clerke', whose 'servyce' is to be rewarded. Is this not conclusive proof of a patronage link between the poet and

[28] See Scattergood, pp. 312–57, 359–71, 372–86, 110–11, 121–33, 29–35; *The Garlande*, lines 1461–9. One might contrast Skelton's output with that of Alexander Barclay, who was clearly a Howard client during this period. At least four of his known works were dedicated to the Howard dukes. See B. White (ed.), *The Eclogues of Alexander Barclay*, E.E.T.S., 175 (1928), pp. 60–1.

[29] Edwards, pp. 226–7; Ian A. Gordon, *John Skelton, Poet Laureate* (Melbourne and London, 1943) p. 38, Nan Cooke Carpenter, *John Skelton* (New York, 1968) pp. 34, 88; Pollet, *Poet of Tudor England*, pp. 135–44.

the Howards? Clearly a connection of some kind is referred to here, but one must carefully consider what that might be before soaring into flights of fancy about the patronage enjoyed by the poet and the significance which that connection might have for the satires against Wolsey of the 1520s. Again the dating of the text becomes a crucial question, and again the revisionist interpretations of M. J. Tucker provide a useful avenue into this complex problem.

Let us begin, however, with the more commonly accepted dating of the poem, that which assigns it to the year 1523, the year of its publication. Such a dating would obviously have profound implications for the political background to the Wolsey satires. If it could be shown that Skelton was a guest of the Howards, and was referred to as 'my clerke' by Elizabeth Howard (née Stafford), countess of Surrey, only months after the completion of the most uncompromisingly aggressive poem against Wolsey, *Why Come Ye Nat?*, then one would have taken a long stride towards demonstrating a direct factional stimulus behind the satires. If the 1523 dating were accepted, a number of coincidences would, as many critics have cheerfully pointed out, slip neatly into place and appear to present an overwhelming case for the Howard connection. For Elizabeth Howard was, as has already been observed, the daughter of Edward Stafford, duke of Buckingham, whose execution might be blamed on the machinations of Cardinal Wolsey, if Vergil and the French Chancellor, Duprat, are to be believed.[30] It would thus appear no coincidence that Skelton's first satire against Wolsey, *Speke, Parott*, appeared only months after that execution. The hand of the Countess, and of her Howard relatives, might well be perceived behind the project. Such an argument soon gains a momentum of its own and rapidly provides deceptively attractive answers to some of the more practical difficulties of the Skeltonic biography. The fact that Wolsey did not retaliate against the poet after the circulation of the satires, for example, is neatly explained away by the support which the latter was supposedly receiving from the Howards. They, of course, were protecting him, and not even Wolsey dared risk the consequences of an attack on a second great pillar of the nobility so soon after Buckingham's controversial downfall.

The succinct, even glib, manner in which this argument provides answers to some of the pressing problems of Skelton's career has, however, too often concealed the number of equally pressing difficulties which it creates. First, as has been suggested, it relies on the existence of a non-existent feud; for the Howards and Wolsey were not mutually antagonistic in the early 1520s. Second, if Skelton did write the satires at the Howards' behest, why did he not say as much through dedications? It might be possible to argue that the patrons of so contentious a series of works would wish to remain anony-

---

[30] Vergil, pp. 264–5, 277–80; Pollard, p. 316.

mous. But circumstances militate against such an explanation. If the noble patron wished to remain anonymous for fear of the consequences of Wolsey's wrath, how much more likely is it that the poet himself should have wished to have shielded himself with obscurity? Yet Skelton proudly append-ed his name to each of the poems in question. Clearly he wished to proclaim his authorship (for reasons which will be considered in the following chap-ters); a fact which argues against the notion of a secret literary intrigue against the Cardinal. This reveals another obvious flaw in the argument which alleges a factional motivation for the satires. For if, as the Howard school imply, the poet was a recognised client of the Howards of long stand-ing, it would clearly have been necessary for not only the patron but also the client to remain anonymous. If his connections were that well-known (and the implications of the arguments of the Howard school are that they were), then the mere mention of his name would have been sufficient to indicate a Howard involvement. For it to have performed the functions which the Howard school allege, then, the anonymity would have needed to have been total; that it was not argues that it was not a shield for a publicity-shy noble patron. Similarly, if secrecy was the reason for the lack of a dedication to any of the satires, is it not remarkable that within months of the completion of *Why Come Ye Nat?* the poet should have so openly announced his connec-tion with the countess of Surrey through the presses of the King's printer in the text of *The Garlande?* If secrecy were so vital in the autumn of 1522, one would expect it to have remained so in the autumn of the following year. Yet Skelton allowed *The Garlande* to be published, boasting of his sojourn at Sheriff Hutton and of his gracious reception by the Countess.

Evidently there are flaws and inconsistencies in the argument which uses the Howard passages in *The Garlande* to determine the motivation for the poems against Wolsey. Indeed, one need look no further than the text of *The Garlande* itself for a clear indication that all is not well with such reasoning. As has been suggested, for that argument to work it must be assumed that Skelton was the agent through which the Howards expressed their supposed hatred of Wolsey in the period from 1521 to 1522–3, and that in 1523, in *The Garlande*, the poet provided his most obvious gesture of gratitude towards his backers. Yet that text, which supposedly offers Skelton's sincere gratitude towards Wolsey's rivals, is dedicated, not to the Howards, but to Wolsey himself and to the King, and moreover to Wolsey in terms which sug-gest that he is to be afforded an equal reverence to that offered to Henry:

> *Ad serenissimam Majestatem Regiam, pariter cum Domino*
> *Cardinali, Legato a latere honorificatissimo &c*
> *Lautre Envoy*
> *Perge, liber, celebrem pronus regem venerare*
> *Henricum octavum, resonans sua praemia laudis.*

Cardineum dominum pariter venerando salutes,
Legatum a latere (1587–93)

Is it likely that Skelton would dedicate, and in such glowing terms, his most open tribute to his patrons to the very man whom they had employed him to vilify? Clearly such a suggestion is nonsensical. Yet it is necessary to accept it if one defends the notion of Howard patronage.

It is, then, extremely difficult to square the stance of *The Garlande* with that of the satires against Wolsey if one assumes a Howard connection. Yet the only basis for assuming such a connection is the fact that *The Garlande* was published within a year of the completion of *Why Come Ye Nat?*, which allows the inference that both were written at almost the same time. However, M. J. Tucker advances a somewhat different, and rather more helpful, interpretation of *The Garlande*'s origins.[31] Once more through a study of astronomical data, with which he compares Skelton's astrological introduction, Tucker produces just one possible date for the passage's composition: not 1523 but 1495.[32] Again the obvious objections to an attempt to date a text on such, arguably subjective, evidence must be raised. But on this occasion it is possible to call on external evidence to support the assertion. For, as Tucker observes, Thomas Howard II, earl of Surrey, and his wife Elizabeth (née Stafford) were not in residence at Sheriff Hutton during the Christmas and New Year of 1522–3 but at Court, and the Howard household books for 1523–4 make no mention of Skelton.[33] The only occasion on which the astronomical data coincide with a period in which a countess of Surrey was in residence at Sheriff Hutton was New Year 1494–5,[34] when the Countess in question was not Elizabeth Howard (née Stafford), wife of Thomas Howard II, but Elizabeth Howard (née Tilney), wife of Thomas Howard I. This dating, Tucker claims with some justification, also enables a more acceptable identification of those gentlewomen of the Howard household for whom Skelton wrote lyrics with known individuals. It also removes the difficulties surrounding the possible involvement of Elizabeth Howard (née Stafford) in the Wolsey satires. For there would thus be no possible reason to assume a connection between the Countess and the poet.

Is it possible, then, that Tucker is correct, and that it was the household of Thomas Howard I and Elizabeth, countess of Surrey, that received Skelton into its midst for a Christmas celebration? Fortunately there is one further piece of evidence which supports him.

[31] M. J. Tucker, 'The ladies in Skelton's *Garland of Laurel*', *R.Q.*, 22 (1969), pp. 333–45.
[32] Tucker 'The ladies', pp. 334–5.
[33] M. J. Tucker, 'California MS Ac.523, formerly Phillips MS 3841', *Notes and Queries*, 209 (1964), pp. 374–6.
[34] Tucker, 'The ladies', pp. 333–4; and O. Gingerich and M. J. Tucker, 'The astronomical dating of Skelton's *Garland of Laurel*', *H.L.Q.*, 32 (1969), pp. 207–20.

Skelton makes reference in *The Garlande* not only to the eleven gentle-women of the Howard household to whom he addressed lyrics but also to one man. 'Castyng my syght the chambre about', he wrote,

> To se how duly ich thyng in ordre was,
> Towarde the dore, as he were comyng oute,
> I sawe maister Newton sit with his compas,
> His plummet, his pensell, his spectacles of glas,
> Dyvysynge in pycture, by his industrious wit,
> Of my laurell the proces every whitte
> (1093–9)

Such a description clearly suggests a draughtsman, or as Scattergood notes, someone whose duties included scrivening, illuminating or painting,[35] and implies the existence of a real individual. Whereas Scattergood can only observe that Newton has not been identified but was probably a Howard servant, it is possible to suggest a more definite identification. Throughout Payne Collier's edition of the *Household Books* for the period 1481–90 one finds references to one John Newton who was clearly a Howard household servant. On 9 October 1485, for example, one finds, 'Item, to Jhone Newton his wages Xs', an item which recurs throughout the volume.[36] On another occasion Newton was given one penny 'for baytyng', or maintenance, whilst away from the Howard seat on an errand. And during April 1482 he was sent on two occasions to London, given a (liveried?) jacket, and paid 'be his owne hands' by lord John Howard.[37] The evidence of the *Household Books*, then, clearly suggests that a man called Newton was a member of the Howard retinue throughout the decade prior to Skelton's composition of *The Garlande*. What is required is some indication that this man and 'maister Newton' the scrivener or illuminator were one and the same. The following item in the household accounts seems to provide such an indication:[38]

> The XXij yere of the King (1483) and the XXj
> day of Feverer . . .
> (John Newton) Item, the same day, paied to John
> Newton, be the handes of Thomas Seynclow, for
> to have owt a pardon xxvjs viijd

The reference is not conclusive. But, if the phrase 'to have owt' is taken to mean to copy, or to illustrate, then it would seem that Newton was indeed the sort of craftsman that Skelton described. That he was a probable candidate for the illustration or design of Skelton's ornate laurel crown is also suggested by the cost of the work entrusted to him on this occasion: a manuscript costing 26s 8d would have been lavish indeed.

[35] Scattergood, p. 507, n. 1096.   [36] *Household Books*, p. 466.
[37] *Ibid.*, pp. 454, 263.   [38] *Ibid.*, p. 356.

There is then a good deal of evidence which favours the 1495 dating for the composition of the poem. Both Tucker's identification of the ladies of the lyrics and the suggestive existence of a Newton in the Howard household in the period immediately prior to the astrological date referred to in the prologue support it. Indeed the text itself, taken as a whole, suggests a long period of construction rather than a hasty composition in 1523. The lyrics and the main vehicle of the narrative, the dream-allegory, seem to be works of the 1490s. Yet there are other sections of the text which can only have been written at other times. The extended defence, in lines 1254–1375, of the poet's mock-elegaic lyric *Phyllyp Sparowe* (written *c.* 1509) against 'sum jangelyng jays' who 'discommende' it can only have been relevant at the time of Alexander Barclay's attack on that poem in his *Shyp of Folys*, published in 1509.[39] Equally, the bibliographical section of the poem, in which that defence is inserted, can itself not have been completed prior to 1522, for it includes *Speke, Parott* and *Collyn Clout* among Skelton's works.[40] Thus what appears to have been the case is that Skelton began the work during 1494–5, either at Sheriff Hutton, or immediately prior to or following his visit there, as an aureate celebration of his own talent and a monument to his lasting fame, which included verses written about his stay at the castle both as a literary repayment for the Howard's hospitality and as an advertisement that the poet had friends in high places. The poem was not printed however, and the poet kept it about him, adding sections and updating it, preparing it as his own *apologia* until the opportunity came to publish it in 1523. It thus tells us nothing about the poet's relationship with the Howards in 1523, and nothing about the Wolsey satires, only that Skelton was a guest of the Howards in 1494–5.

Is this enough to suggest long-standing patronage? Surprisingly, it has been argued that it is. Tucker uses this inference to resolve the crucial question of why the poet ceased writing against Wolsey after *Why Come Ye Nat?* and began to praise him in subsequent works. *The Garlande*, he asserts, reveals that Skelton wrote his satires as a client, not of Thomas Howard II, earl of Surrey, but of his father, the Duke of Norfolk (Thomas Howard I): hence his visit to Sheriff Hutton in 1494–5, and hence the sudden ceasefire in his literary attack on Wolsey in 1523, the year in which the Duke retired from an active role in national politics and removed himself from Court to his East Anglian estates. This retreat, it is argued, left Skelton defenceless and without a patron and forced him to make suit to Wolsey for forgiveness through the dedication to *The Garland*.

Such an argument seems totally contrary to the revisionary drift of Tucker's earlier arguments. If his work on *The Garlande* has proved any-

---

[39] Alexander Barclay, *The Shyp of Folys*, ed. T. H. Jamieson 2 vols., (London, 1874), II, p. 331.
[40] *The Garlande*, lines 1187–90 and 1234.

thing it is not that Skelton was entirely dependent on Thomas Howard I for his living and protection, but that he had no significant links with the Howards at all. At a stroke, through the reassignment of *The Garlande* to 1494–5, Tucker has removed the only substantial support from the argument that the Wolsey satires were factionally motivated.

That Elizabeth Howard invited Skelton to the family residence in 1494 is an entirely different prospect to her namesake's having done so in 1523. On the latter occasion, as the following chapters will demonstrate, the poet was in a very isolated position, both politically and socially. For the Countess to have announced her support for him through an invitation to her home in the public manner which the poem suggests would indeed have far-reaching implications for a study of the history of Skelton's patronage. For the same invitation to have been made in 1494 would, however, have involved no such political implications. At that time Skelton was seemingly enjoying a successful career at Court and was clearly of sufficiently high standing and merit in the eyes of the Crown for him to be appointed tutor to Prince Henry within the next three years.[41] The Countess's invitation under those circumstances probably says less about her desire to court Skelton's favour than her desire to remain abreast of the fashions at Court and attract the favour of the Countess of Richmond. If Skelton was well thought of by the Crown, and more particularly by the influential Countess of Richmond, at this time, it is not surprising that he was so publicly entertained by the wife of a nobleman whose political rehabilitation after the miscalculation of Bosworth was still not fully confirmed and who was still earnestly seeking the restoration of his lost dukedom. Such an expedient interest in the poet's career need have had no lasting implications for his future patronage. And thus one ought also to experience no surprise at the discovery that there is no further reference to Howard hospitality or interest in the poet to be found in his works after this event.

Tucker's persuasive case for the redating of *The Garlande* has thus done much to remove the spectre of the Howards from the Wolsey satires. Hence the incongruity of the continued insistence on a Howard hand on Skelton's shoulder, albeit from a different Thomas Howard. The insistence is made doubly incongruous when it is set against the rest of the available evidence, or lack of evidence, on the subject. If Howard was the poet's lifelong patron, and so important to the poet's well-being that the moment that he retired permanently from Court the latter had to run immediately for shelter into the arms of his erstwhile target, the question of why there are so few references, and not a single dedication, to the man and his son in the canon becomes all the more relevant. Why, for instance was there no funeral elegy for the Duke on his death in 1524, of the sort which Skelton provided for

---

[41] See chap. 2, below.

Henry VII, the Countess of Richmond, the fourth Earl of Northumberland, and even for William Bedell, Adam Uddersall and John Clerk, whom he immortalised in ridicule? Why also is there no reference to him in Skelton's earliest extant poem, *Upon the Dolorus Dethe . . . of the Mooste Honorable Erle of Northumberlande?*[42] In this text Skelton seems to reveal some insight into the political situation in the north, as he is the only commentator to suggest the existence of an intrigue between the Earl's retainers and the unruly Commons who slew him.[43] In his elegy he berates the populace for the 'Godless' folly of their rising, and prays for the future of the Earl's son and heir. He tells the nobility to grieve over their costly inaction during the rising, and calls on God to bring Percy's soul to salvation. In all this there is no mention whatever of lord Thomas Howard's having been sent north to quell the rebellion. If Skelton was a Howard client is it likely that he would have missed the opportunity to record and celebrate his patron's role in the putting down of John à Chambre and the rebels, particularly as the loss and restoration of order was so crucial a concept in the poem? Again, how does one account for the number of references to the dead Percy's incomparable stature as a nobleman 'whos pere is hard to fynd, / All gyf Englond and Fraunce wer thorow sought' (lines 178–9)? At one point it is even explicitly noted of Percy that 'Surmountinge in honour *all erlis* he did excede' (line 135, my italics). Praise of the dead Earl is clearly required of his elegy, but if Howard dominated Skelton's life in the way in which the Howard school suggest, the poet might have chosen not to emphasise the deceased's qualities in quite these terms.

The passages in *The Garlande*, then, cannot be seen to provide evidence of any significant patronage for Skelton. Moreover, after their completion in 1495, there is not one reference to the Howards to be found in the canon for the next eighteen years, until Thomas Howard I's victory at Flodden in 1513 was celebrated in the poem's *A Ballade of the Scottysshe Kynge* and *Agaynst the Scottes*, and in the hymn *Chorus de Dys contra Scottos*.[44] The victory was, of course, the zenith of the senior Thomas Howard's military career, the event which signalled his formal reacceptance into the nation's social and political elite through his consequent restoration to the dukedom of Norfolk. Yet it would be extremely difficult to gain that impression from a reading of Skelton's poems. It will be helpful to quote in full the passage which contains

---

[42] Scattergood, pp. 29–35.

[43] Edwards, p. 42; M. E. Hicks, 'Dynastic change and northern society: the career of the fourth earl of Northumberland, 1470–89', *Northern History*, 14 (1978), pp. 78–107, 80; M. E. James, 'The murder at Cocklodge', *Durham University Journal*, 57 (1964–5), pp. 80–7. It is possible of course that Skelton was simply using his imagination, or was mistaken, or that he was simply following an elegiac convention. For this last possibility see J. Scattergood, 'Skelton and elegy', *Proceedings of the Royal Irish Academy*, 84 C, no. 10 (1984), pp. 333–47, esp. 340–1.

[44] Scattergood, pp. 113–15, 115–21; Dyce, I, p. 190.

the reference to Howard in *Agaynst the Scottes*, both because it conveys the tone and direction of the whole piece, and because it is so short. In a poem of 184 lines, not counting the supplementary blast against its detractors, Howard is mentioned but once, in a passage directed against the Scots in general and King James IV in particular.

> Unto the castell of Norram,
> I understand, to sone ye came.
> At Branxton More and Flodden hylles,
> Our Englysh bowes, our Englysh bylles,
> Agaynst you gave so sharpe a shower,
> That of Scotland ye lost the flower.
> The White Lyon [Surrey], there rampaunt of moode,
> He ragyd and rent out your hart bloode;
> He the White and ye the Red,
> The White there slew the Red starke ded.
> Thus for your guerdon quyt ar ye,
> Thankyd be God in Trinyte,
> And swete Saynt George, our ladyes knyght!
> Youre eye is out; adew, good nyght! (130–43)

Thus in a poem celebrating the Earl's greatest feat of arms there is no praise of him whatever, and certainly no hint of a patron–client relationship between Surrey and the poet. There is merely an impersonal and somewhat gory metaphor which manipulates the two opposing commanders' heraldic emblems for descriptive effect. Here, as in the remaining two Flodden pieces, Skelton's aim is to revile and ridicule the dead James IV and the defeated Scots, not to praise the Earl, any more than he praises 'Our Englysh bowes, our Englysh bylles'. Indeed, one wonders whether, had there had not been the poetically useful coincidence of lion emblems, Skelton would have found it necessary to mention Surrey at all. It is a national effort which the poet portrays, and a national victory reflecting the virtues of a national character which he praises. It is God, the English character and the King who represents both, that take the credit for the victory, not Howard.

This is made even clearer in *A Ballade of the Scottysshe Kynge*, which was effectively a first draft of *Agaynst the Scottes*, in which Howard gains a reference of only two lines in length in a poem of seventy-five lines. There it is simply stated of James IV that 'That noble erle, the Whyte Lyon, / Your pompe and pryde hath layde a downe' (lines 68–9). Interestingly, however, Howard's son, lord Thomas II, makes an appearance in this text. He, like his father, is afforded a single couplet.

> His sone the lorde admyrall is full good,
> His swerde hath bathed in the Scottes blode.
> (70–1)

When it came to the final draft this reference was excised in favour of further stress on the discomfiture of the Scots. But its original inclusion is indicative of Skelton's method of composition. In the first draft, when the poet had to hand virtually no detailed news concerning the battle, he was clearly casting about for 'safe' information which would give his text authenticity, but which would not later prove to be erroneous. The only sure knowledge which he had received was that James IV was dead and had been taken to Norham Castle ('For a prysoner there now ye be / Eyther to the devyll or the trinite' (lines 40–1)). Thus the entire poem is constructed around that fact. It is quite evident that Skelton was not even aware of the result of the battle, so all the emphasis is placed on the personal downfall of the Scots King (it is *his* ballad, whereas the later version of the text is despatched against the entire defeated nation). What other information the text contains is there because it was felt to be incontrovertable. The Scots–Danish alliance prompts the poet to refer to the 'ranke Scottes and dronken Danes' (line 64) (a reference later removed once it became clear that the Danes played no part in the battle), and the fact of the siege of Norham Castle leads Skelton to refer to that site as the location of the engagement.[45]

Thus it is that the couplets referring to the Howards are appended to the tail-end of the ballad, because, if anything was certain information, it was the fact that the English Commander and the Lord Admiral would have been involved in the battle and, regardless of the result, could be said to have bathed their swords in Scot's blood. When he came to write the final draft of the text the poet was fully conversant with the facts of the engagement, and so could vaunt the Scots' 'overthrow / At Branxton More' (lines 10–11), and remark that 'At Floddon hyllys, / Our bowys, our byllys / Slew all the floure / Of theyr honoure' (lines 25–8). With this new information available he no longer needed the general references to the Howards and so removed completely the couplet on the Lord Admiral, developing the lines concerning Surrey into the heraldic metaphor cited above.

Thus *A Ballade* is the most pro-Howard version of the narrative (albeit pro-Howard by default). When Skelton became aware of the full extent of Surrey's victory he actually reduced the emphasis placed on the Howards' contribution to the battle and chose to stress instead the folly and pride of the Scots. Again, this is hardly the approach which one might expect from a poet who was applauding his patron's greatest military achievement.

After the Flodden poems it was another nine years before a Howard appeared in Skelton's verses again, and here again his appearance was determined by the poet's treatment of national issues rather than any apparent desire to mention a Howard *per se*. On this occasion it was Thomas Howard

[45] Pollet, *Poet of Tudor England*, pp. 70–6.

II, by this time Earl of Surrey,[46] who was mentioned in Skelton's survey of
the ills of the Realm in *Why Come Ye Nat?*. This reference is more substantial than those in the Flodden poems and might, at first glance, suggest, something of the personal involvement between the poet and the Earl which the
Howard school allege. Certainly the passage is overtly complementary.

> . . . the good Erle of Surray,
> The Frenche men he doth fray,
> And vexeth them day by day
> With all the power he may.
> The French men he hath fayned,
> And mad theyr hertes attaynted.
> Of chevalry he is the floure:
> Our lorde be his soccoure!
> The French men he hathe so mated,
> And theyr courage abated,
> That they are but halfe men (153–63)

It is, however, important to note exactly what it is that Skelton is commend-
ing and in what terms. In this text, just as was the case in the Flodden poems
concerning his father, the inclusion of Surrey and the manner in which he is
treated is determined by the general argument which the poet is advancing.
Skelton is contrasting the lack of the purposeful initiatives against the Scots
('Our armye waxeth dull, / With, "Tourne all home agayne!" / And never a
Scot slayne!' (lines 150–2)) with the vigorous action taken against the French
('Yet the good Erle of Surray / The Frenche men he doth fray'). The point
made here is that the Scots hold the English in contempt because of the
'worthy truce' arranged by lord Dacre, with Wolsey's connivance,[47] whilst
the French have been taught to fear the rightful superiority of English arms
and of the English character and so cower,

> Lyke foxes in theyr denne,
> Lyke cankerd cowardes all,
> Lyke urcheons in a stone wall,
> They kepe them in theyr holdes
> Lyke hen-herted cokoldes (164–8)

The Surrey passage is a continuation of the attack on Dacre and Wolsey's
truce, not a gratuitous eulogy on Surrey. Skelton is simply using the Earl's
French campaign of 1522 as an example of truly honourable behaviour with
which to contrast all the more starkly what he portrays as the craven and
treacherous policies pursued on the northern border. If Surrey had not existed, the poem would have necessitated his invention, and in the place of this

---

[46] He succeeded to his father's title on the latter's elevation to the dukedom of Norfolk on 1
February 1514.

[47] For a fuller consideration of Skelton's treatment of this subject see G. Walker, ' "Baytyng The
Bochers Dogge": a study of John Skelton's satires against Cardinal Wolsey as a source for the
politics of the 1520s', University of Southampton Ph.D. thesis, 1985, chap. 5.

passage one would have found a reference to a warrior of classical or biblical provenance performing the same function. Skelton's argument relies on the contrast between active and passive policies, and Surrey provided an ideal and readily available model for that purpose. Moreover, what made the Earl particularly valuable as an exemplar was that mention of his French campaign also enabled the poet to launch a further attack on Wolsey's foreign policy. He sets up the Surrey/Dacre contrast in order to reflect shame on the latter and, by implication, on his backer, Wolsey. But he is then able to suggest that even Surrey's martial achievements have been undercut and devalued by Wolsey's policies. For, despite the Earl's victories, the French are able to buy themselves security by offering Wolsey bribes ('They shote at him with crownes. / With crownes of golde enblased' (lines 178–9)).

Thus, having used Dacre's alleged failures as a stick with which to beat Wolsey, Skelton is able to perform an identical feat with Surrey's successes. His allegation is that Wolsey's regime is emasculating the nation's foreign policy, entangling it in 'A webbe of lylse wulse' (line 131), producing truces with the Scots when a war ought to have been fought and won, and allowing the French to buy their salvation despite their parlous military position. Again it was the fact that a Howard was in the field and winning victories that necessitated his inclusion in the text, not any more personal ties which he might have had with the poet. This fact is clearly suggested by the terms in which Skelton describes the campaign in France. He evidently has no idea precisely whom or where Howard is fighting, simply that it is against the French. Thus a whole string of generalised insults is aimed at the enemy, which imply that they are utterly defeated, but which contains no concrete details of battles, sieges or victories. Had Skelton been praising his patron one might expect rather more by way of detail than is evident here. Alternatively, if it was the case that he simply did not have the information to hand at that moment, one might expect a later poem to make good the lapses, as *Agaynst the Scottes* had done for *A Ballade of the Scottysshe Kynge*. No such supplementary work was, however, forthcoming. Thus the generality of these comments also argues against Howard patronage.

But what of the comment on Surrey that 'Of chevalry he is the floure' (line 159), and the later remark 'God save my Lorde Admyrell!' (line 376)? Do these suggest such ties? Once again it has to be concluded that they do not. The former phrase is the most obvious cliché taken from the medieval manuals of style,[48] whilst the use of the term '*my* Lorde Admyrall' in the

---

[48] See Stephen Hawes' use of these and similar phrases in 'The example of vertu', in F. W. Gluck and A. B. Morgan (eds.), *Stephen Hawes: The Minor Poems*, E.E.T.S., 271 (1974), lines 654, 1259, 1557, 1739; and in W. E. Mead (ed.), *The Pastime of Pleasure, by Stephen Hawes*, E.E.T.S., original series, 173 (1928 for 1927), lines 657–8, 2268, 2986, 4141–2. Similar phrases are used by Geoffrey of Vinsauf, an authority from whom Skelton is known to have borrowed (see Edwards, pp. 26–8, for Geoffrey's influence on *Phyllyp Sparowe*). See N. F. Nims (trans.), *The Poetria Nova of Geoffrey of Vinsauf* (Toronto, 1967), p. 92.

latter need not indicate any personal relationship. In the same text Skelton refers to 'my lorde of Canterbury' (line 1120) and, in a weary commentary on the actions of those noblemen who have 'gone' without a struggle, to 'My lorde . . . and syr knyght' (line 915) as representative figures. Skelton, it seems, used 'my lorde' to denote anyone with whom he has no particular quarrel as well as those whom he seems to admire. It is only the spineless and the treacherous that do not deserve the title, such as '*The* lorde Dakers' (line 272, my italics), 'the lord Rose' (line 286), and 'The Erle of Northumberlande' (line 290).

Thus the poet's use of the phrase 'my lorde' need not mean that he was singling out Howard for special favour. Indeed, if that had been his intention, Skelton would surely have indicated the Earl's case as an exception when he constructed his carefully worded criticisms of the nobility as a class. The poet declares that Wolsey can 'outface' '*All* noble men' (line 623, my italics), that '*No* man dare come to . . . [his] speche', 'Of what estate he be / Of spirituall dygnyte; / Nor duke of hye degre, / Nor marques, *erle* nor lorde' (lines 615–20, my italics), and that none of them, 'Duke, erle, baron, nor lorde' (line 342), has the courage to stand up to the Cardinal's bullying. If Skelton had wished to indicate that a particular nobleman was exempt from such charges (as he surely would have done if one were his patron), he would have said so, perhaps in the conventional and anonymous way in which he had excused some clerics from his charges of ecclesiastical shortcomings and immorality in *Collyn Clout*:[49]

> Of no good bysshop speke I,
> Nor good preest I escrye,
> Good frere, nor good chanon,
> Good nonne, nor good canon,
> Good monke, nor good clerke,
> Nor of no good werke;
> But my recountynge is
> Of them that do amys (1095–1102)

And yet there is no equivalent retraction in *Why Come Ye Nat?* excluding 'good' lords or earls, which again suggests that the poet was under no constraint to maintain amicable relations with a noble patron.

The third and final poem to refer to a Howard earl directly, *Howe The Douty Duke of Albany*,[50] followed *Why Come Ye Nat?* in the succeeding year. This poem is a vicious attack upon John Stuart, duke of Albany, and his abortive invasion of England of November 1523. The main thrust of the text, which reviles Albany and the Scots, is largely negative and recalls the Flodden poems. It does, however, contain two very definite references to

[49] For other examples of this conventional device see chap. 6, below.
[50] Scattergood, pp. 359–72. For a detailed study of this text see chap. 6, below.

Thomas Howard II, earl of Surrey. The first is similar in tone and content to *Agaynst The Scottes*, in that it is a perfunctory rehearsal of facts with only implied praise and no aureate embellishment. 'He', Skelton observes of Albany, 'reculed backe',

> To his great lacke,
> Whan he herde tell
> That my Lorde Amrell
> Was comyng downe
> To make hym frowne
> And to make hym lowre,
> With the noble powre
> Of my Lorde Cardynall (52–60)

Immediately a flaw appears in the traditional model of Howard–Wolsey rivalry. If Surrey was the fierce enemy of Wolsey that some writers have claimed,[51] how is it that Skelton felt able to refer to them both with implied praise in the same passage, and thus remind Surrey of the contribution made to his victory by his 'enemy' Wolsey? And how is it that the poet was able thus to imply praise for Surrey in a poem commissioned by and dedicated to Wolsey? Again a piece of evidence frequently cited by the Howard school in support of their arguments, actually proves inimical to those arguments when considered in its correct context. Clearly the notion that monolithic factional blocs led by Wolsey and the Howards existed in a state of continual mutual hostility does not adequately describe the situation at Court in the 1520s, and thus cannot explain the motivation behind the Wolsey satires.

To return to the text of *Howe the Douty Duke*, however, the second reference to Surrey in that poem deserves rather more attention than the first, as it seems, from a superficial reading, to be precisely the sort of thing which one might expect to have littered the poet's works were he a Howard client, namely a poetic 'puff' for a Howard. 'On the[e] must nedes lyght', begins Skelton, addressing Albany and the Scots,

> That durst nat byde the sight
> Of my Lorde Amrell,
> Of chivalry the well,
> Of knighthode the floure
> In every marciall shoure,
> The noble Erle of Surrey,
> That put the in suche fray.
> Thou durst no felde derayne,

[51] Vergil, p. 265; *L.P.* II (i) 1959 (Talbot Papers, College of Arms A 39, cited in G. W. Bernard, *The Power of the Early Tudor Nobility: A Study of the Fourth and Fifth Earls of Shrewsbury* (Brighton, 1985), pp. 20–1); Edwards, pp. 170, 200–4; Pollet, *Poet of Tudor England*, pp. 81, 119; Scarisbrick, *Henry VIII*, p. 229.

> Nor no batayle mayntayne,
> Against our stronge captaine;
> But thou ran home agayne (235–46)

A careful reading of the text reveals, however, several qualifying factors which disqualify this passage as evidence of a patron–client relationship between the poet and the Earl. Once again the main thrust of the text, and of these lines, is not directed at the eulogising of Surrey's martial prowess but at the ridiculing of the Scots' cowardice.

From the manner in which praise is bestowed in the poem, it is evident that by no means is all of it directed at Surrey. It is another national victory which Skelton is portraying, and the poet again adopts a national perspective. Surrey is '*our* strong captaine', he is admired as a figure representative of the English character, and as the King's lieutenant, not as an individual. In a poem of 535 lines King Henry, who was not present at the siege, gains the lion's share of the praise, receiving in excess of one hundred lines of flattery from a pen 'insufficient . . . / His grace to magnify' (lines 401–2). Surrey, by contrast, gains merely nineteen. The only participant in the campaign actually to gain praise for his personal courage and martial ability is not Surrey but the Captain of the beleaguered garrison of Wark, Sir William Lisle, of whom Skelton observes,

> . . . Sir William Lyle
> Within shorte whyle,
> That valiaunt knyght,
> Putte you to flyght
> By his valyaunce. (38–42)

Thus this apparent paean of praise to Surrey is already critically flawed, as Skelton states that it was Lisle and not the Earl whose contribution to the victory was the most significant. His garrison had actually fought and defeated the invaders, whereas Surrey's subsequent arrival with the English army had merely frightened off the already halted enemy. Had Skelton been intent on constructing the poem as a vehicle for praise of Surrey, he would have presented the Earl in a somewhat more central role. As it is all one sees here is a lampoon of Albany for his cowardice when faced with the prospect of fighting Surrey's army, and a description of the Earl constructed of two stock aureate phrases (Surrey is the flower of knighthood and the well of chivalry). Those phrases are, moreover, an obvious recycling of the description of Surrey in *Why Come Ye Nat?*, in which he had been described as the flower of chivalry. Such uncritical use of cliché hardly suggests a concern on the poet's part to convey sincere praise of the Earl's character. If that had been the intention one would expect to find the flattering comparisons with classical and biblical heroes which Skelton uses elsewhere to convey praise, (in this same text, for example, Henry VIII is compared to no less than eight such 'worthies'). Again, the impression gained is hardly one of patron-worship. As chapter 6 will demonstrate the purpose behind the writing of *Howe the Douty Duke* can be determined by a close reading of the text, and transpires to have nothing to do with any admiration for Surrey on the part of the poet, and everything to do with the needs of English foreign policy. In writing the poem Skelton praised those individuals who were involved in the Scottish campaign: the actual combatant on the spot, the Commander of the royal army in the region, and the King in whose name the victory was won. He allotted praise to each in proportion to their respective national importance. There is no suggestion in the poem that the Earl was anything more than a hero of a national victory for which God and the King should be praised.

How then is one to treat the widely accepted notion of a Howard–Skelton connection after this review of the evidence?[52] Have we been too single-minded in our policy of applying rigorous doubt to each reference and to each text and, in the process of questioning individual details, ignored an overwhelming general picture greater than the sum of its parts? Or does it seem that there is indeed very little substance to sustain the 'Howard myth'? It may be that there is further evidence to be (re)discovered which will allow the development of a more convincing case by the Howard school. But, whilst all that their case rests on is a scattered handful of highly dubious coincidences and references wrenched from their context in the poems, the notion of Skelton as a Howard client, and more specifically of the Wolsey satires as being covertly commissioned by the Howards, must surely be regarded with the utmost suspicion.

But if the 'Howard myth' is indeed merely mythical, from where might it have originated? Only with H. L. R. Edwards' biography of the poet did the idea of Howard ties become important, and this may have been as much due to mistaken identity as any more concrete evidence. For Edwards and subsequent scholars may well have been misled by the peculiar mutations of the Skeltonic biography in the hands of sixteenth-century writers, and by the existence of another John Skelton, whose life and career curiously overlap those of the poet. This latter coincidence may well have given rise to some of the less than helpful assumptions made about the poet's political allegiance.

It is clear that even before his death Skelton's public reputation was diverging markedly from the private reality.[53] *The Hundred Merry Tales* of John

---

[52] The only dissenters from the Howard school consensus have simply questioned the duration of this period of patronage (William O. Harris, *Skelton's* Magnyfycence *and the Cardinal Virtue Tradition* (Chapel Hill, 1965), for example, has argued that it might only have begun after 1513–15. All critics accept that it was the Howards who prompted the satires against Wolsey.

[53] See Pollet, *Poet of Tudor England*, chap. 10.

Rastell, published in 1526, seem formally at least to have begun this process, although seemingly an aural tradition must have preceded this publication.[54] There Skelton is portrayed, in Tale LI, as a buffoon in the 'Scoggin' mould, a character of low comedy, ready with a jest or witticism to confound his superiors and amuse the multitude. This tradition of 'Merry Skelton', noted in the chronicler Edward Hall's description of the laureate as 'a mery Poet',[55] developed into the 1530s and beyond, through the, now lost, *Jests of Skelton* of *c*. 1530–2,[56] Thomas Bertelet's (?) publication of *Tales and Quick Answeres, Very Mery, and Pleasant to Rede* (*c*. 1535),[57] and the apocryphal *Merie Tales, Newly Imprinted & Made by Master Skelton Poet Laureat* of 1567,[58] until it formed the basis of all opinions of the poet until the last century.

Linked with this tradition was the development of another mythical Skelton: Skelton the proto-protestant. This tradition, which developed after his death, was based largely on a misreading of *Collyn Clout* and the other Wolsey satires as anti-Catholic invective, and on the assumption that the bawdy goings-on at Diss and Westminster described in the 'Merry Tales' tradition were real, and constituted a serious stand on the poet's part against the Church's strictures against clerical marriage. It is in this guise that Skelton is referred to as the author of the anti-clerical *Vox Populi, Vox Dei*, which is clearly a work of the Reformation,[59] and in which the poet attracted the attention of his earliest biographers.[60] To these traditions might be added the notion of Howard patronage, which seems also to have been based on coincidences and mistaken assumptions. For, just as it is possible to find the origins of these other myths, indications can be found of a possible source for the Howard connection. There is a fleeting reference in the work of the twentieth-century biographer Dr Ian Gordon, to the existence of a Sir John Skelton, of Shelton and Snoryng Magna in Norfolk (the county in which some scholars have attempted to locate Skelton's birthplace and family),[61] and a little research in the calendars of *Letters and Papers* gives rise to the suggestion that this John Skelton, rather than the Laureate Poet, was the source of the Skelton–Howard myth.

Sir John Skelton/Shelton conforms to all the assumptions made by biographers concerning his more famous namesake. He was clearly an adherent

[54] W. C. Hazlitt (ed.), *A Hundred Merry Tales: The Earliest English Jest-Book* (London, 1887).
[55] Edward Hall, *The Union of the Two Noble Families of Lancaster and York*, (ed.) Henry Ellis (London, 1809), p. 657.
[56] *L.P.*, V 923 (vii).
[57] *S.T.C.*, 23665, sigs A3v–A4. Printed in Dyce, I pp. lxxv–lxxvi.
[58] *S.T.C.*, 22618, sigs A–C8, D6. Printed in Dyce, I pp. lvii–lxxiii.
[59] Printed in Dyce, II pp. 400–13; and in F. J. Furnivall (ed.), *Ballads from Manuscripts* 2 vols. (London, 1868), I pp. 108–51.
[60] See Bale, *Scriptorum*, pp. 651–2.
[61] Gordon, *Poet Laureate*, p. 11.

of the Dukes of Norfolk and of sufficient standing in his locality to warrant an official invitation to Court on important state occasions.[62] Skelton the poet possessed neither of these qualifications after 1502 (except perhaps during a brief period around 1513). The existence of an exact namesake of the poet's at Court and in London,[63] at the same time as the Laureate (and hailing from the same county as the poet's benefice at Diss), who was firmly connected with Wolsey's apparent rivals the Howards, at precisely the time that the poet was launching his literary attack on the Cardinal, seems almost designed to cause confused conflations of their characters and histories in the minds of subsequent writers anxious to simplify and explain that remarkable outburst of invective. Indeed, an example of apparently just such a con-flation can be found in the *Merie Tales [of] . . . Skelton* of 1567. There, in Tale XII, the hero, Skelton, encounters a recalcitrant cobbler whilst he is rais-ing troops for the King's 'warres byyonde the sea' in his parish.[64] Now, this latter activity is a very peculiar responsibility to have devolved on John Skel-ton, the local parson (who was an absentee at Westminster during all Henry VIII's wars), but quite a natural one for the local sheriff, Sir John Shelton, who had, in 1513, raised and led twenty men to fight in the French War.[65] If the two individuals were being confused in 1567, within forty years of the poet's death, it is perhaps no surprise that later writers should fall into the same error and create from the *pot-pourri* of myths and traditions surround-ing the poet a Skelton who was a Howard client, who was of sufficient stand-ing in his own right to warrant a regular place at Court, and who could treat, almost on equal terms, with nobility and royalty alike.[66]

But if Skelton did not enjoy significant noble patronage, how did he manage to survive, and at times prosper, in a society of which it is usually observed that the patronage system was the only ladder to success? And more immediately how was it that the young student made that initial and crucial move from academic success at Oxford to Court service under Henry VII, if he was not carried along in the train of Thomas Howard I? H. L. R. Edwards was the first to note the suggestive correspondence between the poet's fortunes and the career of John Blythe, later bishop of Salisbury (from

---

[62] For Shelton's career in Crown service see, for example, *L.P.*, I (i), 20, 81; II (i), 703; (ii), 2288, 2020, 2662, 2737; IV (i), 133, 2002; (ii), 2672; V, 166 (12), 1694. See also the Sheriff's Rolls in P.R.O. *Lists and Indexes*, no. IX (London, 1895). For a fuller account of his career, see Walker, '"Baytyng"', chap. 1.

[63] The Royal Pardon Roll of 1509 lists Shelton's second residence as London. P.R.O. Supple-mentary Patent Rolls, C 67/52/2 f.31 (*L.P.*, I (i), 438).

[64] 'Howe the Cobler tolde Maister Skelton, it is a Good Sleeping in a Whole Skinne', printed in Dyce, I pp. lxv–lxvi.

[65] *L.P.*, I (i), 1176, 1453.

[66] Note Edwards, pp. 146–55 and *passim*, Pollet, *Poet of Tudor England*, p. 104 and *passim*, concerning Skelton's supposed familiarity with nobility and King alike, and *D.N.B.*'s remarkable assertion that 'many noble patrons remained faithful to him till the end'.

1494).[67] For Blythe was taking his MA at Oxford in 1480, and so may well have been lecturing, as the MA syllabus required, and moving in University circles at the time that Skelton was working towards his laureation. Thereafter Blythe became a King's Chaplain in 1488, just before Skelton was to arrive at Court, whilst, four years later, Blythe was Chancellor of Cambridge University where, either in that or the following year, Skelton was honoured with the grant of an honorary degree, thus making him Cambridge's only laureate. It would be tempting to think that it was Blythe, perhaps a former tutor to the poet, who aided Skelton's rise to royal service by pointing out a promising scholar to the King, or suggesting to the former that he might try his luck at Court, and subsequently using his influence at Cambridge to gain him the laureate degree.

This is of course the purest speculation, based on what could simply be coincidence. However, as Edwards notes, there exists one piece of documentary evidence which demonstrates that Blythe and Skelton were at least known to each other, and may well have been close acquaintances. For in the accounts of John Suckling, Master of Godshouse, Cambridge, there is reference to a meal provided two years after Skelton's second laureation, for both the new bishop of Sarum and the poet.[68]

ITEM: Tuesday, for dinner and supper with magistro Skelton, because he was with the Bishop of Sarum . . .vd

That Skelton was with Blythe on this occasion does not, of course, prove a close friendship, but the fact that the Bishop was prepared to impose the poet's company on the hospitality of a colleague suggests a relationship stronger than simply casual acquaintance. Edwards uses this information to claim a long friendship between Blythe and Skelton. That clearly overstates the case: the simple concern of a senior academic for a promising pupil's career might well be sufficient to account for their relationship. But whether one or neither of these explanations is correct, it is evident that the poet did not need to be the client of a noble house to gain his place at Court. Perhaps as the result of influence exerted by an academic acquaintance, perhaps simply as a result of his own academic reputation, at some time during 1488 or 1489 Skelton made his way to London, and to the Court of Henry VII. It will be the task of the following chapter to follow him there, to examine his career at Court and to consider how his success or failure in that environment may have stimulated the creation of the Wolsey satires.

---

[67] Edwards, p. 40.
[68] *University of Cambridge, Grace Book B*, (I), p. 92; printed in Edwards, p. 287.

The Court career of John Skelton, King's Orator

If Skelton cannot be seen as the direct spokesman for a politically influential family (and thus by implication for a whole section of the noble community which has variously been dubbed the conservative or traditionalist nobility[1]) then, it might be argued, the value of his satirical utterances as historical source material must be markedly reduced. The views of a powerful family, it might be felt, are of more consequence to the study of the politics of a period than those of an individual poet, no matter how influential that poet may have been. Thus it is perhaps unfortunate that the present chapter must, in some ways, continue the erosion of the traditional view of Skelton's social and political credibility. Having dispensed with the notion of Skelton the Howard-poet, it is now necessary to re-evaluate his role as a Court poet, in order to understand the background of the Wolsey poems; and to answer the question, if connections with noble backers did not give an extra significance to Skelton's opinions, could his own social position as a poet at Court and as a former tutor to Henry VIII provide him with an independent political insight which warrants our respect?

Inevitably, any attempt to tackle this problem, faces the block created by the lack of clear, undisputed evidence. The particular function which John Skelton performed at Court during his two prolonged stays in Westminster is not always easy to discern. Nor is it any simple task to decide on what precisely his status there might have been. From his own self-aggrandizing autobiographical comments within his poems, from his claims to be England's Adonis, her Catallus and her Homer, whose famous name should be echoed to the skies[2] and from his free use of the terms 'Poet Laureate' and, after 1512, '*Orator Regius*' the impression could easily be gained (and often has been gained[3]) that the poet was an extremely substantial figure on both the social and political stages. Was he not, one might be tempted to suggest, the

---

[1] See, for example, M. Pollet, *John Skelton, Poet of Tudor England*, trans. from the French by J. Warrington (Lewisberg, 1971) pp. 119–20; Edwards, pp. 200–8.

[2] *The Garlande*, Introduction and lines 519–32.

[3] See, for example, Edwards, p. 160; Nelson, p. 29; Pollet, *Poet of Tudor England*, pp. 104, 124.

official poetic mouthpiece of the Crown and the broadcaster of its opinions to the world; as it were, the King's Champion in the literary lists? As with most of the accepted Skeltonic biography however, as soon as the available evidence is examined closely, a number of serious objections begin to suggest themselves. In fact, just as the search for 'the Howard connection' yielded very little obvious evidence to support such a notion, so any analysis of the King's Orator's career seems to reveal surprisingly few occasions on which the King gave him leave to speak on his behalf. A brief consideration of Skelton's career at Court at this point might serve to indicate just when he could have made that significant contribution to Court culture which he so often cites as his claim to immortality.

As will become clear from what follows, the period from the early 1490s until 1502, the year of the death of Prince Arthur, was the high-watermark of Skelton's career. But even here it is evident that he did not enjoy anything approaching the monopoly of royal favour and recognised academic pre-eminence which the title 'King's Orator' might suggest.

When Henry Tudor won his crown in 1485 Skelton was not, it seems, at Court, but was still pursuing his academic career at Oxford. The major literary figure in the newly established Tudor Court was the blind French poet Bernard André (or Andreas). In 1486 André was granted an annual pension of ten marks 'in consideration of the increase in virtue and learning coming to many at Oxford and elsewhere from his teaching', a grant in which he was referred to as 'Poet Laureate'.[4] He is subsequently to be found referred to as 'Royal Historiographer'[5] and 'King's Poet',[6] and when, in 1496, it was necessary to appoint a supplementary tutor to assist in the education of Arthur, Prince of Wales, it was to André that the King turned. Thus, however significant Skelton's position at Court may have been during his most successful years, he has always to be considered in the context of a far brighter light; that of André's career.

Skelton was never publicly recognised as the single greatest poet and scholar at Court, whether in the 1490s, or later during the reign of Henry VIII, a failure which, it will be suggested, was of no small importance in the eventual genesis of the Wolsey poems. When Skelton arrived at Court, possibly as the result of John Blythe's influence, André was already there and enjoying a royal pension purely for his literary and scholarly merits, something which, it seems, the former was never to receive. When Skelton was made Laureate by his university, it was in the knowledge that André already held that honour, and when Skelton gained the high distinction of being ap-

[4] W. Campbell, *Materials for a History of the Reign of Henry VII*, (London, 1873–7) 1x (ii), p. 62. Cited in Nelson, p. 25. For André, see also G. Kipling, *The Triumph of Honour: Burgundian Origins of the Elizabethan Renaissance* (Leiden, 1977), pp. 16–20.

[5] Kipling, *Triumph of Honour*, pp. 19–20.

[6] *Hymni Christiani Bernadi Andreae* (Paris, 1512), introduction; cited in Nelson, p. 25.

pointed tutor to Prince Henry (*c*. 1498), he would have been fully aware that André had already held the highest tutorial appointment, that of schoolmaster to the heir apparent, for two years. Financially, too, André totally eclipsed Skelton's fortunes. For, whilst the latter can only definitely be seen to have received a single royal gift of twenty shillings on 11 November 1497 at his first mass,[7] and possibly to have received a further payment of £3 6s 8d on 3–4 December 1497 as 'my lady the Kinges moder poet',[8] André's earnings can be readily observed in contemporary records, amounting as they did to a £24 annual pension, in addition to a 100s payment each year after 1500 on the receipt of an annual chronicle commissioned by the Crown.[9] Whatever Skelton achieved from his first sojourn at Court, whether in terms of reputation or reward, he achieved whilst playing a distinctly second fiddle (or, more accurately, second lute) to André.

A fairly accurate estimate of when Skelton's Court career began can be gleaned from the subject matter of his extant poetry, and from the references to the titles of other, now lost, works to be found in *The Garlande*. For whilst only the other, foreign, Court poets celebrated political events and state occasions in 1486 and 1487,[10] Skelton was among those celebrating events in 1489. This, added to the fact that the poet's personal calendar, by which he dated many of his poems, has been shown to have begun in 1488,[11] clearly suggests that he began to write at Court in that year. Thereafter Skelton can be seen sporadically contributing writings on if not for Court occasions. He and André, and probably others, wrote an elegy on the death of the fourth Earl of Northumberland, and celebrated Prince Arthur's elevation to the title of Prince of Wales. When the Court poets were invited to retaliate in verse against the French emissary Robert Gaguin, who had penned some disparaging lines concerning England and her King, not only these two but also de Giglis, Carmeliano and Vitelli rose to the occasion.[12] The need was clearly

---

[7] P.R.O. E101/414–16; cited in Edwards, p. 288.

[8] P.R.O. E101/414–16; printed in Edwards, p. 288, although it is not certain that this designation, and therefore this payment, refer to Skelton.

[9] For a full account of records pertaining to André in the P.R.O., see Kipling, *Triumph of Honour*, p. 20.

[10] For an introduction to the personnel and work of the continental scholars working at Henry VII's Court, see Nelson, chap. 1, and Kipling, *Triumph of Honour*, 1. That circle included André, Pietro Carmeliano, Giovanni de Giglis, Polydore Vergil, Quentin Poulet, Giles Dewes and Cornelio Vitelli amongst others. In 1486–7 the coronation of Queen Elizabeth was celebrated, certainly by André, and probably by others. The birth of Prince Arthur called forth verses from André, Carmeliano and de Giglis, whilst de Giglis' own arrival in England as papal Legate, and Henry VII's victory over Lambert Simnal had also been lauded by André. There is no indicated of Skelton having written for a Court occasion in this year.

[11] Edwards, p. 193; H. L. R. Edwards and W. Nelson, 'The dating of Skelton's later poems', *P.M.L.A.*, 53 (1938), pp. 601–11, 611–14, 614–19, 620–2.

[12] Nelson, pp. 25–6; Edwards, pp. 43–4. See also the latter's 'Robert Gaguin and the English poets', *Modern Language Review*, 32 (1937), pp. 430–4.

for Court solidarity in the face of a foreigner's insult, and the fact that Skelton contributed to this retaliatory broadside is a good indication that he was a member of the Court circle by that time. However, it is perhaps an interesting indication of his position within that circle that we do not hear of his contribution either from his fellow poets or from the chroniclers, but merely from his own personal bibliography in *The Garlande*, which lists amongst his works, 'The Recule ageinst Gaguyne of the Frenshe nacyoun' (line 1187). This, as Edwards has asserted, seems clearly to refer to the incident of 1498 noted above. What his contemporaries thought of Skelton's contribution is not known. In his *History*, André himself notes the 'Gaguin incident', but makes no reference to Skelton's 'Recule', despite listing most of the other Court poets involved. 'Giovanni Gigli, of happy memory', André notes,[13]

a man most learned in things human and divine, made a witty satire and replied in the King's name to the orator . . . Pietro Carmeliano of Brescia, famous poet and orator and most worthy King's secretary, in a witty poem (which I cannot reproduce owing to his absence at this time) poured scorn to perfection on the sour French jester: to say nothing of the biting epigram of that most eloquent orator, Cornelio Vitelli . . . We ourselves being sealed of the poet's tribe, raved upon the fellow not (as they say) in a few lines, but in almost two hundred: truly there is nothing bolder than a bad poet! . . . Thus hooted and hissed at by these and many other like compositions, he departed in great rage.

The offering of John Skelton, Poet Laureate, was, it seems, just one of the crowd of 'many like compositions'. However, is this necessarily surprising? It must be remembered that Skelton was a native-born scholar (and a notably xenophobic one, if his later works are any indication) who was trying to establish himself in a poets' 'tribe' consisting entirely of foreign scholars, most of whom held significant papal offices and clerical appointments in this country. It would not be unreasonable to suggest that a newly arrived poet may have encountered some animosity from this 'closed shop' of continental *literati*, especially at a time when Burgundian and Italian letters were the vogue of Europe, and England was considered a cultural backwater.[14] Professional jealousy or elitism might then account for Skelton's omission from André's account, particularly as it seems to have been written not at the time, when a fresh-faced graduate might be ignored, but some years later when Skelton's reputation had increased and he would thus be more difficult to omit without a conscious determination so to do.

But, whether it was through intentional omission or lapse of memory that André did not mention Skelton's writing on this particular occasion, it is evident, in general, that Skelton's academic qualifications – his degree and his Laureate crown – need not have automatically set him apart from the schol-

[13] B. André, *Vita Henrici VII*, trans. in Edwards, 'Robert Gaguin', p. 431.
[14] Kipling, *Triumph of Honour*, p. 20.

arly crowd and guaranteed his eminence at Court in quite the way which one might imagine. For, as indicated above, André possessed the same title, albeit from a continental university, as did Carmeliano and the John Kay (or Caius) who translated *The Siege of Rhodes* into English in about 1483. The laurel crown was not a royal award, merely an academic qualification gained for conspicuous achievement in the fields of Latin and Rhetoric.[15] Thus, to be a Laureate did not guarantee any particular status at Court for, in Edwards' somewhat overstated assertion, 'the early Tudor Court was soon crowded with them'.[16]

By 1490 however, the first suggestion that Skelton had become a figure worth noting in literary circles emerges. For in that year, on 22 June, William Caxton, the printer, published a translation of the *Eneydos*, a French bastardisation of the *Aenead*, dedicated to Prince Arthur, and in his introduction he chose to beg for scholarly advice and correction, as tradition demanded, not from André or Carmeliano but from Skelton.[17]

I praye Mayster John Skelton, late created poete laureate in the Unyversite of Oxenforde, to oversee and correcte this sayd booke and t'addresse and expowne where as shalle be founde faulte to theym that shall requyre it. For hym I knowe for suffycyent to expowne and englysshe every dyffyculte that is therin, for he hath late translated the Epystlys of Tulle, and the Boke of Dyodorus Syculus and diverse other werkes oute of Latyn into Englysshe, not in rude and olde langage but in polysshed and ornate termes craftely, as he that hath redde Vyrgyle, Ovyde, Tullye and all the other noble poetes and oratours to me unknowen. And also he hath redde the ix muses and understande theyr musicalle sceyences and to whom of theym eche sceyence is appropred. I suppose he hath dronken of Elycon's well. Then I praye hym and suche other to correcte, adde or mynysshe where as he or they shall fynde faulte

Critics have made much of Caxton's apparent eulogy, and have claimed that it reveals that Skelton was 'the Finished Scholar', universally admired for his accomplishments, and even that he was a tutor at this time to Prince Arthur.[18] It is conceivable however, that this dedication is rather less effusive than it seems. Certainly parts of it seem to ring less than true. Is Caxton perhaps not entirely sure of what Skelton has written? He is on safe ground with Tully and the *Diodorus*, but does not the 'and diverse other werkes' suggest, in an age noted for its lengthy lists of authors read or translated, that the printer is merely covering up a gap in his knowledge? His list of the works which Skelton 'hath redde' would certainly confirm such suspicions, as, after he has rehearsed Virgil and Ovid, the set texts for every scholar in the land,

[15] Edwards, pp. 34–7.
[16] *Ibid.*, p. 37.
[17] W. Caxton, *The Boke of the Eneydos Compyled by Vyrgle*, W. T. Culley and F. J. Furnivall (eds.), E.E.T.S., Extra Series, 57 (1890), pp. 3–4.
[18] Edwards, p. 34; Ian A. Gordon, *John Skelton: Poet Laureate* (Melbourne and London, 1943) pp. 16–17; Pollet, *Poet of Tudor England*, pp. 21, 164.

he can only refer back once again to Tully with the admission that all else is unknown to him.

What this passage surely suggests is that, by 1490, Skelton had made a name for himself, in some quarters at least, as a translator and Latinist, and that his reputation as such was sufficient to merit reference, but he was not yet sufficiently well known for Caxton to be entirely familiar with his work. Thereafter Skelton continued to write verses for state occasions, most of which, like 'The Triumphs of the Red Rose' mentioned in *The Garlande* bibliography,[19] are now lost, and at some time around 1498 he was appointed tutor to Prince Henry, the second son of Henry VII. Clearly this appointment was a great honour and advancement for the poet and indicates that he was sufficiently highly thought of by the Crown, or more specifically by Margaret, countess of Richmond,[20] to be thus singled out. It may have been, as Edwards suggests, that it was a recognition of Skelton's innate piety that caused his selection, and led to his successive elevation through the minor clerical orders to the priesthood between March and June 1498.[21] More plausibly it was his reputation as a solid Latinist in the classic, medieval, aureate mould, coupled with the fact that he was one of the few able men of English birth without Italian and papal connections, which attracted the Crown's attention, particularly if it was the case, as Lord Herbert of Cherbury alleges, that Prince Henry was marked out from an early age as a future Archbishop of Canterbury.[22] But, plausible as such suggestions might be, the lack of evidence makes it impossible to advance any more than purely provisional statements about Skelton's elevation to the tutorship.

That Skelton was indeed tutor to Prince Henry for some years is made clear, not only by the poet's own claims to this effect (his famous remark that 'The honor of England I lernyd to spelle' being the most obvious[23]) but by no less a witness than Desiderus Erasmus. Erasmus, during a visit with his patron lord Mountjoy and Thomas More to the royal household at Eltham in 1499, was called upon to produce something in writing as a gift for the Prince. Thus commissioned he ran up a hasty eulogy which found time to praise not only the wondrous learning of the Prince, but also that of his schoolmaster. 'You have with you', the scholar observed, 'Skelton, that incomparable light and ornament of British Letters, who can not only kindle your studies but bring them to a happy conclusion.'[24]

Once again, this is not quite the sincere appreciation of Skelton's talents which one might imagine. As Edwards observes, Erasmus could read no

[19] *The Garlande*, lines 1223–5.
[20] Edwards, pp. 55–7.
[21] *Ibid.*, p. 57.
[22] Lord Herbert of Cherbury, *The life and Reigne of Henry VIII* (London, 1672), p. 12.
[23] *Agenst Garnesche*, v, lines 95–6.
[24] Preserved Smith, *Erasmus* (New York, 1923), p. 62; cited in Edwards, pp. 66–9.

English at this time and so could hardly be praising Skelton's 'British Letters' from first-hand knowledge. Indeed it is unlikely that the humanist was even familiar with Skelton's work or career, for in the surviving manuscript of the royal eulogy he has misspelt the poet's name.[25] His praise was merely an attempt to please and to win favour from the princely household; it consists of the sort of phrases which he was to apply to others, high and low, during his career, when in search of an avenue towards patronage. It is hardly a sincere appreciation of the poet–tutor's skills and ought not to be taken as an indication of an international reputation.

It has been suggested that Skelton must have been an active participant in the production of Court entertainments during his period as tutor to Prince Henry. There is, however, little evidence to support such an assertion. It is true that William Cornysh (who undoubtedly did write, design and perform such plays and pageants[26]) set at least one of Skelton's ballads to music,[27] and that the only surviving manuscript of the poet's *Diodorus Siculus* was copied out for Robert Pen, another Gentleman of the Chapel Royal,[28] but it is unwise to assume from this that Skelton was closely linked to the Chapel, still less to assume that he was a guiding light in its productions. Such thinking has done untold damage to our conception of Skelton as an historical figure. For contemporary evidence is eloquent in its silence about such a connection. It is surely wise to ask whether it is likely that a poet who had been a royal tutor could contribute material to pageants and plays for a total of three decades or more without anyone ever recording his name as a contributor, whether in the royal account books, in the ambassadorial correspondence, or in the accounts of the various chroniclers and writers such as Hall, Vergil, Fabyan and Cavendish, who so delighted in listing the very closest details of the pageants and disguisings which they witnessed. The likelihood shrinks even further when the poet in question was one who was otherwise so enthusiastic in proclaiming his authorship of everything which he wrote for public consumption.

Skelton's own testimony on this point is also revealing. For, in *The Garlande*, he provides a list of his works which refers to a number of apparently

25 Edwards, pp. 67–9. On 23 July 1519, when Erasmus drew up a list of the most notable English scholars, he cited 'such men as More, Linacre, Pace, Colet, Stokesly, Latimer, Tunstall and Clerk' as 'credit[s] to the Court of Henry VIII'. No mention was made of the erstwhile 'light and ornament'; *L.P.*, III (i) 394.

26 For Cornysh's career, see S. Anglo, 'William Cornish in a play, pageants, prison and politics', *Review of English Studies* (1959), pp. 347–60.

27 *Manerly Margery Mylk and Ale* appears in B.L. MS Additional 5465 (Fayrfax MS), fos. 96v–99r, as the lyric accompanying Cornysh's score.

28 Corpus Christi College Cambridge MS 357, printed in F. M. Salter and H. L. R. Edwards (eds.), *The Bibliotheca Historica of Diodorus Siculus translated by John Skelton*, E.E.T.S., Old Series, 233, 239 (1956–7). For the assertion that these references demonstrate a close link between Skelton and the Chapel, see N. C. Carpenter, 'Skelton's hand in William Cornish's musical parable', *Comparative Literature*, 22 (1970), pp. 157–72, and Edwards, p. 47.

dramatic pieces. *Magnyfycence* is the only text which survives, but the list also refers to other works seemingly designed for public performance. One finds, for example, reference to 'Vertu . . . the soverayne enterlude' (line 1177), to 'his Commedy, Achademios callyd by name' (line 1184), to *Magnyfycence* itself, called simply 'a notable mater' (line 1192), and to 'pajauntis that were played in Joyows Garde' (line 1383). Such a list provides a helpful indication of the extent of the poet's role as a 'courtly maker'. It is clear, for example, simply from its length, that Skelton's dramatic output cannot sustain the claims made by his biographers for a long association with Court entertainments. Four works cannot be stretched into a whole career, even before the most generous of audiences. The point is reinforced by Edwards' convincing assertion that the 'Commedy' *Achedemios* was probably written and performed during the poet's days at Oxford as part of his work towards the Laureate award,[29] and the likelihood that *Magnyfycence* and *Vertu* were designed for performance in merchants' halls.[30] This leaves merely the reference to the 'pajauntis' played in 'Joyows Garde' which, from internal evidence, seems to suggest that the poet played a minor role in the celebrations surrounding the marriage of Prince Arthur and Catherine of Aragon in 1501.[31] Beyond this possibility there is nothing to link Skelton with Tudor Court festivities and ceremonies during the reign of Henry VII.[32]

Indeed, the wider picture of the poet's life at Court during the reign of Henry Tudor is one of extremely limited royal support and preferment. After the gift given by the King at Skelton's first mass,[33] it seems that the royal tutor was entirely overlooked by his sovereign for advancement or reward. Perhaps symbolically, even the records of his tutorial wages are now lost. Indeed, he was eventually to be unceremoniously dropped from the royal household in 1502, as soon as the death of Prince Arthur made it clear that his princely charge was to be the new heir apparent.

For all that might be suggested to the contrary,[34] the loss of the royal tutorship, and the subsequent move to the rectory at Diss in Norfolk were clearly a dramatic demotion for the poet and stand as evidence of a significant loss of favour. That he was to be offered no replacement household or Court office must have come as a bitter blow, and Skelton, being in his forties, may well have feared that his career was effectively over. That he was to describe himself, when at Diss, as 'a man utterly doomed to oblivion and, so to say, dead in his heart', and refer to himself, alluding to Ovid's exile, as biding his time beside Eurotas, gives the lie to the claim that he would not have been

[29] Edwards, p. 36.
[30] See P. Neuss (ed.), *Magnificence* (Manchester, 1980), pp. 42–5.
[31] For a detailed discussion of this case, see G. Walker, '"Baytyng"', pp. 98–103.
[32] For a fuller account of Court events in this period, see Walker, '"Baytyng"', chap. 2.
[33] P.R.O. E 101/414/16; cited in Edwards, p. 288.
[34] See, for example, Edwards, p. 78.

unduly disappointed by his move to Diss. This is particularly obvious when one notes that these comments were made in a petition sent to the newly crowned Henry VIII, in an attempt by the poet to gain a swift recall to Court on the death of Henry VII. Moreover it was the Countess of Richmond who arranged for Skelton's presentation to the living at Diss, not the King.[35] Thus this solitary, distant, prebend may actually have been offered in an attempt to rescue the poet from complete unemployment. There is no evidence to suggest that Skelton was actually resident in Diss until 4 April 1504, almost two years to the day after he was paid off with a 40s 'golden handshake' from the Crown.[36] Whether the poet had to wait for two years before the Countess took pity on him, or whether he stayed on in London after receiving the benefice in the vain hope of gaining some more prestigious reward is in doubt. Whichever is the case, the incident is a clear reflection of the status at Court of the erstwhile light and ornament of British Letters.

Thus ended Skelton's first 'coming to Court' on a distinctly dying fall, with the unrecorded retreat to a modest Norfolk rectory. During his stay in the capital he had enjoyed some success, but, significantly, this was due to his Latin and Greek scholarship rather than his poetry. Whilst at Court Skelton was a tutor rather than a poet, and although he produced some poetry his attention was concentrated on the education of his royal pupil. He was not, then, a Poet Laureate in anything approaching the modern sense of the term. What poetry he wrote, he produced as a side-line to his duties, not, as some critics have suggested, as a commissioned poet, kept at Court on an indefinite royal stipend, free to write on whatever topic suited either his sovereign or him. If there was a true 'King's Orator' at the Court of Henry VII, that man was Bernard André, not John Skelton.

It was, however, during Skelton's second period at Westminster, that which began *c.* 1512, that his claim to the title of *Orator Regius* was first advanced. So is it possible that his return involved a marked improvement in his status and fortunes? It must be noted that during his absence the poet had not been entirely forgotten in London. His *Phyllyp Sparowe*, written in Diss, gained sufficient notoriety for Barclay to refer to it, albeit disparagingly, in his *Shyp of Folys*, published in 1509,[37] whilst *The Great Chronicle of London* referred, perhaps rather idiosyncratically, to Skelton, Thomas More and William Cornysh as 'poettes . . . of fame' for their satiric wit.[38] Furthermore, around 1513 the poet was honoured by the Benedictine monk Henry Bradshaw of Chester who, in his *Life of Saynt Werburge*, referred to 'inven-

[35] *Ibid.*, p. 78.
[36] *Ibid.*, p. 78.
[37] Alexander Barclay, *The Shyp of Folys*, S.T.C. 3545 (1509) fo. cclxxii, and T. H. Jamieson (ed.), *The Shyp of Folys*, 2 vols. (Edinburgh, 1874), II p. 331.
[38] A. H. Thomas and I. D. Thornley (eds.), *The Great Chronicle of London* (London, 1938), p. 361

tive Skelton and poet laureate' among those poets, both ancient and modern, of whom he asked pardon in the prologue to his work.[39] Bradshaw, at least, seems to have been particularly impressed with Skelton's erudition, for in his later *Life of Saynt Radegunde* he again cited the poet as one of those writers to whose talents he could not aspire, this time referring to him, with Chaucer, as 'fathers of eloquens'.[40] But despite such complimentary references Skelton's second stay in Westminster brought him rather less in terms of reward from the Crown and recognition from the literary community under Henry VIII than he had enjoyed in the reign of Henry's father.

The most obviously striking fact about Skelton's second period at Westminster is the length of time that it took for him simply to regain a place in or around the Court. As soon as it had become known that Henry Tudor was dead, he had written and despatched a verse tribute, his *A Lawde and Prayse Made for Our Sovereigne Lord the Kyng*, to the new King. And when this failed to gain him an immediate summons to Court from his old pupil, he despatched as a birthday gift in 1511, a copy of his *Speculum Principis*, the guide to princely behaviour he had written for his young charge around 1500, as a jog to the royal memory of past services rendered. In case there should be any doubt as to the message which this gift was intended to impart, the poet added a new *Palinode* and *Soliloquy* to make the matter unmistakably clear. In these, having described himself as 'a man wholly given over to oblivion', he proceeds to complain that he is one upon whom 'neither the King's munificence nor Fortune's blessing has so far designed to smile more richly'.[41] The text is an obvious lament and complaint that Skelton has not received the rewards which he deserved; it is an almost insolent hint that he felt that it was time that the situation was changed. It is perhaps the sort of ironic supplication which only an old schoolmaster writing to a former pupil could attempt without risking some unpleasant reaction. How should he account for his lack of favour, he asks.

Shall I impute it to the gods, angered with me perchance? Let me not commit so great a folly. But shall I then impute to so mighty and generous a king the conspicuous blemish of inadequate liberality? From such a thought may that God preserve us who, best and greatest, weighs all with the most scrupulous justice in the scale of his inexhaustible liberality, and likewise dispenseth all things with a lavish hand.

Given the character and reputation which Henry VIII was to acquire over the succeeding decades, this 'supplication' reads as a quite remarkable document, coming as it does from the rector of a country parish to his sovereign.

---

[39] Henry Bradshaw, *The Holy Lyfe and History of Saynt Werburge*, ed., C. Horstman E.E.T.S., 88 (London, 1887), p. 199.

[40] Henry Bradshaw, *The Lyfe of Saynt Radegunde*, ed., F. Brittain (Cambridge, 1926), p. 37.

[41] B.L. Addit. MS 26787 fos. 26v–30v, printed in F. M. Salter, 'Skelton's *Speculum Principis*, *Speculum*', 9 (1934), pp. 25–37.

Skelton, however, with his mixture of personal bluntness and almost manic professional self-confidence, clearly felt that his relationship with his king was a special one. In *A Lawde and Prayse* his confidence that 'the foxis chare / The wolvis, the beris' that had troubled the realm 'shall wirry no mo' was an indication that the poet felt that better days were coming now that Henry had succeeded and that 'the yeris of grace / And welthe ar come agayne, / That maketh England faire'.[42] Certainly in 1511 he still felt that the promise remained of his own personal restoration to fame.

For all his apparent confidence, however, the expected summons did not arrive, and soon another literary offering had to make its way to Court. Again it was a schoolroom favourite rededicated to the new King; this time the *Chronique de Rains*, a French version of the life of Richard I and an account of his battles against the Saracens, with hostile marginal comments provided by the Poet Laureate directed against the French author and his nation.[43] It was only after the arrival of this further work at Court, in 1512, that the poet seems to have gained his recall. For it is at approximately this point that the first mention is made of the *Orator Regius* tag, in the short poem *Calliope*. Possibly the King had been swayed by nostalgia to recall his old tutor. What is perhaps more likely is that the swaying of the Crown's foreign policy towards a strongly anti-French stance brought with it the possibility that Skelton could be useful at Court once more. For, if there was to be war with France, the strongly Francophobic poet might prove a useful propagandist for the cause, as indeed he did in 1513. As the reference in the *Great Chronicle* reveals, he was known and respected in the City as a satirist,[44] thus his pen was a useful weapon to employ, particularly given that, as Henry would know, the poet had little sympathy with the somewhat ambivalent attitude towards war adopted by some of the humanists. Indeed Skelton was careful to emphasise that very point in his dedication attached to the *Chronique*, which reiterated his own desire for a recall to Court, and clearly suggested his enthusiasm for an aggressive foreign policy.[45]

Go, my book, in haste: prostrate yourself before the King and commend me to him, his humble poet Skelton. Above all, recount to His Majesty the famous battles waged by England's greatest hero, Richard, first of our race . . .

Whatever the reason for which the summons came, it seems to have come in 1512. Thereafter Skelton was at Westminster, sporting the title of 'King's Orator', wearing green and white livery with the name of Calliope, the Muse

---

[42] *A Lawde and Prayse*, lines 22–3, 40–2.
[43] Corpus Christi College, Cambridge, MS 432 fos. 4, 7, 13v; cited in Edwards, p. 310, trans. pp. 131–2.
[44] This was probably as a result of the publication of *The Bowge*, and perhaps the circulation of the Diss manuscripts.
[45] Trans. Edwards, pp. 131–2.

of Epic Poetry, embroidered on the back, and providing Latin verses for Abbot Islip of Westminster which were to be hung in the newly constructed Henry VII chapel.[46] A brief flirtation with royal favour followed, and brought with it a period of almost frantic activity.

It may have been, as Pollet and Nelson suggest, that Skelton actually accompanied the royal army to France, along with the scholars Ammonio and Carmeliano, and the King's minstrels and players.[47] But, whether he followed the King or remained at Court, the xenophobic poet was in his element during the war. As has been described, he produced a series of verses to celebrate the various victories, major and minor, of the Scots and French campaigns: a *Chorus de Dys Contra Gallos*, followed by a *Chorus de Dys Contra Scottos*, two Latin hymns of triumph, and in the vernacular, first the brief *A Ballade of the Scottysshe Kynge*, then the fuller, better informed narrative entitled *Agaynst the Scottes*. Yet the signs are that Skelton's period of favour was over almost as soon as it had begun. In 1512, in *Calliope*, he had boasted of his Tudor livery with its golden embroidery,[48] but by late 1513 it seems that those who had before merely questioned his flamboyant reappearance at Court (he had written *Calliope*, he stated, to answer the question 'Why were ye Calliope, enbrawdred with letters of golde?'), were now openly critical of his verses. He felt it necessary to add a postscript to *Against the Scottes* to justify his invective to

> . . . Dyvers People That Remord This Rymyng
> Agaynst the Scot Jemmy

And from this point onwards a number of critical attacks seem to have been aimed at him.[49] It seems clear that he had upset Court sensibilities with his vicious lines against a dead monarch who was, after all, Henry's brother-in-law.[50] It may also have been that the poet had overstepped the mark in his keenness to publish the *Ballade*, and had irritated his rivals with his ostentatious self-publicity. Certainly after *Agaynst the Scottes* Skelton no longer occupied the

---

[46] These verses were his *Eulogy Upon His Own Times*, and elegies for Henry VII and the Countess of Richmond.

[47] Pollet, *Poet of Tudor England*, pp. 68–9; Nelson, pp. 125–7.

[48] This livery may have been granted by Letters Patent in the same year, but the reference to the, now lost, document by Abbe De Resnil (cited Dyce, I p. xv) is doubtful.

[49] See Alexander Barclay's vicious lines against the 'rascolde' Poets Laureate in green garb, who attempt to instruct princes and 'Which voyde of wisedome presumeth to indite, / Though they have scantly the cunning of a snite', which is clearly aimed at Skelton. B. White (ed.), *The Eclogues of Alexander Barclay*, E.E.T.S., 175 (1928), *Eclogues, Prologue*, lines 100–114; and *Eclogue IV*, lines 664–693.

[50] Queen Catherine herself fell foul of this feeling when she proposed to send the corpse of the dead king to Henry as a grisly token of the English victory. 'I thought to sende himself to you', she informed Henry, 'but our Englyshemens herts wold not suffre it. [They thought] it shuld have been better for hym to have been in peax than have this reward.' B. L. Cotton MS Vespasian F III, fo. 15.

limelight, and his career seems to have suffered another decline in material terms.

It seems that while the Crown thought that the poet's antagonistic muse might prove useful Skelton could find an audience for his invectives, and commissions for more reflective pieces, such as the elegies for Henry Tudor and lady Margaret hung in the Henry VII Chapel, Westminster, at the request of Abbot Islip. But once the King's mind, and public policy, moved on to other things, Skelton was forgotten and left to fend for himself, with only his income from Diss, less the wages paid to his deputy, who is known to have been in residence by 1515 at the latest,[51] to support him. With no immediate call for his talent for invective once peace with the former enemies was concluded, Skelton's fortunes were to fall significantly, as a brief examination of events during the next decade will reveal.

It is curiously symbolic of the poet's fortunes that, in 1514, whilst the Epiphany entertainments were graced by the anonymous play *Beauty and Venus*, Skelton was called on 'By the kynges most noble commaundment' to enter into a comic mock-duel in verse, or *flytyng*, with one of Henry's Gentlemen Ushers, Sir Christopher Garnesh. Whilst the major Court commissions were passing elsewhere, the 'King's Orator' was being called on to enter into an undignified bout of name-calling with a Court officer. The inspiration for this event was the Scots *flytyng*, between the poets Dunbar and Kennedy, the results of which were published in 1508. But, unlike that affair, the English Laureate was not vying here with a rival poet for any recognition of superiority, but merely wasting his pyrotechnic invective on a courtier with no proven academic or literary ability. It may even have been that Garnesh had to rely on a 'ghostwriter' for his part of the duel.[52] Although Garnesh's contribution to the contest no longer survives, it seems clear from Skelton's verses that there could only have been one winner. How could any opponent have matched the exuberant, vitriolic prolixity of such passages as the following?

> Now Garnyche, garde thy gummys;
> My serpentens and my gunnys
> Agenst ye now I bynde;
> Thy selfe therfore defende.
> Thou tode, thow scorpyon,
> Thow bawdy babyone,
> Thow bere, thow brystlyd bore,
> Thou Moryshe mantycore,
> Thou rammysche, stynkyng gote,
> Thou fowle, chorlyshe parote,
> Thou gresly gargone glaymy,
> Thou swety sloven seymy,

---

[51] Norfolk Archdeaconry Register, 1523, fo. 220; printed in Edwards, p. 292.
[52] Note lines 90–4 which refer to 'thy scryb[e]' and see Edwards, pp. 152–3 for the suggestion that Garnesh's second was Stephen Hawes.

> Thou murrioun, thow mawment,
> Thou fals, stynkyng serpent,
> Thou mokkyshe marmoset,
> I will nat dy in thy det. (iii, 158–73)

That Skelton threw his considerable talent earnestly into the endeavour cannot, however, disguise the essential triviality of the contest, and thus what it reveals about the opinion held of Skelton by the King at whose 'commaundment' it was instigated. When the opportunity arose to be diverted by some boisterous entertainment, it seems that Henry and the Court would find the time to listen to something in the style of *Agenst Garnesche* from Skelton. But when refinement or cultured tones were called for, as was the case with the allegorical Epiphany or Christmas revels, or with those pageants, disguisings and plays performed to honour a significant diplomatic or national occasion, then it seems that the royal eye would fall elsewhere. By 1512 Skelton's aureate, scholarly style was seemingly overlooked and his public image was that of the caricatured 'merry' satirist. Thus 'England's Homer' was never offered the chance to show a royal audience what he could do with the dramatic form, and *Magnyfycence*, his masterpiece in that genre, was probably performed in a merchants' hall, whilst lesser works represented English Court culture to the assembled ambassadors of Europe.

As time passed the same names reappeared in the records of Court entertainments. The Epiphany revels of 1516 were the occasion for the play *Troylus and Pandar*, performed, and probably written, by William Cornysh, accompanied by the children of the Chapel, whilst the Christmas revels of that year featured Henry Medwall's *Of the Finding of Truth*. The following Epiphany it was Cornysh once more who provided the entertainment, a service which he seems to have repeated at the festivities held to mark the signing of the Treaty of London, in 1518. It was a 'goodly Comedy of Plautus' which the King requested for his amusement in March 1519, but Skelton, despite his earlier fame for Latin translation, was not called on to provide it. It is, however, to the following three years, the very period which was to produce his bitterest and most significant political verses, to which one must look to see the most obvious examples of Skelton's exclusion from the mainstream of Court patronage.

The honour and prestige to be gained from an involvement in the sumptuous diplomatic festival of 1520 that has become known as the 'Field of Cloth of Gold' must have been obvious, even to a Francophobe such as Skelton. It was to be the most remarkable public display of English ceremonial and spectacular culture in a reign noted for such events, and with so magnificent an audience in prospect and so generous a budget to tempt them, the competition among the artists, scholars and craftsmen to gain a commission for the project must have been keen indeed.[53] One might imagine, therefore, the feelings of the *Orator Regius* when he saw his former pupil and nominal patron prefer, as a deviser of 'Histories and convenient raisons' to adorn the English pavilions, not 'England's Homer' but,[54]

Maister Mayn who dwelleth with the bushope of Excester, and maistre Barkleye the blacke monke and poete.

For Skelton to have been overlooked would probably have seemed to him a betrayal, particularly if he had indeed accompanied the Court on its last triumphant French jaunts, but to have been overlooked in favour of Barclay, his sternest and bitterest critic, must have been almost intolerable.

Worse, however, was to follow. As the Crown's foreign policy began to revert once more to an anti-French stance, Skelton may have hoped to see his fortunes rise once more, as they had in 1512–13. This was not to be. It was Stephen Hawes who was to receive £6 13s 6d 'for his play' in January 1521,[55] and it was John Rastell, the humanist, and his fellow 'Greek' William Lily (significantly the author of the infamous jibe against the Laureate, 'Skelton thou art / Let all men know it, / Neither learned, / Nor a poet'[56]), who were commissioned to devise verses to accompany the pageants which greeted Charles V on his visit to London during March 1522. Similarly it was to Cornysh, not Skelton, that the chance fell to write the anti-French play to be performed before the imperial party at Westminster during the succeeding June.[57]

It is a fact of no little significance for any study of the outburst of satires against Wolsey which the poet created in 1521–2 that there is no evidence to suggest that Skelton received any royal commissions for the entire seven-year period from the completion of *Agenst Garnesche* to the emergence of *Speke, Parott*. Thus, not only was the poet without support from any noble source in 1521, and isolated from the influential sections of the scholarly world, especially after his involvement in the, so called, Grammarians War of 1518–21, in which he opposed the ultimately successful humanists,[58] but the prospect of royal favour which had seemed so promising in 1509 had proved to be an equally barren hope.

Thus it is extremely misleading to assume that Skelton's titles of *Orator Regius* and Poet Laureate imply an exalted position at Court. In the past, all

---

[53] J. G. Russell, *The Field of Cloth of Gold: Men and Manners in 1520* (London, 1969), pp. 22–47 and *passim*.
[54] B.L. Cotton MS Caligula D VII fo. 202 (*L.P.* III (i) 737).
[55] *D.N.B.*, Hawes, Stephen.
[56] '*Et doctus fieri studes poeta, / Doctrinam nec habes, nec es poeta.*' The translation is Fuller's (cited Dyce, I p. xxxviii).
[57] Anglo, 'William Cornish', pp. 357–60.
[58] See chap. 3 below.

manner of claims have been made for Skelton's status at Court, and these have influenced the manner in which the poems written against Wolsey have been regarded. Skelton was not, contrary to traditional assumptions, a close confidant of Henry VIII, fulfilling some hybrid role of poet, minstrel, teacher and counsellor.[59] Neither was he a substantial figure at Court, capable of observing and criticising Wolsey at close quarters. Only during a brief period during the heady days of 1512–13 did the poet carry anything resembling a franchise to speak for the Crown, and then only on the specific issue of the war with France and Scotland, and even here that franchise was no monopoly, for others, including the King's Latin secretary, Ammonius, are known to have written their own propaganda pieces.

This, then, seems to have been the limit of Skelton's appointment (if appointment it was) as *Orator Regius*; a limited commission to provide propaganda for the war. Thereafter the title has a hollow ring to it, and the poet's continued reference to it says more for his own desire for fame than for any continued Crown patronage. This much is evident from the references to the poet in the work of other writers after 1513. Barclay, Whittington, Hall, Lily and Bradshaw all refer to Skelton, the first two named even refer to his title of Poet Laureate, but none so much as mention the *Orator Regius* tag. This clearly suggests that its significance was more personal than public after 1513. Thereafter the story of the poet's first period at Court, the story of a loss of favour and increasingly obvious royal indifference, repeats itself. As *Orator Regius* he was indeed a champion without a cause: a King's Orator with nothing to say.

The ambiguities and apparent contradictions which suggest themselves in any study of Skelton's historical and literary reputation seem thus to reflect a genuine ambiguity which surrounded, indeed dogged him during his lifetime. It is certainly difficult for the modern reader to reconcile the irreverent rogue of the *Merrie Tales*, who 'dyd shite upon the freer' who would not vacate the poet's bed,[60] with that 'incomparable light and ornament of British Letters' chosen by the pious lady Margaret of Richmond to educate her grandson. But it is evident that this same difficulty confronted his contemporaries. At Court, after 1504, it seems that he was, by and large, known as the author of coarse invective and ribald comic verse. He was attacked for poor taste over his vicious lampoon of the dead Scots King after Flodden, and for his apparent satire of the Mass for the Dead in *Phyllyp Sparowe*, and this reputation for sharp satire seems to have stuck to him. Hence the references, from the more generous commentators such as Hall and Fabyan,

---

[59] For such views of Skelton's role at Court, see Pollet, *Poet of Tudor England*, p. 125; Gordon, *Poet Laureate*, p. 29; and Edwards, p. 160 and *passim*.

[60] *Merie Tales*, IX, 'How Skelton Handled the fryer that woulde needes lye with him in his inne'; printed in Dyce, I pp. lxiii–iv.

to him as a 'merie poet' and a satirist of fame, and also the less charitable descriptions of the 'rascolde', wanton graduate of 'stinking Thais'. There were those academics who, like Bradshaw and Whittington, appreciated his traditionalist erudition, his learning and his fierce if idiosyncratic piety, but for each voice that was prepared to speak up for his talent there was always it seems another, closer to the Court, a Lily or Barclay, prepared to dismiss his talents.[61] Whether this sprang from a general contempt for his peculiarly rebarbative character and genius, from the concerted hostility of an influential literary clique, or simply from the estrangement from the New Learning of an old man with more grandiose ideas than substantial achievements to his name is unprovable. Whatever caused Skelton's lack of favour, it is clear that one cannot avoid its implications when one comes to consider the Wolsey poems.

In the past two chapters the traditional picture of the Skelton who began to write *Speke, Parott* has been radically revised, to replace the model of a well-to-do, highly respected Court poet, a confidant of kings and noblemen, and a man with a close knowledge of the innermost decisions of high politics, with that of a freelance poet and scholar who had enjoyed the peak of his career in the 1490s and who never, despite his best efforts, recovered that lost vestige of greatness, and who, but for the resurgence of his fortunes during 1512–13, was on the fringes of Court life. To call him a Court poet, except for brief periods during the 1490s and 1512–13 is thus misleading. Skelton was not a regular contributor to Court events, nor a fixture in the social life of the Court; there is no indication, for example, that he enjoyed '*Bowge* of Court' himself after his dismissal from the tutorship. He was rather a Westminster or London poet, than a Court poet. He lived at Westminster on his comfortable but by no means grand income from Diss and gained much of what reputation he enjoyed from City chroniclers. There is nothing to suggest that he followed the Court on progress when it left the capital. The main part of his work seems also to have been designed for London or Westminster audiences. *Magnyfycence*, as has been noted, was most probably performed in a merchants' hall, and even his elegies for Henry VII and lady Margaret were commissioned by the Abbot of Westminster, not the Crown. And, as the following chapters will reveal, the insights demonstrated in many of his works, and particularly the poems against Wolsey, are very much those of a Londoner rather than a regular courtier.

Clearly this revision of our view of Skelton has important implications for our understanding of the Wolsey poems. If Skelton neither spoke for a noble

---

[61] The literary world had its own factions and not simply such divisions as 'Greek' against 'Trojan', New against Old learning. For Barclay was as traditional in his ideas as Skelton, but probably despised him more than anyone.

faction, nor was cognisant of decisions of policy made in Court and Council, then his political statements in the poems are far less privileged than has usually been thought. Similarly, the motivation behind the writings must be open to reinterpretation as those factors which have hitherto been seen as prompting them; the influence of the Howards and the insights into the effects of Wolsey's policies provided by an intimacy with the sovereign can no longer be accepted. Indeed, would Skelton have been tempted to launch his literary assault on the Cardinal at all had he enjoyed that patronage of the Crown or influencial noblemen which has previously been supposed? It is this question, amongst others, that shall now be considered.

❦ *3* ❧

'Speke, Parott' and 'Why Come Ye Nat To Courte?': the context and evolution of a satiric stance

'SPEKE, PAROTT', THE MAIN TEXT

In the previous chapter it was suggested that, contrary to the traditional view, it was not as a result of Skelton's patronage that the Wolsey-satires came to be written but as a result of his lack of patronage. The man who began to compose *Speke, Parott* in September 1521 was neither the tool of a powerful noble faction, nor the elected mouthpiece of a disaffected Court intelligentsia; he was a struggling academic and poet who was far from well placed. He probably had not had a work published since 1513 and was in heated dispute with the humanists who dominated the scholarly establishment. He was thus in need both of patronage and of recognition, and had seemingly tried many methods of courting both. He had turned his hand to Morality Drama with *Magnyfycence*, but apparently gained little appreciation for it. And he had tried ribald verses like *Elynour Rummynge*, but these had seemingly succeeded only in endorsing the poor opinion which his critics held of him. To another poet such reverses might have been merely minor frustrations, but to Skelton they were clearly serious and somehow almost incomprehensible threats to his professional pride. For he is perhaps unique amongst poets in the depth of his concern for his own status and reputation. It is not simply that, like Chaucer, he sought to explore and advance the role of the Poet in society, but that he consciously strove to justify himself to an audience and to achieve a universal recognition of his own excellence in that role. Throughout his career one witnesses his conscious efforts not only to become a great poet, but to be seen and appreciated as one in his own life-time. Hence the number of his poems which were written 'against' another individual, or constructed as defences against, and refutations of, criticisms of his work. A brief consideration of such works will serve to illustrate the point.

As early as 1495–7 Skelton's tendency for literary self-defence had become evident when *Agaynste a Comely Coystrowne*, and its accompanying Latin stanzas *Contra alium Cantirantem et Organisantum asinum*, had been com-

53

posed 'against another singer and doltish musician who criticised the muse-like Skelton'.[1] *Ware the Hauke*, written in Diss *c.* 1505, contained similar declarations of the poet's own pre-eminent worth, in addition to obser-vations concerning the role of the Poet-Satirist in society. There it is observed that,[2]

An ancient privilege is given to pious poets, that of saying what they wish in a way which will delight, either whatever is effective in defending just causes, or whatever is necessary for stinging obtuse wantons.

That Skelton felt himself more than worthy of this privilege is indicated by a series of cryptically encoded lines in the body of the poem which can be re-solved to read,[3]

> Just like the phoenix of Arabia,
> A bird not like any other,
> The land of Britain has produced
> Its own poet Skelton.

Skelton's self-confidence and self-assertiveness seemingly knew few bounds, as is made clear by the series of poems devised immediately before and fol-lowing his second 'coming to Court' *c.* 1512. He had despatched his *A Lawde and Prayse* to Henry in 1509 subscribed 'by me, Laureate poet of the Britons'. And, once recalled, he had immediately proclaimed himself a favourite of the Muses by having the name 'Calliope' embroidered on his Tudor livery, an action which he subsequently justified with the claim that he was indeed enrolled of the Muse's household, as she had given him,[4]

> The high degre
> Laureate to be
> of fame royall.

Once under criticism Skelton defended himself in an even more assertive manner, as is evident from his aggressive envoy to *Agaynst the Scottes*, and the *flytyng*, *Agenst Garnesche*. In the latter work his lack of patience with the jibes of lesser men is fully revealed. 'How may I your mokery mekely tol-lerate(?)' (ii, line 1), he asks, in the second round of verses, subscribed with the retort to the 'mere' Gentleman Usher, 'Loke nat to[o] hy' (ii, line 44). In the third round his defence is more explicit and illuminating. 'I am laureat, I am no lorell' (iii, line 14), he observes,

> Lytyll wyt in your scrybys nolle
> That scrybblyd your fonde scrolle,

[1] Translated in Scattergood, p. 392.
[2] 'Epilogue' to *Ware the Hauke*, trans. in *ibid.*, p. 405.
[3] *Ware the Hauke*, lines 239–42, trans. in *ibid.*, p. 404.
[4] *Calliope*, lines 6–8. The subscription to *A Lawde and Prayse* is translated in Scattergood, p. 420.

Upon hym for to take
Agennst me for to make,
Lyke a doctor dawpate,
A lauryate poyet for to rate.
Yower termys ar to grose,
To far from the porpose,
To contaminate
And to violate
The dygnyte lauryate. (iii, 90–100)

The fifth text of the contest elicits further elaboration.

What eylythe the, rebawde, on me to rave?
A Kynge to me myn habyte gave
At Oxforth, the universyte,
Avaunsid I was to that degre;
By hole consent of theyr senate,
I was made poete lawreate.
To call me lorell ye are to lewde
Lythe and lystyn, all bechrewde!
Of the Musys nyne, Calliope
Hath pointyd me to rayle on the.
It semyth nat thy pyllyd pate
Agenst a poyet lawreat
To take upon the for to scryve;
It cumys the better for to dryve
A dong cart or a tumrell
Than with my poems for to melle.

The honor of England I lernyd to spelle,
In dygnyte roiall that doth excelle.
Note and mark wyl thys parcele;
I yave hym drynke of the sugryd welle
Of Eliconys waters crystallyne,
Aqueintyng hym with the Musys nyne.
Yt commyth the wele me to remorde,
That creaunser was to thy sofreyne lorde;
It plesyth that noble prince roiall
Me as hys master for to calle
In hys lernyng primordiall.
Avaunt, rybawde, thi tung reclame! (v, 79–106)

It ys for no bawdy knave
The dignite lawreat for to have. (v, 114–15)

It is clear that Skelton felt himself to be deserving of respect and acclaim above the common lot for a number of reasons. Chief amongst these was his academic and literary merit, symbolised by his laureate crown, which not only indicated the esteem owed to him by the highest circles of academia ('At Oxforth the universyte, / Avaunsid I was to that degre: / By hole consent of theyr senate'), but also symbolised his status as one of the great, or 'Master Poets';[5] the universally acclaimed exponents of the poetic art. The laurel was thus a potent metaphor for Skelton, which both recalled the greatest triumphs of his early career and stood for his continued faith in his ability and hope for a return to public respect. But not only did he feel that he ought to receive the intellectual and spiritual respect which is due to the great poet, but there ought also to be a corresponding social esteem, manifested in more obvious gestures of favour due to him. Additionally, besides these claims to respect which were the product of his vocation, he clearly cites in the stanzas quoted above a more immediate claim to honour which stemmed from his special relationship with Henry created by his previous tutorial duties. Even if his sovereign had managed to forget these, Skelton had not. Thus he lectured Garnesh on manners, stating that, if the King had been pleased at one time to call Skelton 'master', his subjects ought to treat the poet with an even greater respect. This sense of his own social and artistic worth is a constant sub-text to all Skelton's poems.

Perhaps nowhere is his determination to justify himself as a poetic master-craftsman more obvious than in the text of *The Garlande*, and in its history prior to publication.[6]

In *The Garlande*, which is reliant to no small degree upon Chaucer's *House of Fame* for its framework and imagery, there is none of Chaucer's poetic modesty. In *The House of Fame* the poet-dreamer had been content merely to witness the happenings in Fame's court, and when specifically asked whether he had come there to win fame for himself, he had replied in the negative, and indicated a desire merely to hear,[7]

> Tydnges, other this or that,
> Of love, or suche thynges glade.

In *The Garlande*, the entire poem is a glorification of the dreamer Skelton's career and talents: an *apologia* aimed at justifying his inclusion 'with laureate tryumphe in the Courte of Fame' (line 63). The claims made within it are totally at odds with the medieval modesty convention which dominated Skelton's sources,[8] as the representative Latin *Epigraph* makes clear.[9]

---

[5] R. Skelton, 'The Master Poet: John Skelton as conscious craftsman', *Mosaic*, 6 (1973), pp. 67–92.

[6] *Ibid.*, p. 91. Also note Lily's criticism of Skelton's desire for fame as a poet, 'Whilst thou to get the more esteem, / A learned poet fain would seem' ('*Doctrinae tibi dum parere famam / Et doctus fieri studes poeta*'), printed in Dyce, I p. xxxviii.

[7] *The House of Fame*, 1888–9; F. N. Robinson (ed.), *The Complete Works of Geoffrey Chaucer*, 2nd edn (London, 1957), p. 300.

[8] For an examination of the conventions of dream-allegory prior to Skelton, see A. C. Spearing, *Medieval Dream-Poetry* (Cambridge, 1976), chap. 1–3.

[9] Trans. in Scattergood, p. 497.

While the stars shine remaining in everlasting day, and while the seas swell, this our laurel shall be green; our famous name shall be echoed to the skies, and everywhere Skelton shall be remembered as another Adonis.

In the text the poet establishes his lineage by citing all the previous great poets, writers and orators, both mythical and historical, whose number he is to join. He names, among others, Phoebus, Orpheus, Amphion, Quintillius, Theocritus, Cicero, Sallust, Ovid, Lucan, Statius, Persius, Virgil, Livy, Ennius, Poggio, Macrobius, Petrarch, Plutarch, Lucileus, Vincent of Beauvais, Terence and Gaguin. Finally appear the three great masters of the English language, Chaucer, Gower and Lydgate, who all praise Skelton's skills and speak up for his inclusion among their ranks. In response, Skelton's praise of this awesome trio is respectful, yet not so dominated by humility that he cannot find the time to observe that 'thei wantid nothyng but the laurell' (line 397) to complete their perfection: a suggestion seemingly designed to suggest his own superiority. After this exchange the poet is then presented with his laurel crown, and all the other Laureates give precedence to him, as

> All other [laurels] besyde were counterfete they thought
> In comparyson of that whiche I ware (1105–6)

> They sayd my lawrell was the goodlyest
> That ever they saw. (1112–13)

That Skelton began to write so manifestly self-assertive a poem during his first period at court in the 1490s is remarkable enough,[10] that he thought it sufficiently important to keep it with him for over a quarter of a century as he adapted and updated it as a continuing, expanding *apologia*, is surely indicative of the paramount importance which he placed upon the advancement of his own reputation. And, as time passed, far from muting the arrogant assertions of youth, the ageing poet seems to have actually increased the self-vaunting content of the text. He retained passages attacking his rivals (such as the 'interpolated satire on the poet's rival' to be found between lines 741 and 753) long past the time of their usefulness, and inserted the strident defence of *Phyllyp Sparowe* into the growing bibliographical section. He may also have added the Latin epilogue to the main text, which despatched the vision without the traditional modest apology for its shortcomings:[11]

Skelton speaks to his book. Go shining light of the Britons, and celebrate our songs,

---

[10] It is, however, conceivable that he began it even earlier, to celebrate his Laureation, and then subsequently adapted it for the occasion of his visit to Sheriff Hutton. This might explain the inclusion of the verses against one 'Rogerus Statham', and the comments on the hard-heartedness of Mistress Gertrude Statham (lines 1038–61), which Edwards suggests are evidence of a love-triangle involving the poet. It is far more likely that such sentiments stem from the poet's youth than from his time as a priest and tutor.

[11] Trans. in Scattergood, p. 512.

your worthy British Catallus! Say Skelton was your Adonis; say, Skelton was your Homer. Though barbarous, you now compete in equal race with Latin verse. And though for the most part it is made up of British words our Thalia [the Muse of Comedy] appears not too rude, nor is my Calliope [Epic Poetry] too uncultured. Nor should you be sorry to suffer the intrigues of malice, nor to endure the attacks of a mad dog: for Virgil himself bore similar threats; nor was Ovid's muse spared them.

One might well agree with Skelton the critic when he comments that the poet's arrogance seems appalling,[12] but it is possible nevertheless to observe the theoretical basis for such obvious self-confidence.

Clearly Skelton held very definite views about the role and importance of great, or in his own word 'laureate', poetry, specifically satirical poetry, in society. In his last poem, the *Replycacion*, written, at Wolsey's behest, against the heretical scholars Bilney and Arthur, in the year before the poet's death, he was to produce a remarkable defence and justification of his art and of his own status and worth as a poet–satirist. There one finds, in the manner of the earlier aggressive envoys to *Agaynst the Scottes*, or *Speke, Parott*,[13]

A confutacion responsyve, or an inevytably prepensed answere to all wayworde or frowarde altercacyons that can or may be made or objected agaynst Skelton laureate, devyser of this Replycacyon.

In this supplement, the poet confronts his critics directly.

> Why fall ye at debate
> With Skelton laureate,
> Reputyng hym unable
> To gainsay replycable
> Opinyons detestable
> Of heresy execrable?
>   Ye saye that poetry
> Maye nat flye so hye
> In theology,
> Nor analogy,
> Nor philology,
> Nor philosophy
> To answere or reply
> Agaynst suche heresy. (300–13)

In defence of poetry's capacity to deal with matters both human and divine Skelton cites King David, 'Poete of poetes all / And prophete princypall' (lines 321–2), as the ultimate example of a poet invested with, not only artistic skills, but also with prophetic power and divine inspiration. Poetry is thus, he states, a revelatory vehicle, a 'harpe of prophecy', which transcends all other arts and sciences. And it is the Laureate Poet who is entrusted with the full power and responsibility of that prophetic role.

[12] R. Skelton, 'The Master Poet', p. 92.
[13] Scattergood, p. 382.

> ... there is a spyrituall,
> And a mysteriall,
> And a mysticall
> Effect energiall,
> As Grekes do it call,
> Of suche an industry
> And suche a pregnancy,
> Of hevenly inspiracion
> In laureate creacyon,
> Of poetes commendacion
> That of divyne myseracion
> God maketh his habytacion
> In poetes whiche excelles,
> And sojourns with them and dwelles. (365–78)

> ... [and] he our penne dothe lede,
> And maketh in us suche spede
> And forthwith we must nede
> With penne and ynke procede. (385–8)

The Poet is thus seen as a prophet, and his words as a direct representation of the divine will. Perhaps no greater claim could be made by an artist for the metaphysical status of his art. But the argument is brought back to more earthly considerations in an *Epilogue*, described as,[14]

The epitome of Skelton, the laureate poet ... about the rarity of poets and about the infinite abundance of gymnosophists, philosophers, theologians and the rest of the learned sort. Infinite and innumerable are the sophists, infinite and innumerable are the logicians, innumerable are the philosophers and theologians, infinite the doctors and innumerable the masters; but poets are few and rare. Thus everything that is rare is precious. Therefore, I think that poets, before all others, are fitted with divine inspiration. Plato prophesies thus, and thus Socrates, thus the great Macedonian, thus Caesar, and the greatest of Roman heroes, always honoured famous poets.

The argument, although somewhat unorthodox, is easy to follow, and the conclusion is clearly that poets, as visionaries, should be listened to with respect and should be afforded the highest honours that the realm could offer. The idealistic optimism of the theory casts into bleak contrast the reality of Skelton's career as outlined in the previous chapter, particularly given the special claim to favour which the poet felt that he possessed due to his role in the 'creation' of the sovereign. Psychoanalysts would no doubt find interesting the strange irony by which the poet whose concern for his reputation amongst his readers was so intense that it reached almost manic proportions, should be the one man who was shunned by those whom he most desired to applaud him.

It is perhaps unsurprising, then, given the poet's enduring belief in his own

[14] Trans. in *ibid.*, p. 520.

worth, and this history of failure on the part of the Court and the academic community to live up to what he saw as its responsibility to honour him, that Skelton should have begun to despair for the future of his career, and should have decided that the desperate situation of his lack of favour required a dramatic solution to resolve it. This, I should like to suggest, is what prompted the creation of that hybrid vehicle *Speke, Parott*. For, as with the earlier supplications of the 1509–12 period, it is clear that, on the political level at least, the most important reader for whom *Parott* was intended was King Henry himself, and its aim was to prompt the King once more to summon the *Orator Regius* to Court. Simultaneously on the broader intellectual level the purpose of the text was to (re)establish Skelton as a major scholar–poet in the eyes of the London and courtly intelligentsia. In short, just as *The Garlande* had been in the 1490s (and was to be again in 1523), *Speke, Parott* was an *apologia*, albeit a subtler one; an attempt to glorify Skelton by the display of the full range of his poetic talents and the full depth of his learning and ingenuity. Its aim was to prompt, in as dramatic a fashion as possible, the resurrection of his Court career.

Thus on one level the poet provides a contemporary satire; on another he explores and expounds on what satire is and how it works, what is necessary for good scholarship and what scholarly values ought to be. The aim of the first level of the exercise was to win the favour of the King or the leading courtiers by echoing what the poet perceived as royal opinion. The aim of the second was to win Skelton the respect and acclaim of the scholarly community, and effectively to refute the allegations of that section within it which had hitherto rejected and reviled him. The former objective determined the political subject matter of the text and the inclusion of Wolsey as its chief target. The latter objective in great part determined the choice of poetic form and the persona of Parott as narrator.

The very first lines proclaim the purpose of the text.[15]

> *Lectoribus auctor recipit opusculy huius auxesim*
>
> (By his readers an author receives an amplification of his short poem)
>
> *Crescet in immensem me vivo pagina presens*
> *Hinc mea dicetur Skeltonidis aurea fama*
>
> (The present book will grow greatly while I am
> alive; thence will the golden reputation of
> Skelton be proclaimed)

Skelton is openly staking his reputation on the reception of the poem by his intended audience, and is attempting, through *Parott*, to gain the fame which he clearly feels that he deserves.

---

[15] *Speke, Parott, Epigraphs*, trans. in *ibid.*, p. 454.

There then follows the lengthy twenty-one line description of the text's narrator,

> My name ys Parott, a byrde of Paradyse,
> By Nature devysed of a wonderowus kynde . . . (1–2 *passim*)

Had the intention been only to produce a shield behind which to launch the satire, as some critics have suggested, no such elaboration of detail would have been necessary. But three stanzas are devoted to a description of a parrot's cage, his mirror and his 'beke, bente, and . . . lytell wanton iye' (lines 8, 10, 12). What Skelton is doing is both subtly defining the attributes which allow Parott to act as a satiric narrator (indeed, which make him the satiric narrator *par excellence*), and revealing his own learning by creating a poetic persona which draws on a whole range of literary traditions. The figure of Parott absorbs and adapts not only classical parrot-lore, such as that to be found in Ovid's *Amores*, and the more recent *Epitres de l'amant verd* of Jean Lemaire, but also that of the medieval bestiaries and such works as the Epistles of St Paul, which describe the nature of divine insight and prophecy. In short, Skelton has created in *Speke, Parott* a living advertisement for his own talents, a text of intricate complexity in which every word, every phrase, is carefully chosen, and every implied cross-reference a potential source of illumination. The text is indeed phenomenally complex and obscure in places, as many critics have pointed out, but what such critics fail to observe is that not only is the obscurity a product of Skelton's satiric intentions; a smoke-screen to conceal his attack on Wolsey, but it is also a necessary function of his literary intent. The text is intended to be a clear demonstration to a sceptical audience that he is not simply a wanton, ribald rhymer. Hence the subtlety and complexity are deliberately emphasised. This was intended to be a satire the very intricacy of which would astound its audience. The reader's confusion is thus intentional. One is supposed to be initially baffled by Parott's apparently rambling monologue, only for the text gradually to untangle and resolve itself as one reads it, and as later remarks clarify earlier obscurities. Thus the 'Muse-like' intellect of its creator, Skelton, would be made manifest, and his 'golden reputation' would be proclaimed by everyone.

The creation of Parott as the narrator is evidence enough of the care invested by the poet in his text. He is 'a byrde of Paradyse' and so, as an eye-witness to the perfect, pre-lapsearian world, an ideal judge of the present fallen state of humanity. Yet he is of a profoundly ambivalent nature. He is 'devysed' by nature, yet also outside nature, immortal.[16] He is a fool and thus able to speak without caution, yet he is also wise beyond the intelligence of

---

[16] The best exposition of these introductory stanzas is in Heiserman, pp. 129–30, but see also Edwards, pp. 182–5.

men, as he has witnessed the entire history of mankind since 'Dewcalyon's flood' and knows the danger of loose talk.[17]

He is an exile, cast out of Paradise by Fortune, and thus forced to dwell in the mortal world, and specifically in the world of the Court, for it is 'to greate ladyes of estate' that he is sent. His cage is a symbol of his ambivalent status. It identifies his separation from the frivolity of the ladies, and thus suggests the detachment of the Prophet, yet it is also a part of the ladies' world, designed to delight the senses. It is 'curyowsly carven, with sylver pynne / Properly paynted': a description which prefigures the revelation, not afforded until line 93, that Parott gains much of his prophetic 'jacounce' not from God, but from 'auncyent Aristippus', the pleasure-loving pupil of Socrates. He is thus an indulged sinner, living in luxury and fed with sweetmeats by ladies, yet is also distanced from sin and aware of its folly, a Christ-like figure, like the Pelican of *Pierce The Ploughman's Crede*, who 'shall lepe from this lyfe as mery as we be' (line 222). He can thus view the world on which he comments from every possible perspective and draw wisdom from both human and divine sources. The details of his description are carefully chosen and are part of the intricate cross-referential pattern of the text. The 'myrrour of glasse' in which he 'totes' is not only a detail appropriate to the parrot of the bestiaries who is said to mimic Narcissus in adoring its own image,[18] but is also utilised by Skelton as a symbol of Parott's satiric-cum-prophetic capabilities. It is the mirror which Parott will hold up to nature, and is the glass through which, as St Paul declared, the truth is seen but darkly in the material world,[19] as the text suggests,[20]

> The myrrour that I tote in, *quasi diaphanum*
> *Vel quasi speculum, in enigmate* . . .
> [Is] For logicians to loke on, somewhat
> sophistice.

Thus the apparently neutral details of Parott's cage are subsequently revealed to possess great significance. And it is in this manner, with later passages investing earlier lines with meaning, that the text must be read.

As Skelton continues to outline Parott's appearance and attributes his significance becomes apparent. Such attributes make him an ideal plaything for Court ladies, a 'lytell pratye fole', and an ideal 'mynyon to wayte upon a quene', yet also give him the licence to speak truth prophetically, to be literally the most valuable minion for a prince. He is learned in many

---

[17] The legend of Pittacus, son of Deucalyon, states that he was turned into a parrot by the gods at his own behest after a long and much travelled life. This is clearly part of the heritage of Skelton's bird.

[18] Alexander Neckham, *De Naturis Rerum*, cited in Edwards, p. 184.

[19] I Corinthians, xiii, 12.

[20] Lines 190–3, Heiserman, p. 153, gives 'as though transparent, or like a looking-glass in a riddle'.

tongues, he can imitate the cries of animals, and has also learnt Latin, Hebrew, Chaldean, Greek, French, Dutch, Welsh, Castilian and Irish, which make him an entertaining pet, but which also reveal him to be a prophet in the Pauline model, who speaks in tongues, 'pronownsyng my purpose after my properte' (line 30).

Clearly this is not a text to be read once only and then discarded. The poet requires as great an effort on his reader's part as he himself has invested in the poem. Parott is consciously designed to be the perfect prophetic narrator, yet his authority, like much of his meaning, is concealed. On the surface he is simply a pet owned by ladies, as his monologue is merely a 'wanton' nonsense. Skelton leaves the revelation of his narrator's true worth, like the revelation of his true political intentions, to his readers' ingenuity, even though he continually leaves heavy hints to lead them on their way. The poem is written for those capable of decoding it, with the intention that thereafter reader and poet will achieve a mutual respect.

What, then, of this monologue which Parott was so painstakingly created to deliver? Let us examine its *content*. Before considering the political side of the satire it is perhaps opportune briefly to examine the second level of the text, the attempt to re-establish Skelton's literary career and reputation. For, although the political aspects of the poem have attracted by far the greatest critical attention, *Speke, Parott* itself, before the addition of the envoys, is only partly concerned with criticism of Wolsey. Taken as a whole the original text is far more a product of Skelton's involvement in the Grammarians' War than of any dissatisfaction with the Cardinal. Seemingly the poet felt that his veiled criticism of Wolsey, in keeping as he felt it to be with the prevailing mood of the Court, was sufficient to achieve the political purpose of the text. Its literary purposes required greater elaboration and greater clarity of comment, intended as they were both to reveal the full scope of the poet's talents and to conclude the long-running scholarly feud between the 'Trojans' and the 'Greeks' in favour of the traditionalists. Perhaps a brief summary of the background to the relevant skirmish in this strange war between schoolmasters is thus necessary, in order that Parott's terms of reference can be clearly understood.[21]

In 1519 William Lily, headmaster of St Paul's School, had adopted a new Latin grammar, the *Vulgaria* of the humanist William Horman, as the standard classroom text at St Paul's, in the place of the older *Vulgaria* of John Stanbridge, headmaster of St Mary Magdalen's School, Oxford. The traditionalist grammarian Robert Whittington took exception to the change and

---

[21] For the following paragraph I am indebted to Heiserman, pp. 150–2; Nelson, pp. 148–57; and M. Pollet, *John Skelton, Poet of Tudor England*, trans. from the French by J. Warrington (Lewisberg, 1971), pp. 113–18.

published his own *Vulgaria* in response, in the evident hope that a revision of the traditional methodology advocated by Stanbridge, his former tutor, would be readopted in the place of Horman's more radical ideas. This, however, was not to be, and so Whittington took the dramatic step of nailing a Latin poem, which lauded the superiority of his own grammer over Horman's, to the railings of St Paul's school. This action prompted both Horman and Lily to compose a series of defences of their own methods, and attacks on Whittington's in the form of pamphlets and epigrams. In the exchange of insults and allegations which followed, Whittington called upon the aid of Skelton, who wrote at least one invective against Lily, and who received in return a retaliatory text (including the 'neither learned, nor a poet' jibe, cited earlier), and pupils of Horman's joined in the fray.[22] At issue were the respective merits of two very different methods of teaching the classical languages. The traditionalists, dubbed the 'Trojans' simply for their opposition to the Greek learning of the humanists, favoured a bricks-and-mortar approach, similar to that by which all contemporary languages were learnt, in which the rules of syntax and the tried and trusted grammatical formulae were conned before the pupil progressed to read the major Latin authors. Horman and the 'Greeks' favoured a more textually based style, which taught basic rules but which advanced a pupil quickly to the reading of selected classical authors in order that the rules of grammar might be learnt from their writings rather than by rote. Mastery of the basic elements was the key to the Trojan system, the appreciation and adoption of an elegant style that of the Greek.

It is this debate, and the wider context provided by the struggle between the humanists and the traditionalists in the universities and at Court,[23] which forms the background to *Speke, Parott*. Hence the second part of Parott's monologue is concerned with his comments on contemporary trends in classical scholarship. It has been suggested that the intervention of Henry and Wolsey on the side of More, Pace and the humanists, in defence of Erasmus' *New Testament*, had brought about 'the decisive victory of the new learning [over the "old"] in England by 1519'.[24] It is clear, however, that Skelton felt the struggle to be far from over and sought both to rally the traditionalists, and to find favour with the 'humanist' King, with his poem. He begins with a succinct summary of the 'Trojan's' arguments:

> Let Parrot, I pray you, have lyberte to prate,
> For *aurea lyngua Greca* ought to be magnyfyed,

---

[22] See Pollet, *Poet of Tudor England*, p. 229 for a list of the various pamphlets known to have been included in these exchanges.

[23] For this wider context, see M. Dowling, *Humanism in the Age of Henry VIII* (London, 1986), chapter 1.

[24] *Ibid.*, p. 57.

> Yf it were cond perfytely, and after the rate,
> As *lyngua Latina*, in scole matter occupyed;
> But our Grekis theyr Greke so well have applyed
> That hey cannot say in Greke, rydynge by the way,
> 'How, hosteler, fetche my hors a botell of hay!' (141–7)

The study of Greek, Parott asserts, is a good thing, provided that it is learned in the traditional manner, based on a sound knowledge of vocabulary and syntax, as Latin *used to be* in schools (a pointed reference to the change at St Paul's). However, nowadays the Greeks are so hasty in their progression to the reading of the major authors that they omit all the essential groundwork. Hence, as the ironic example makes plain, they cannot even construct so basic yet essential a sentence as to ask for hay for their horses. And so, by implication, although they may make a promising start with their studies, they are unlikely to get much further.

Here Skelton dispenses almost entirely with the *alegoria* which make the first portion of the text so apparently ambiguous. Once away from the politically sensitive ground of the attack on Wolsey, Skelton drops the crypticism completely. What remains is an explicit, often tedious, attack on the methodology of the humanist schoolmasters, interspersed occasionally with comments on their dominance over the academic community and the harmful effects on scholarship which this creates:

> In *Achademia* Parrot dare no probleme kepe,
> For *Greci fari* so occupyeth the chayre,
> That *Latinum fari* may fall to rest and slepe,
> And *silogisari* was drowned at Sturbrydge Fayre;
> Tryvyals and quatryvyals so sore now they appayre,
> That Parott the popagay hath pyte to beholde
> How the rest of good lernyng is roufled up and trold. (162–8)

The classic texts are being introduced too early into the curriculum ('Plautus in his comedies a chyld shall now reherse / And medyll with Quintylyan in his *Declamacyons*' (lines 176–7)[25]). The traditional textbooks are forgotten ('Albertus *De Modo Significandi* / And Donatus be dryven out of scole' (lines 169–70)) and humanist translations, such as Erasmus' *New Testament* of 1516, are replacing sound works with mere corruptions of the original texts ('For ye scrape out good scrypture, and set in a gall: / Ye go about to amende, and ye mare all' (lines 153–4)). All of this makes Parott long for the

---

[25] The first line of this couplet may also be an ironic reference to the performance of the 'goodly Comedy of Plautus', noted in chap. 2 above, which was likely to have been performed by Cornysh and the children of the Chapel in 1520. This conclusion, I have since discovered, was also arrived at by L. F. McGrath, see McGrath. *Speke, Parott* and Plautus', *Notes and Queries*, 214 (1969), pp. 452–3.

unchanging purity of Paradise, or at least for something to clear his head,

> Now a nutmeg, a nutmeg, *cum gariopholo*,
> For Parott to pyke upon, his brayne for to stable,
> Swete synamum styckis and *pleris cum musco*!
> In Paradyce, that place of pleasure perdurable,
> The progeny of Parrottis were fayre and favorable;
> Nowe in valle Ebron Parrot is fayne to fede;
> 'Christecrosse and Saynt Nycholas, Parrot, be your good spede!' (183–9)

The paying off of recent academic scores was thus a major motivation behind *Parott's* appearance in 1521. And yet it was not only a destructive work, despite its attacks on Wolsey and humanist scholarship. It was also intended to fulfil a constructive purpose. As the second epigraph reveals, the text was devised to proclaim 'the golden reputation of Skelton'. It was intended to demonstrate the poet's learning and his capacity as an innovator (the two traits which, as Robin Skelton remarks, mark out the master poet), to justify his role as a satirist and to demonstrate the value to society, both of satire in general and of himself in particular. It is not possible here to do anything approaching justice to the full complexity and dazzling brilliance of the text, but a brief summary of the more obvious ways in which it acts as a showcase for Skelton's talents should serve to illustrate the point.

Through the mouthpiece of Parott the poet displays his learning as the ideal refutation of his critic's allegations of triviality and wantonness. In the poem proper he suggests the depth of his reading with a pyrotechnical display of citation (Parott alludes to, or quotes from, amongst others, the medieval bestiaries, from Lydgate, from Statius, Ovid, Reuchlin, Lemaire, Horace, Migne, Aristippus, Martial, Ptolemy and Haly, Cicero, Erasmus, Albertus Magnus, Donatus, Priscian, Plautus, Dionysius Cato and Juvenal, from Exodus, Genesis, I and II Kings, Samuel, Numbers, Jeremiah, Judges, I Corinthians, I Thessalonians, and from the Book of Psalms). He reveals his knowledge of languages and his mastery of Latin grammar and demonstrates his intricate knowledge of the Bible by producing the obscure alias 'Jerobesethe' for Gideon, which first appeared only in the Venice Bible of 1519, and there only once in II Kings, xi, 21.[26] He reveals his talent for punning and ability to juggle with biblical and classical exempla for allegorical effect by neatly conflating the stories of Aram and Aran, and the cities of Baldock and Baldac, first to suggest the provenance of the threat which Wolsey poses, and second to prefigure his fall, and suggest its liberating effect on the realm.[27] He mixes a topical satire with a reproof of his scholarly rivals, all within the confines of a visionary monologue spoken by a ladies' pet. He concludes this phenomenally eclectic work with a return to Parott himself, a

[26] See Edwards, p. 187.   [27] See Heiserman, pp. 138, 142.

series of further hints about the satirical and allegorical nature of the preceding stanzas and a reflection on the nature and role of satire itself.

Parott, Skelton reminds his readers, hails from Paradise, but is exiled in the human world. 'The myrrour that I tote in', the bird remarks, is as though transparent, or like a looking-glass in a riddle, which is a further indication, if any is needed, that he is speaking with hidden significance. Hence his call for support is aimed at the most learned readers. The text, he observes, is,

> For logicions to loke on, somwhat *sophistice*;
> Rhetoricyons and oratours in freshe humanyte,
> Support Parrot, I pray you, with your suffrage ornate,
> Of *confuse tantum* avoydynge the chekmate.
> (193–6)

These learned men must avoid the apparent block, the 'chekmate', posed by the seeming confusion of Parott's monologue, and look beyond. For they must realise that such confusion is merely a stratagem:

> But of that supposicyon that callyd is arte,
> *Confuse distributyve*,[28] as Parrot hath devysed,
> Let every man after his merit take his parte;
> For in this process, Parrot nothyng hath surmysed,
> No matter pretendyd, nor nothyng enterprysed,
> But that *metaphora, alegoria* withall,
> Shall be his protectyon, his pavys and his wall. (197–203)

It is a message which the envoys will strive to make painfully plain. By reading beyond the ordered confusion of the surface narrative one will find something of greater importance to be uncovered. The point is made from a different perspective in the pious conclusion to the text, in which Parott observes that his monologue, like all satire, can only obliquely point out the path to salvation by ridiculing the opposite. He can suggest criticism, and chide sinners, but it is the readers who must pierce the allegory and it is they who must act to reform the evils represented. The widened, Christian perspective of these final stanzas is traditional enough, but even here the poet cannot resist introducing a last word, which points the reader back once more to the text and indicates its multiple levels of meaning, should anyone have missed the earlier observations to this same effect. In a Latin epilogue he adds the words 'Fair readers, understand skilfully, cherish your Parott'.[29] Such labouring of the point is perhaps excessive, but as will become apparent, Skelton's pessimism regarding his readers' ability to appreciate his allegory was well-founded.

[28] 'Methodical confusion' (Heiserman, p. 153), or 'ordered confusion' (Scattergood, p. 459).
[29] *Speke, Parott*, line 232b, trans. in Scattergood, p. 460.

What, then, of the *political* level to Skelton's poem? The claim advanced above that the poet wrote an attack on Wolsey in order to attempt to win favour from the King and Court might initially seem a strange one, but it is one which seems fully borne out by a careful reading of the text. However, before beginning to speculate on *why* Wolsey might have been attacked in the poem, it is perhaps wise to offer a demonstration of *how* he was attacked, and how what Skelton describes as his strategy of '*confuse dystributyve*', *metaphora* and *alegoria* operates.

On any reading of *Speke, Parott* it soon becomes clear that the intention behind the satire is not that it should stand as a rationalised omnibus of indictments against Wolsey, as, for example, the Lords' articles of 1529 were to do.[30] In many ways this is an experimental work. It is certainly an experiment in literary form – but it is also a political experiment, an experiment in terms of tactics. It is a testing of the water of reaction, an attempt to see just how far one could go in writing an attack on the chief minister of the realm, even one written in what was felt to be a favourable political climate, without having to do so from the relative safety of complete anonymity or exile – both of which were impossible, given the self-advertising function of the text. William Cornysh, Polydore Vergil, and perhaps by this time the future Baron North also, had all been imprisoned for writing against principal ministers within the preceding two decades, the last two named by Wolsey himself.[31] Thus the poet intent on a satiric assault on so august a target would have to be extremely careful in treading a path across the minefield which lay between fruitless obscurity and the sort of overconfident iconoclasm which would provoke a disastrous official reaction should he overstep propriety, or should Wolsey survive what Skelton clearly perceived as a period of royal displeasure. In many ways Skelton was therefore caught in a cleft stick of his own making. To be a successful satirist would involve striking home at the target in the way most designed to provoke retaliation; yet to hope to avoid that reaction, he would have to blunt the literary barbs almost to the point of impotence. This was the dilemma which *Speke, Parott* was designed to overcome, but which was ultimately to frustrate it. For Skelton, as will become apparent, both misread his audience and, for all his continual, unsubtle, reminders to his readers of the subtlety of his satire, chose to err too far on the side of crypticism.

---

[30] For a transcript of these articles, drawn up and signed by many of the nation's leading noblemen, see lord Herbert of Cherbury, *The Life and Reigne of Henry The Eighth* (London, 1649), pp. 263–74.

[31] See S. Anglo, 'William Cornish in a play, pageants, prison and politics', *Review of English Studies*, 59, for an account of Cornysh's verses, for Vergil see D. Hay (ed. and trans.) *The Anglica Historia of Polydore Vergil* (Camden Society, 1950) 74, Introduction. North's apologetic verses to Wolsey from his prison cell can be found in F. J. Furnivall and W. R. Morfill (eds.), *Ballads from Manuscripts*, Ballad Society (London, 1868–73), pp. 336–9.

One intention behind the subtlety of the poem is clearly that, through *metaphora* and *alegoria*, a protective shield will, as Parott claims, be raised between the poet and any possible punishment. Not, as some critics have suggested, the shield of total obscurity, but of definite, if guarded, allegorical allusions which it is quite possible to trace out, but which are none the less sufficiently removed from actual names and events to allow the poet, if taxed on the subject, to deny a specific intent. That Skelton passionately desired his readers to follow exactly what he intended is clear from his continual insertion into the text of instructions as to how it should be read, some of which have already been noted while others will be encountered below. But what he also wished was to be able to prevent the maliciously motivated reader from proving beyond doubt that such an intention existed. As he makes Collyn Clout, the eponymous narrator of his subsequent, more explicit, satire, remark,

> . . . no man have I named
> Wherefore shulde I be blamed. (1111–12)

This defence, of course, makes a rather telling assumption. For it seems to rely on that very scrupulous adherence to the letter of the law on Wolsey's part which Skelton was to deny that he practised. If Wolsey was the tyrant that Skelton put such a great deal of invention and effort into claiming, why was it that the poet felt safe behind so flimsily 'legalistic' a shield? That he should have such apparent confidence in so subtle a defence must surely undercut the apparent authenticity that critics have seen in his allegations of Wolsey's tyranny.

Such considerations are, however, the concern of the following chapters. The major thesis advanced in the main text of *Speke, Parott* is not the charge of tyranny but the supposed identification of an excess of futile activity which, Parott suggests, characterises Wolsey's regime. At first, as one would expect in a text which only gradually lifts its 'pavys' of metaphor and allegory to admit a clear view of its target, the references to Wolsey and his mission to Calais are vague and concealed amongst other matters. So much so that it is only a retrospective reading that reveals a particular relevance in them at all. Thus it is only in terms of a generalised futile activity that the specific example of Calais begins to show through. Parott's unnamed inquisitor broaches the issue with the weary question,

> Besy, besy, besy and besynes agayne!
> '*Que pensez voz* Parrot? What meneth this besynes?'
> *Vitulus* in Oreb troubled Arons brayne;
> Melchisedeck mercyful made Moloc mercyles.
> (57–60)

Apparently something is going on, the purpose of which is unclear to the
questioner. But Parott's assessment of the situation specifically equates the
'besynes' with Wolsey's activities in a covert yet definite manner.[32] Just as his
inquisitor is confused by this business, Parott suggests, so was Aaron confused by the creation of the idolatrous golden calf (here simply the '*Vitulus*')
on Mount Horeb,[33] whilst the abominable Molech[34] is encouraged to greater
evil by the ill-considered licence granted him by King Melchisedek.[35] At this
point the association between Melchisedek/Aaron and Henry, and the
Vitulus/Molech figure and Wolsey seems, even at best, extremely tenuous,
but subsequent stanzas serve to confirm the political intention behind these
lines.

That the *Vitulus* or golden calf is a figure for Wolsey is made clear at line
348 in the *Dysticon Miserabill*, and in the subsequent *Testrasticon*, both of
which occur amongst the envoys. The first of these Latin stanzas refers to an
elevated and tyrannical figure who dominates a sovereign, and who is
referred to only as the *Vitulus bubali*,

> *Altior, heu, Cedro, crudelior, heu, leopardo;*
> *Heu, vitulus bubali fit dominus Priami.*

> (Higher, alas, than the cedar, more cruel, alas, than the leopard;
> Alas, the bull-calf of the ox has become the master of Priam.)[36]

Thus the 'bull-calf', earlier associated with a false idol through the association with Aaron, is now given a personality as a cruel and unnaturally elevated politician. The figure's precise analogue has not been revealed
(although the previous envoy had clearly referred to Wolsey). But this omission is made good in the lines of the *Testrasticon* which follow, and which
clearly equate the Priam of the *Dysticon* with Henry VIII, and thus the
Vitulus with his chief minister,

> *Non annis licet et Priamus sed honore voceris;*
> *Dum foveas vitulum, rex, regeris, Britonum;*
> *Rex, regeris, non ipse regis, rex inclite, calle;*
> *Subde tibi vitulum ne fateut nimium.*

> (Granted that it is not because of your age
> but because of your rank that you are called Priam;
> as long as you cherish the bull-calf, King of Britain, you are ruled;
> King, you are ruled, you do not yourself rule,

---

[32] All the major critics attempt glosses of these political stanzas. For a representative sample, see
Heiserman, pp. 133–49; Edwards, pp. 184–90; Pollet, *Poet of Tudor England*, p. 122.

[33] Exodus, xxxii, 1–24.

[34] The bull-god venerated by Solomon in I Kings, xi, 7 and II Kings, xxi, 6 (not as Scattergood,
p. 455, gives, I Kings, xi, 5, and II Kings, xiii, 13).

[35] The Priest-King of Salem in Genesis, xiv, 18–20.

[36] *Speke, Parott*, lines 347–8, trans. in Scattergood, p. 462.

> celebrated King, learn by experience;
> make the bull-calf subservient to you,
> lest he become too foolish.)[37]

If any doubt as to the validity of the *Vitulus*/Wolsey association remains, one need only refer to the latin *Decastrichon Virulentum* appended to *Why Come Ye Nat?*, in which the bull-calf reappears, and is referred to as a '*butcher's* bull-calf' (Wolsey's father was, of course, a butcher), a 'wolf of the sea' (hereafter a favourite pun on 'Wolsey'[38]), and a 'Thomas who rides a mule'.[39]

Thus at the very outset of Parott's political ramblings there is the suggestion that the *Vitulus*, which stands for Wolsey, 'troubled Arons brayne', which suggests that, just as one false idol confused Aaron in biblical times, so another now attempts to do the same to Henry, and also, significantly, that Henry is himself 'troubled' by Wolsey's activities. The following line advances a view of the harmful effects of what Skelton suggests is Henry's refusal to keep Wolsey on a tight leash, by warning of the effects of Henry's too lenient mercy;[40] and this trend is continued throughout the text. The selfsame point is reiterated two stanzas further on, at lines 76–7; 'Some run to far before, some run to far behynde, / Some be to churlysshe, and some be to kynde.' Skelton implies that the entire realm laments the ill-effects of Wolsey's unchecked dominance. The Church is placed in jeopardy ('Rachell ruly doth loke' (line 114)), good leadership and good judgement are banished ('Gideon is gon' (line 116)), as Henry spends his time away from government ('Madionita Jetro, our Moyses kepyth his shepe' (line 115)), traditional houses of religion and sanctuary are under threat ('and *assilum, whilom refugiam miserorum / Non phanum, sed prophanum*, standyth in lytyll sted' (lines 124–5)), and law is in decline ('*Ulula*, Esebon, for Jeptc is starke ded!' (line 126)). Such claims of misery and decay are interspersed with further hints of Wolsey's dominance over Henry ('Bo Ho doth bark wel, Hough-ho he rulyth the ring' (line 130)), and warnings that unspecified enemies are gathering and preparing to attack (see, for example, lines 118–9, 'Oreb et Zeb, of *Judicum* rede the boke / Now Geball, Amon and Amaloch . . . ', which allude to the warnings of the gathering of the enemies of Israel to be found in Psalm 83).

And yet, despite the claims that metaphor and allegory were necessary as a

---

[37] *Speke, Parott*, lines 349–52, trans. in Scattergood, p. 462.
[38] See W. Tyndale, *The Practice of Prelates*, ed. H. Walter, Parker Society (London, 1849), p. 37.
[39] *Decastichon*, lines 1, 2, 6, 7, trans. in Scattergood, p. 495.
[40] Melchisedek had already been used as a figure for Henry in *Agaynst the Scottes*, lines 115–16. Skelton had said of Henry, in an apostrophe addressed at the dead Scots King, 'In him is fygured Melchisedec, / And ye were disloyall Amalec'. Wolsey reappears as Moloc in *Speke, Parott*, line 402.

shield for the satire, which imply that Skelton was saying things which were too controversial to be said openly, the poet largely restricts himself to such general denunciations of Wolsey's governance as these, which suggest that he is a dangerous force in the commonwealth, due to his predeliction for excess. Too much power is in too few hands. There is too much reliance on one man's activities and too much business excludes good sense and kills good laws. This Skelton summarises in the mock-proverbial declaration that

> ... reason and wytte wantythe theyr provynciall,
> When wylfulnes ys vicar generall (53–4)

The rest of the satiric game, which Parott refers to in the envoys as the 'ryche jacounce', seems to involve Skelton simply alluding to the Cardinal in more and more circumlocutionary ways, tempting his educated readers to tease out their relevance and share the joke. It is a game of 'catch-as-catch-can' ('let every man after his merit take his parte' (line 199)), in which the poet draws a diverse and diffuse web of allegory into a collage, visible only when viewed *in toto*, that denounces Wolsey as a foolish, arrogant and wasteful tyrant. The charges themselves take second place to the overall effect, in great part, as shall be suggested, because Skelton had few effective charges available to him and few critical points which he felt it safe to make. The text is thus an effective marshalling of the resources which the poet could muster at short notice, when the opportunity to write seemed to present itself.

But why should Skelton have felt that an attack on Wolsey's dominance of affairs and on his handling of the Calais conference of 1521 might win him the favour at Court which he had sought throughout his career? To discover this we will need to examine those aspects of Parott's monologue which reveal how the relationship between Henry and Wolsey was viewed from the poet's position on the sidelines of the political arena during the late summer and autumn of 1521. For what the structure of *Speke, Parott* allows the attentive reader to do is not only follow Skelton's gradually more obvious focusing of the satire on the person of Wolsey and the occasion of the Calais conference, but also follow a surprisingly simple series of arguments at work behind the attacks. This in turn permits a clearer view of the sort of audience at which the poet aimed, and of the sort of response which he hoped to elicit from them.

The fact that Skelton chose the Calais conference as the subject matter for his political satire of 1521 is unsurprising. The Court and City would have talked about little else that summer and autumn than the Cardinal's magnificent departure for Calais, his chances of success there and the consequences for international trade of either a resumption or a complete cessation of the Franco-Imperial conflict which had begun earlier that year. Wolsey's visit made Calais the centre of European attention for the entire period of the conference, as he ostensibly acted as a mediator between the French and Imperial delegates in order to prevent, or simply postpone, a war in which the unprepared England would be forced to participate, owing to the obligations created by the Treaty of London of 1518.[41]

Skelton's treatment of that conference, given what can be discovered of its public justification, is also, despite its inconsistencies, far from surprising. For the poet was trying to win the favour of the King, and of the Court which mirrored his opinions, and was attempting to do so by telling the sovereign exactly what he thought that the latter wished to hear.

By the late summer of 1521 there were obvious signs of a rift between Henry and Wolsey over relatively minor issues, which were likely to have given rise to all manner of rumours at Court concerning the future of the realm's chief minister. In particular such signs, or whatever account of them was carried to the outer reaches of the Court, and thence to Skelton's ears, might well have suggested a general royal dissatisfaction with Wolsey's handling of the Calais conference to one who, like the poet, was not privy to the Cardinal's secret brief for his visit to Calais. This brief stated that he should not, in effect, secure a peace at all but should, if possible, conclude a separate, aggressive, Anglo-Imperial treaty against France during his visit to the Emperor at Bruges, whilst delaying the outbreak of war, via the arrangement of a truce at Calais, until England was ready to participate in a joint invasion.[42]

During September, the month in which Skelton seems to have begun *Speke, Parott*,[43] Henry had a lengthy disagreement with his chief minister, through the correspondence of his secretary Richard Pace, over whether or not to despatch English merchant vessels to Bordeaux to purchase the year's wines.[44] The King, concerned for the safety of his subjects, and their ships, should the French decide to take pre-emptive action against English traders as a preparation for war, was convinced that the journey ought not to be taken. Wolsey, conversely, was anxious that the French should not be pushed into a premature abandonment of the conference and a declaration of war by any precipitate English action, and so recommended that the pretence of normality should be maintained and the journey proceed as normal. At the outset this disagreement was simply another matter for consul-

[41] For a study of English foreign policy and Wolsey's objectives at Calais, see P. Gwyn, 'Wolsey's foreign policy: the conferences of Calais and Bruges reconsidered', *Historical Journal*, 23 (1980), pp. 755–72. See also J. G. Russell, *Peacemaking in the Renaissance*, (London, 1986), pp. 93–132.

[42] Gwyn, 'Wolsey's foreign policy', pp. 765–71.

[43] The convent at Bromhall, to which Parott refers in lines 127–9 of the poem, was first prepared for dissolution on 12 September 1521, when the Prioress resigned. See H. L. R. Edwards, 'The date of Skelton's later poems', *P.M.L.A.*, 53 (1938), pp. 601–19.

[44] For a discussion of this argument, and of the rift between Wolsey and Henry at this point, see J. J. Scarisbrick, *Henry VIII* (London, 1968), pp. 86–92.

tation between the sovereign and his leading adviser. The subject was broached cordially enough by Henry, who, in a despatch dated 1 September, summarised what he perceived to be the various advantages and disadvantages of the journey for his minister's benefit and declared that he desired Wolsey and the counsellors in Calais 'diligently and maturely to examine and debate the forsayde doubtes and to advertise hym wyth diligence of your opinion and mynde therein'.[45] In response Wolsey returned the recommendation that the voyage should proceed as planned but stressed as he did so that this, possibly unpopular, advice was not his own consideration alone, but that arrived at by,[46]

the whole number of suche your counsillors as be here with me, after long reasoning and debating of the said matter, finally concluded by one assent.

That the Cardinal was, even before this disagreement began, anxious concerning his continued favour with the King, after his prolonged absence from Court, can be ascertained from his declaration, relayed through Pace, that it would be to his

cumforthe to have sum wrytynge off the Kyngis owne hande, declarynge hys contentacion wyth [my] . . . paynes and labors susteignydde there [Calais], in the bryngynge of hys affayris to the desyridde ende.

The depth of his desire for a reassuring word from the source of his power and influence can also be ascertained from Wolsey's request that Pace move the matter to the King 'as off [himself]'. At the same time he requested that the secretary keep him informed, in a separate letter, of all matters of interest occurring at Court, presumably so that he might keep one step ahead of any attempts to undermine his influence during his absence.[47]

During the following week the difference of opinion between King and Chancellor over the Bordeaux voyage became more obvious, as can be inferred from Pace's letter of 9 September, from Oking, in which he informed Wolsey that the King[48]

gretly doubtith off the sendynge off hys navye and merchiantes to Bordeaux thys yere, and much studyeth theruppon for the welth and suertie off his subjectes, as he sayth, and thys hath movydde hym so to dispute that matier wyth Your Grace, as he doith.

As time passed, however, neither party, for all their moderate language, was

---

[45] B. L. Cotton MS Titus B I fo. 290 (*St. P.* I 30), Pace to Wolsey from Guildford.
[46] J. Strype, *Ecclesiastical Memorials*, 4 vols. (London, 1721), I p. 42, Wolsey to Henry VIII, 4 September 1521.
[47] *St. P.* I 33, Pace to Wolsey, 4 September 1521.
[48] *St. P.* I 34.

prepared to alter their opinion,[49] and Henry clearly soon began to feel that Wolsey's continued advocacy of the voyage betokened a serious misjudgment of the French King's trustworthiness, and that his attempts to induce Henry to place his trust in the goodwill of the French was nothing more than a slight to his royal honour. No one, he felt, was more inclined to place trust, where it might honorably be applied, than the King of England. As Pace informed Wolsey on 20 September,[50]

as towchynge the sendynge off his navye to Burdeaux, His Highnesse doith sumwhatt marvayle that Your Grace haith founde so goodde fayth in the sayde Frenshe Kynge, and that the same fayth is by hys mystruste and diffidence exilidde, not wyth stondynge your wrytynge affore . . . agaynst the sayde kyngs fayth and breche off promise in strykynge bataiyle wyth the Emperour. And Hys Hyghnesse supposith that Yo[ur Grace] doith well knowe that he haith as goodde [fayth] as an other Prince, and that itt is nott [his] acustumate maner to mystruste wyth owte cause evident, but rather to trust when other men haith grete diffidence, seyng reason whye he schulde so do. And he dotith nott, but yff Your Grace, and othre his Counsailors there, hadde hadde so large knowledge off the juperdye off sendynge hys sayde navye to Burdeaux, at that tyme ye debatidde the matier there amongst you, as he haith s[ent] unto you synse the same debatement, ye wolde all have agreede wyth hym in oon opinion.

The King completed this indignant declaration with a long recitation of the perfidies of the French and the consequential dangers to England arising from French treachery.

On his receipt of this despatch Wolsey clearly realised how close he was to exciting Henry's anger through his continued opposition to clearly stated royal opinions. Hence, at some point around 28 September, he composed a long and apologetic letter, in which he humbly submitted that he had not thought to question either Henry's views or his faith in his previous despatches. Yet he still felt it necessary, for the greater good of the realm's foreign policy, to express his doubts as to the wisdom of abandoning the Bordeaux voyage, once again using the collective responsibility of the Councillors in Calais to shield himself from the full force of any royal outbursts. 'Lyke as we heretofore confoure our opinions and myndes touching the voiage to Bordeaux, to your high pleasure', he declared,[51]

soo we remitte the same to your grete wisdome, notwithstandyng, uppon our fidelities and duties towardes your Grace, we persist in our former opiniion for the passing of your subjectes to Bordeaux at this first vintage.

Fortunately for Wolsey, Henry was not given too much time to meditate on his minister's continued disagreement with a decision which seemed self-

---

[49] See, for example, B.L. Cotton MS Caligula D VIII fo. 150 (*St. P.* I 37), Wolsey to Henry VIII, 15 September.
[50] B.L. Cotton MS Caligula D VIII fo. 153 (*St. P.* I 38).
[51] B.L. Cotton MSS Caligula D VIII fo. 157 and Galba B VII fo. 55 (*St. P.* I 39).

evidently wise to the royal mind. For the King was presented with something of a *fait accompli* in the matter within days of his receipt of the Cardinal's letter. As Pace informed the latter on 4 October,[52]

Concernynge the sendyng off Hys Graces subjectes and schyppis to Burdeaux [for] the vintage, Hys Hyghness sayth, that [in] asmuche as, whils he and you were in disputacion by wrytynge, wither itt were meate they schulde or myght suerly repare thydre, or nott, by the reason off the evidente daungers of these warres, they ar departidde wyth the numbre off 20ti schyppis [as Hys Grace is informydde], he wull no further dispute in that that is past.

The secretary's evident relief at this cessation of royal argumentativeness can be judged from a second despatch sent to Wolsey on the same day, in which he declared that, although it was lately the King's pleasure to dispute with the Cardinal, now it was his pleasure to hold his peace, whereof Pace, for his part, was right glad. Clearly this dispute was perceived by Pace to be of no small significance. Equally evidently, any dispute which would have kept the merchants concerned uncertain as to the future of their trade for over a month after their initial petitioning of the King for his pleasure in the matter,[53] would have been of great interest in the City and the Court, and thus was likely to have been known of, although probably not in detail, by Skelton. In addition, such royal displeasure with Wolsey as could be inferred from this dispute might have appeared the more serious because this was not a solitary example of such a disagreement. It followed close on the tail of an earlier debate between King and minister which concerned the despatch of a company of 6,000 archers to Calais as an escort for the Emperor. Initially the grounds for disagreement on this occasion concerned who should be appointed to command the troops, but subsequently the disagreement spread to the more fundamental question of whether they should be sent at all.[54]

It is possible, with hindsight, to dismiss these differences of opinion between Henry and Wolsey as merely passing questions of detail of the sort which would inevitably arise periodically between two strong minds concentrated on complex matters of grave concern, and thus of no import to their long-term relationship. But, however secure hindsight reveals Wolsey's position to have been during 1521, the Cardinal himself clearly experienced some anxiety over his sovereign's temporary displeasure. In his concern to maintain his position of favour, he began to suspect a deliberate attempt to tarnish his reputation with Henry, and to lash out against a phantasmal conspiracy involving the unfortunate Richard Pace. This prompted the latter, when informed by Thomas More of Wolsey's displeasure with him for alle-

[52] B. L. Cotton MS Galba B VII fo. 119 (*St. P.* I 40 and *L.P.* III (i) 1629).
[53] As B.L. Cotton MS Titus B I fo. 290 reveals, it was a suit made to Henry by the wine importers, 'for to knowe hys mynde and pleasure, wither they schall so doo thys yere or nott', which precipitated the disagreement.
[54] For this dispute see B.L. Cotton MS Caligula E III fos. 7–8; *St. P.* 23–7, 31, 34.

gedly misrepresenting his letters to the King, to write in some evident distress to the Cardinal to defend himself against such charges. In the process he thus provides us with further evidence of Henry's very real displeasure during the Bordeaux dispute. Evidently Wolsey had decided that Pace must have been providing the King, whether wilfully or through negligence, with only edited versions of his carefully worded letters, for the secretary is at pains in his explanatory letter to deny that he had read the Cardinal's despatches 'directydde to the Kyngis Grace, diminutely, and that I do nott well informe the Kynge of the same'. Such misrepresentation, claimed Pace, would only be,[55]

to myne owne evident ruine; for Hys Grace doith rede them all hys selffe, and examine the same at laysor, wyth grete deliberacion, and hath better wytte to understonde them, than I to informe hym.

Whether or not such explanations convinced Wolsey of Pace's honesty is unknown. But it is interesting to note that almost immediately on the Cardinal's return Pace was sent to Rome, to further Wolsey's pursuit of the papal Tiara on the death of Leo X. The Cardinal's harshest contemporary critic, Polydore Vergil, makes much of this fact, alleging in his *Anglica Historia* that it was to remove Pace from Henry's side rather than to make use of his linguistic and diplomatic skills that the secretary was chosen for the mission, and subsequently kept on the Continent.[56]

For our present purposes, however, a more illuminating aspect of Pace's letter is the secretary's refutation of the assertion that he was responsible for the working of a certain royal despatch which had particularly aroused Wolsey's concern. This letter, which as Pace declared 'was unto Your Grace verraye displeasant', far from being a form of words imposed on Henry by his scribe, was, if the latter is to be believed, the result of direct dictation from the King. Exactly what the document contained cannot be gauged from Pace's despatch, but it seems likely to have been one of those letters written at the latter end of the dispute over the Bordeaux voyage, in which Henry expressed his indignation at what he perceived as Wolsey's questioning of his honour. By Pace's account, he had begun to draft a form of words for the letter 'farre discrepant from that ye recevidde',[57]

but the Kynge wolde not approve the same, and sayde that he wolde hym selfe devyse an answere to Your Graces letters . . . and commaundydde me to brynge your sayde letters in to hys Pryveye chiambre, wyth penne and inke, and there he wolde declare unto me what I schulde wryte. And when Hys Grace hadde your sayde letters, he redde the same 3 tymes, and markydde suche places as itt pleasydde hym to make answere unto, and commaundydde me to wryte and to reherse, as lykede hym, and

[55] *St. P.* I 47.   [56] Vergil, p. 293.   [57] *St. P.* I 47.

nott further to medyl wyth that answere. So that I [t]herin nothynge dydde, but obeyede the Kyngis commaundment, as to my dewtie apparteignyth, and especyally at such tyme as he wolde, upon goodde growndys, be obeyede, whoo so ever spake to the contrari.

If, as Pace clearly implies, Henry was here amending a moderately worded despatch into a more forceful and critical declaration, the force of his, albeit temporary, anger with Wolsey is readily apparent. It might be that the secretary, here and elsewhere, exaggerates Henry's displeasure to secure Wolsey's greater confidence and favour (a practice which Wolsey himself often performed with other individuals), but that he exaggerated too greatly, or even fabricated the King's anger, is extremely unlikely. It is one thing for Wolsey to create imaginary disputes for his own purposes when dealing with correspondents for whom he is the only source of information from the Court;[58] it is quite another for Pace to do so when writing to a man so much his superior, who possessed the ability to verify such accounts from numerous other sources. Thus when Pace informs Wolsey of Henry's being in a mood that 'he wolde . . . be obeyede, whoo so ever spake to the contrari' and that his anger was such that the secretary was right glad when it abated, one ought to give his account some credence. Clearly Wolsey's position as the King's most intimate counsellor had, for a time, seemed under threat.[59]

It was precisely this apparent threat to Wolsey's position, and hints of such royal displeasure, mixed with the disagreements over matters public as well as secret,[60] which, I would suggest, prompted Skelton's outburst of anti-Wolsey writing, rather than any more personal or factionally inspired motives. Hence the terms in which the attack on the Cardinal is worded.

Significantly, Parott's first statement of political import is a clear declaration that, for all his international origins, he is loyal to the English Crown. He greets his author's former pupil with a bow,

> In Englysshe to God Parott can supple:
> 'Cryste save Kyng Herry the VIIIth, owur royal Kyng,
> The red rose in honour to flowrysshe and sprynge!'
>
> 'With Kateryne incomporabyll, owur royall quene also,
> That pereles pomegarnat, Cryste save hyr nobyll grace!' (33–7)

Immediately after this loyal utterance Parott makes his first enigmatic com-

---

[58] See chap. 5 below for an account of such occasions.

[59] Peter Gwyn is sceptical about the importance of these disagreements. But, however temporary they were, it seems that Henry's annoyance was, for a time, very real, and Wolsey's anxiety was correspondingly serious. As it is the specific topicality and public appearance of his royal displeasure which is the crucial point here, rather than its long-term consequences, the case advanced above remains a valid one.

[60] Scarisbrick, *Henry VIII*, p. 87.

plaint, significantly, spoken prophetically 'in tongues', and thus demanding the readers' interpretation.[61]

> Parott *save habeler Castylyano,*
> With *fidasso de cosso,* in Turke and in Trace:
> *Vis consilii expers,* as techythe me Orace,
> *Mole ruit sua . . .*

Why the Queen should be told in her own tongue to 'have faith in yourself', and why Turkey and Thrace should be mentioned here is indicated by Heiserman, who observes that the reference alludes to the Turk's seizure of Thrace, and thus to the danger which is presented to Christendom by the Turks, whom the Christian states have the force but not the unity to oppose.[62] This failure to provide the 'plan', the unity of purpose, which will give strength to the 'brute force' available in the realm and in Christendom, is at the centre of Parott's attack. And it is made clear that it is Wolsey's 'besynes' which provides the major distraction from that unity. The theme is further advanced in lines 78–81 following,

> *Ic dien* serveth for the estrych fether,
> *Ic dien* is the language of the land of Beme;
> In Affryc tongue *byrsa* is a thonge of lether;
> In Palestina there is Jerusalem.

Initially this stanza seems to be a further nonsensical demonstration of Parott's linguistic talents. But gradually a political significance begins to crystallise. The text has already implied criticism of an overpowerful counsellor leading an over-generous monarch astray and of senseless activity performed, by implication, by a cleric, which leads only to folly. The clerical metaphor and the reference to the 'vicar general' in the lines 'But reason and wytte wantythe theyr provynciall / When Wylfulnes ys vicar generall' make the allusion to Wolsey all but obvious. Now the consequences of these follies are brought out.

The royal motto '*Ic dien*' is given ironic force by the earlier references to monarchs forced to serve the interests of lesser men, and the irony is reinforced here by the association of the motto with the 'thonge of lether', which suggests not merely service but bondage, and more specifically bondage to a '*byrsa*', which echoes the *burse* in which the Lord Chancellor of England (Wolsey) keeps the Great Seal. Once these allusions are teased out one is able to see that the monarch in question is clearly Henry. The motto was, after all, his own as Prince of Wales, as was the ostrich feather emblem. The subject whom he serves is equally evidently his Chancellor, Wolsey: the message being that the latter is keeping the administration of the realm tied

---

[61] *Speke, Parott,* lines 38–40. Scattergood, p. 454, gives 'Brute force without a plan, as Horace teaches . . . falls by its own weight'.
[62] Heiserman, p. 132.

in knots by his taking of the Great Seal to Calais, and by his dominance over policy-making in general.[63] The full import of Henry's servitude is implied in the remaining lines. *Ic dien*, Parott suggests, is not only the language of the subdued Henry, but also that of Bohemia, and of eastern Christendom generally, which is threatened by the same Turks who had taken Thrace. Thus, he implies, whilst Wolsey beguiles Henry and Christendom falls apart into internal feuds, the Turks will bring Bohemia under their servitude also.[64] The solution to the problem and the ultimate spur to action is provided by the last line of the passage, 'In Palestine there is Jerusalem', which acts both as a reminder that, to all Christendom's shame, the very centre of Christianity is under Turkish control and saying 'I serve' to a heathen master, and as a call to arms for a campaign to throw back the Turk, as Jerusalem is the ultimate goal for a Christian crusade.

But why should Skelton have thought that such references to Wolsey and to crusades would win him royal favour? The answer seems to lie in his perception of high politics at the time. As chapter 2 revealed, the poet was not familiar with the private determinations of either King or Council. He was not a regular courtier, and so had to rely for his information concerning the affairs of Court and State on what was public knowledge and on what could be gleaned from conversations with those closer to the Court. Hence he could easily be forgiven for assuming that the defence of Christendom and a unified Christian attack on the Turk were high priorities in Henry's mind during 1521. The triumphant Treaty of London of 1518 had been signed with the high ideal of uniting Christendom in peace against the Turkish threat paramount among its list of aims, and the London conference had been both the occasion and the justification for Wolsey's elevation to the Legacy *a latere*. The unprecedented number of states eventually involved in that agreement must have made the prospect of a new crusade seem a possibility for the first time in decades and Henry and Wolsey had milked the occasion for all that it was worth.[65] In addition, in a letter which Professor

---

[63] Significantly Henry was to request the Seal's return to England as early as 9 October (*St. P.* I, 22).

[64] For the threat to Bohemia at this time see Karl Brandi, *The Emperor Charles V*, trans. C. V. Wedgewood (London, 1965 reprint), p. 140.

[65] See Scarisbrick, *Henry VIII*, pp. 69–74. Professor Scarisbrick, because he quite rightly does not believe that a crusade was a serious objective of English foreign policy, minimises the emphasis placed on that aim in the public justification of the treaty. Again, the appearance rather than the reality is what concerns us here, and for an impression of how the treaty was presented to the public in England, see *L.P.* II (ii) 4362, and the account in Edward Hall, *The Union of the Two Noble Families of Lancaster and York*, ed. Henry Ellis (London, 1809), p. 595, of a masque which entertained the French envoys, and S. Anglo, *Spectacle, Pageantry and Early Tudor Policy* (Oxford, 1969), pp. 124–69. The treaty was eventually to embrace among its more significant signatories, England, France, Spain and the Empire, the Papacy, Denmark, Hungary, Portugal, the Swiss cantons, Scotland, the Italian states and the Hanseatic towns.

Scarisbrick dates August 1519, Henry himself had declared to the Pope that 'to strike a blow for Christendom has ever been the summit of our ambition', that he was working actively towards a crusade for which he offered and dedicated 'our whole kingdom, our wealth, our authority, our goods, our prestige . . . yes our very blood and body we offer and dedicate to Christ and his vicar'. He had, he claimed, already laid plans for the project with Wolsey and the papal Legate Campeggio and had prepared to raise the finance for it by a levy of a tenth from the clergy and a fifteenth from the laity. He had concluded this remarkable pledge with the assertion that 'we look for a mighty triumph for the faith of Christ and will not spare one drop of blood for him who, to rescue us from our sins, did not spare his son'.[66]

Clearly such a letter reveals more about Henry's desire to keep the Pope's good faith, and to retain the legatine commission for Wolsey, than it does about his actual desire for a crusade on so grand a scale. But, equally, so grand and public a gesture would have left a strong impression on those who had heard of it and were unaware of the more cynical motives which lay behind it. Again the impression could easily have been gained that the defence of Christendom was a crucial element in the Crown's strategic thinking.

The fact that Skelton thought that Henry desired a crusade in 1521 is thus understandable, given these precedents from the preceding years. But more immediately, and more tellingly in the present context, Wolsey's mission to Calais was itself associated with the crusade theme. The conference was, in great part, a product of the 1518 treaty, by which England was obliged to enter any Franco-Imperial conflict on the side of the aggrieved party, and was seemingly aimed at a patching up and renewal of the 'Universal Peace' established in London, which had been the first preparation for a war with the Turk. This certainly seems to have been the popular perception of the mission. Edward Hall, who is usually a reliable witness of popular rumour and opinion in the capital, commented on Henry's motives for despatching Wolsey thus,[67]

The Kynges highness, co[n]sideryng ye murder & effusion of Christen bloud, and the trouble that might ensue to al the princes of Christendome, by invasion of the great Turke, sent the Cardinall of Yorke his Chau[n]cellor by name Lord Thomas Wolsey, to his toune of Calayce to entreate an amitie and peace betwene those two mightie Princes [Francis I and Charles V].

---

[66] *L.P.* III (i) 432; original cited with spelling modernised in Scarisbrick, *Henry VIII*, p. 105.
[67] Hall, *Union*, p. 624. See also *L.P.* III (i) 1270, and *Sp. Cal. 1509–25* 354 for the view recorded by a gentleman-in-waiting to Charles V that it was popularly held amongst the Imperial courtiers that Wolsey had come as a mediator of peace to compose a settlement between France and the Empire.

Such was evidently the public justification for Wolsey's journey.[68] Hence it is no surprise that Skelton should so readily have accepted it, and played upon it. Indeed the need to ensure the unity of Christendom had been given further relevance by the fall of Belgrade on 29 August 1521 (which Pace had informed Wolsey was 'verraye displesante to the Kyngis Hyghnesse') and by the renewed calls for aid from eastern Europe, such as that from the Hungarian envoy who, Hall notes, was 'honorably entertayned [by Wolsey] duryng hys abode in Calyce'.[69] Again, such public events as these, and such public explanations of them, were far more likely to have been known and discussed around the Court and thus known to Skelton, than Wolsey's secret brief to conclude a bilateral treaty with the Emperor during his 'sabbatical' in Bruges, during a break in the conference.

What Skelton is doing then, in the political stanzas of *Speke, Parott*, is, as was suggested above, indulging in the politician's art of telling his intended audience what he believes that they want to hear. Taking his cues from the ostensible purpose of the Calais conference, from Henry's publicly stated desire for a crusade, and from the apparent rift between King and minister, he is suggesting that, whilst Wolsey is controlling policy and the running of the administration from Calais, and whilst Henry is forced to wait at home and to indulge him, nothing profitable is done and the potential for useful action is unfulfilled. This last is effectively symbolised by the reference to redundant artefacts in the lines 'a narrow unfethered and without an hed, / A bagpype without blowynge standeth in no sted' (lines 74–5), which hint at martial implements standing unused and also echo the Miller's bagpipes and the Yeoman's arrows of two of Chaucer's pilgrims, which thus gives to the image religio-military overtones appropriate to Skelton's crusade theme. The implication of all this is that Skelton is pandering to Henry's self-esteem, and suggesting that it would be far more profitable were he to remove the initiative from Wolsey's hands and take control of events himself.

Such an interpretation of these early stanzas of the text might seem overly speculative, but a reading of the succeeding lines and of the envoys serves to confirm such early suppositions. It is quite evident, for example, that Skelton held the bystander's opinion of the Calais conference, that is that it was a genuine attempt to reunite Christendom by reconciling France and the Empire to peace, and thus inevitably doomed to failure owing to the lack of

---

[68] See, for example, *Ven. Cal. 1520–6* 225, 226, 233, 272.

[69] The Hungarian envoy's mission was to request that Wolsey be sent to 'adjust matters between Christians in order that they may turn their weapons against the Turks'. Hall, *Union*, p. 627; *Ven. Cal. 1520–26*, 331. For Henry's displeasure at the fall of Belgrade, see B.L. Cotton MS Galba B VII fo. 1237 (*St P.* I 45). Despite Anglo's doubts (*Spectacle*, p. 177), it is clear that the London mid-summer pageants of 1521 provided an allegorical representation of this siege, and thus acted as a reminder to the public of the crusading theme which had adorned the public face of English foreign policy since 1518. *Ven. Cal.*, III 244.

any desire for a settlement on either side.[70] And his references to the unpursued crusade and to Christendom's inability to defend itself provide the frame of reference within which, he suggests, Wolsey's 'failure' at Calais ought to be judged. Whilst the Turks advance, Wolsey conducts his fruitless business, his 'replicacion restless' (line 282), aimed at reconciling the irreconcilable.

> For Jerico and Jerssey shall mete togethyr as sone
> As he to exployte the man owte of the mone.
> (306–7)

Such points are hinted at, little by little, until finally, in the *dereyn lenvoy*, the poet, in a lengthy diatribe, despatches Parott to expose what he describes as the total futility of Wolsey's mission, and the impossibility of it ever being brought to a successful conclusion.

> Prepayre yow, Parrot, brevely your passage to take . . .
> And sadlye salute owur solen Syre Sydrake,
> And shewe hym that all the world dothe conject,
> How the maters he mellis in com to small effecte;
> For he wantythe of hys wyttes that all wold rule alone;
> Hyt ys no lytyll bordon to bere a grete mylle stone.
>
> To bryng all the see into a cheryston pytte,
> To nombyr all the sterrys in the fyrmament,
> To rule ix realmes by one mannes wytte,
> To such thynges ympossybyll, reason cannot consente;
> Muche money, men sey, there madly he hathe spente;
> Parott, ye may prate thys undyr protestacion,
> Was nevyr suche a senatour syn Crystes
> Incarnacion. (324–37)

What Skelton is reflecting in these stanzas, then, may well be the opinion held of Wolsey's mission by many of those on the fringes of the Court who were not privy to the real terms of the Cardinal's full commission. The prime concern behind the text, however, is to mirror, not popular opinion, but what Skelton perceived to be the King's wishes. So much is evident from the manner in which the envoys continue the satiric charges of the poem proper.

---

[70] *St. P.* I 33. In this letter to Wolsey, dated 4 September, Pace clearly states that 'the communaltie of thys realme, off every sorte, hadde no knowliege off suche secrete matiers, as Your Grace hath treatidde and concludydde wyth thEmperour'. It was commonly surmised that the visit to Bruges was intended simply to reinforce Anglo-Imperial amity. Only for a time, it seems, when royal Letters Patent were issued to raise the 6,000 archers for the Imperial escort, was it rumoured that 'we schalle have warre agaynst Fraunce'. By late September Skelton was clearly of the opinion that a general peace was what Henry intended. See also Richard Lyster's remarks to lord Darcy (*L.P.* III (ii) 1669, 12 October 1521) that he 'trust[ed] the Cardinal will bring a peace home with him', and Wolsey's own remark to Antonio Surian that, because of the failure of the Calais talks to produce a treaty speedily, he would return to England in shame and would be revenged on those who had obstructed the negotiations (*Sp. Cal. 1520–26* 362):

A major purpose of these supplementary verses is certainly to gloss and to clarify the satiric intimations of the poem which preceded them. But what is also significant about them, from a political viewpoint, is the way in which they continue to exhibit a somewhat distorted reflection of the tone of royal despatches, in precisely the manner in which a commentator on the periphery of the Court would be expected to absorb and react to hints and rumours leaking from the royal household.

It is evident that by early October Henry was publicly expressing his expectation of a conclusion to Wolsey's negotiations and was beginning to express the need both for his return and for that of the Great Seal. The Cardinal's main commission had, after all, been fulfilled as early as August, by the conclusion of the Anglo-Imperial agreement. Thus on 9 October Pace can be found writing to Wolsey from Windsor, stating that,[71]

The Kynge signifieth unto [Your Grace] . . . that he thynkyth that the kepynge off the terme nowe, in thys dewe tyme, schulde greatly be to the contentacion off hys subjectes, and also make muche for his owne profecte, and especyally for the bryngynge in off his revenewes, whyche he sayth cumyth in varraye slowly, in so muche that Mr Myklowe haith bin compellyde to borowe money for the payement of hys servauntis wagis. And Hys Grace sayth, that the sayde terme myght be conveniently kepte, yff Your Grace wolde sende home the Master of the Rollys [Tunstall], wyth the Great Seale, for that intent and purpose.

By 15–20 October such expectations had seemingly increased, for Pace was dropping heavy hints in his correspondence which inquired whether the Cardinal would be returning home soon,[72] and suggested that 'Hys Hyghnesse wolde gladly see Your Grace at home, all thyngis concludydde there'.[73] Finally, a week later, on 27 October, the secretary remarked that,[74]

As touchynge Your Graces longe demore there, the Kyng sayth, that thowe he be verraye desirose to have and see you at home, yitt consederynge that your abode there is for so goode, so godly, and necessarie purpose, Hys Grace is well contentydde and pleasydde therwyth: prayynge God to brynge the same to the desyridde effect and ende. Albeitt yff Your Grace schall perceve that the ii Princes intende to make delaye, and not to cum to any goodde and honorable conclusion, then Hys Graces mynde is, ye schall returne home; considerynge that he hath greate neade off yew here, aswell for the administracion off justice, as the orderynge of hys rea[lme] otherwyse.

For all their courtesy Henry's orders are precise and peremptory. Unless a swift breakthrough in the negotiations can be achieved to provide the hoped-for truce, Wolsey is to return home at once and must, if necessary, abandon the conference as a failure. Clearly such a dramatic summons, coming after a

---

[71] *St. P.* I 42.
[72] *L.P.* III (ii) 1691, 20 October. See also *L.P.* III (ii) 1669 for Richard Lyster's remark that 'the time of his [Wolsey's] coming is quite uncertain'.
[73] B.L. Cotton MS Galba B VII fo. 1237 (*St. P.* I 45).
[74] B.L. Cotton MS Galba B VII fo. 133 (*St. P.* I 46).

period of increasing frustration on Henry's part at Wolsey's 'longe demore' in Calais, would have been a matter for discussion at all levels of the Court, and Skelton, ever attentive for news from that direction, could easily have heard word of it. Thus it is of great interest to discover that the first envoy, written just three days after Pace had sent Henry's orders to Wolsey on *Penultimo die Octobris*,[75] should begin with the declaration that Wolsey should return home to England, as everyone, and everything, was weary of his continued negotiations;[76]

> Go little quayre, namyd the Popagay,
> Home to resorte Jerobesethe perswade;
> For the cliffes of Scalope they rore wellaway,
> And the sandes of Cefas begyn to waste and face,
> For replicacion restles that he of late ther made (278–82)

This new message, unmentioned in the poem proper, is repeated in the *Secunde Lenvoy*,

> Passe forthe, Parotte, towardes some passengere;
> Require hym to convey yow ovyr the salte fome;
> Addressyng your selfe, lyke a sadde messengere,
> To owur soleyne Seigneour Sadoke, desire hym to cum home,
> Makynge hys pylgrimage by *Notre Dame de Crome*.
> (301–5)

And in the third Wolsey's return is described retrospectively on 15 *Kalendis Decembris*,[77]

> Prepayre yow, Parotte, brevely your passage to take . . .
> And sadlye salute owur solen Syre Sydrake . . .
>
> Wherfor he may now come agayne as he wente,
> *Non sine postica sanna*, as I trowe,
> From Calys to Dovry, to Caunterbury in Kente.

Here again, then, Skelton's text can be seen to mirror closely the general tone and intent of royal wishes.

Thus it is difficult to escape the conclusion that the poet was deliberately feeding what hints he received of the King's opinions into Parott's repertoire and re-presenting them as satire. Skelton has not designed a consistent pro-

---

[75] Skelton dated most of the envoys individually, which allows one to correlate them closely with events on the political stage.

[76] For a fuller description of these stanzas, see the following section. The references to 'the cliffes of Scaloppe' (line 280) and 'the sandes of Cefas' (line 281) are pointers towards the Calais conference. The former is an anglicisation of Escalles cliff, the latter an allusion, via the pseudonym Cefas for St Peter, to Dampierre-lez-Dunes, both locations bounding the Calais Pale.

[77] *Speke, Parott*, lines 324, 326, 338–40. For '*Non sine postica sanna*', Scattergood, p. 462, gives 'Not without a grimace behind his back'.

gramme of reform, nor even a consistent line of argument with which to attack Wolsey. He seems merely to be making a series of *ad hoc* critical statements which follow slavishly the indications of royal feelings which would have been circulating at Court. Hence, when Henry was in dispute with Wolsey over the practicality of the Bordeaux voyage and the despatch of the English archers,[78] and the issue at stake was whether the King should rely on his own or Wolsey's judgement, Parott can be found praising Henry, indicating that the King has allowed himself to be beguiled into following the Cardinal's wishes for too long, owing to his own innate generosity and because of Wolsey's apparent industry on his behalf, and ridiculing the latter's inability to make reliable political judgements.[79] In addition Skelton cites Wolsey's attacks on the privilege of sanctuary, and his monastic dissolutions simply because they are topical news, as evidence of self-serving decisions, rather than those which, as a Councillor, he ought to make, which benefit the entire commonwealth.

Again, on the specific issue of the Calais mission, one finds Parott attacking the futility of the conference, and implying that it will never unify Christendom against the Turk and so permit a crusade, purely because Henry seemed, at that time, to desire those ends and thus seemed likely to share the feelings of frustration which Parott voices. Skelton does not pursue the implications of his criticism any further than the need to pander to Henry's wishes dictates. Thus there is no analysis of how best the unity of Christendom *should* be achieved, merely criticism of what Skelton felt was Wolsey's inevitable failure to achieve it. The obvious conclusion of Parott's logic, which is that if France and the Empire could never be reconciled then there never could be a crusade and the Turks would make further inroads into Christendom, is not pursued, as such reasoning would obviously lead to the realisation that such a mission as Wolsey's, however seemingly doomed, was the only hope for reconciling the Christian community. Skelton's logic is then, totally *ad hoc*, and based neither on consistent principles nor on sustained argument; it merely trails in the wake of the Crown's publicly avowed policies. Indeed after 1521 Skelton abandoned his crusade-theme altogether and began to argue fiercely for a vigorous anti-French and anti-Scots policy entirely at odds with his earlier suggestions, at precisely the time that Crown policy swung publicly behind the Emperor. Hence, as soon as Wolsey was ordered to return from Calais, Parott began to demand his return in exactly the same terms as the royal summons, citing his retention of the Seal there as the major grievance.[80] The date of this envoy, just three days after the despatch of Wolsey's letter of recall, cannot be mere coincidence.

---

[78] Scarisbrick, *Henry VIII*, p. 86. [79] See *Speke, Parott*, line 126.
[80] *Speke, Parott*, lines 308–12.

The genesis of the political aspects of Speke, Parott, then, stemmed entirely from a desire to reflect HenryVIII's wishes in verse. Wolsey became the poet's target almost by default. It was the political circumstances of the late summer of 1521, when Skelton chose to write his self-justifying and self-advertising masterpiece, that determined the Cardinal's inclusion. For the first time since his remarkably rapid rise to power, Henry's chief minister was kept apart from his sovereign for an extended period of time. And, whilst Calais might not have been the 'early Tudor India' which it has been painted,[81] it is clear that such a lengthy exile from the centre of policy-making and preferment could place severe restrictions on a favoured Crown servant's ability to maintain his position of influence. Hence the difficulties which Wolsey seems to have experienced in his relationship with the King during his mission and which Skelton chose to pick on and exploit for his own ends. The Cardinal had been despatched on a mission the ostensible purpose of which made it appear destined to end in failure. Moreover that failure would be on a grand and humiliating level, given the European scale of the exercise and the magnificent manner in which Wolsey had departed from London.[82] The completion of Henry's own publicly avowed wish for a crusade, however, was seemingly dependent on the mission proving a success. Wolsey's sovereign had had an extended disagreement with him, had expressed 'marvayle' at some of his judgements,[83] and had stated a desire that the Great Seal be returned home and that the Cardinal should follow it. All of this might well have appeared to the uninformed onlooker as evidence of a severe rift between King and Councillor, and as the prelude to the imminent fall of the Cardinal. Such an evaluation of the evidence seems to have been what prompted Skelton's attack on Wolsey in Speke, Parott.

As has been demonstrated, Skelton was ever attentive to what he perceived to be his sovereign's wishes, particularly when he felt that he could play on them to his own advantage.[84] This may well have been the spur which prompted his satiric venture, once his desperation at his lack of recognition and reward had determined him upon a dramatic gesture. The risk was, after

---

[81] D. Starkey, 'From feud to faction', History Today, (October 1982), pp. 16–22, see esp. p. 19.

[82] For Wolsey's departure see Hall, Union, p. 624.

[83] B.L. Cotton MS Caligula D VIII fo. 153 (St P., 38), Pace to Wolsey, 30 September 1521.

[84] Note his timely despatch of the Chronique De Rains to Henry in 1513. It is also possible that Magnyfycence was constructed to shed a favourable light on and invest with an allegorical significance Henry's removal of the 'minions' from his Privy Chamber in 1519. For this incident see Ven. Cal. II 1220; Hall, Union, pp. 598–9. See Maria Dowling's original University of London Ph. D. thesis, 'Scholarship, politics and the Court of Henry VIII' (1981), pp. 104–8, for an embryonic treatment of this assertion. However the possibility that the 'minions' expulsion was a purge of the King's intimate associates instigated by Wolsey and that Skelton was thus writing an allegorical critique of Wolsey's policies, requires far greater evidence than has hitherto been offered to substantiate it.

all, not so great, if the poet had read the signs correctly and Henry had lost faith in Wolsey and was on the point of either severely reprimanding or actually dismissing him. In such circumstances Skelton's satire may well have suited Henry's purposes, just as his war poems had suited the King in 1513. For, in Skelton's scenario, if the Calais conference ended in failure, without a general peace and crusade being agreed on, then Henry risked a loss of face, having seemingly set his mind on such a venture. If, however, the sole blame could be deflected onto Wolsey's personal incompetence rather than any inherent implausibility of the scheme itself, then Henry's honour would emerge untarnished. Such was the role of a Tudor chief minister, to act as a political lightning conductor, who would himself attract any criticism of unpopular or unsuccessful policies, leaving the sovereign free to play the role of impartial judge in such debates. If the Calais conference should prove a failure, then, Wolsey would inevitably have to shoulder the responsibility for it and Skelton's text might aid the Crown in its presentation of Wolsey in the role of failed diplomat. And what better time for the poet to launch the attack could there be than with the 'fals cat' abroad, leaving the poet to play in greater safety in his absence?

From the relative security of his rooms in the Abbey of Westminster, protected by ancient rights of sanctuary, Skelton may have felt that his prospects were good. If the King heard of and liked the piece, as was the poet's intention, Skelton might gain a new recall to Court favour. If he did not, his safe house in the sanctuary precincts would be a convenient place in which to await the cooling of tempers. And his poem would not be open libel. It was to be a subtle, scholarly work, an attack so sophisticated and circumspect that, were Wolsey to survive in his position of power, the poet would be free to deny any critical intentions. It was to be a project worthy of the Master Poet that Skelton felt himself to be, which would, at a stroke, erase the painful memory of the past lean decade and establish him in his rightful place at the centre of literary and scholarly activity.

Any analysis of a poet's motivation, such as the above, will inevitably be speculative to a certain degree. But what is clear beyond doubt is that the traditional explanations for the appearance of *Speke Parott*, in 1521, and the start of Skelton's literary assault on Wolsey will not do. The poem was not factionally inspired, nor was it simply the product of righteous moral outrage on the poet's part. If the text was the result of Skelton's horror at some obvious iniquity which he saw personified in the Cardinal, one wonders why he had not voiced his opinions earlier. He might have criticised Wolsey in *Magnyfycence*, for example, if the play was a parable of the Court politics of 1519. But there, if one accepts Magnyfycence himself to be a portrayal of Henry, and the expelled 'minions' to be figured in the courtly vice characters, Wolsey must be represented by one of those characters who favoured the 'purge', of which the virtue figure Measure is the most likely candidate.[85] The obvious disparity between a portrayal of Wolsey as Measure and Reason in 1519, and as a personification of excess and 'wylfulnes' in 1521 seems totally inexplicable in political terms if one is searching for a sudden change in the Cardinal's actions which might have provoked the poet's change in attitude. The only difference which can be noted is that Wolsey was clearly the repository of Henry's trust and favour in the former year, but the object of criticism and apparent royal displeasure two years later.

It is Skelton's attempt to reflect royal opinions in his political work which determines his approach to Wolsey in the two texts in question, rather than a more principled critique of the Cardinal's character and policies. Similarly, the element of calculation involved in the timing of the attack militates against the suggestion that what one is witnessing here is a spontaneous outburst of indignation. As does the fact that, within two years of the writing of *Speke, Parott*, Skelton was praising Wolsey in terms as fulsome as his attacks had been savage, and writing works commissioned at his behest. All of this suggests most forcefully that the decision to write *Speke, Parott* in 1521, and to write it in part against Wolsey, was more calculating than previous critics have allowed, more freelance, and had far more to do with Skelton's search for patronage than has hitherto been thought.

As time was to show, Skelton had miscalculated. Wolsey did not fall in 1521. But only hindsight portrays the poet's decision to write *Speke, Parott* as a foolhardy gamble. From Skelton's position outside the inner circles of policy-making, prior to Wolsey's triumphal return from Calais, the decision to write against the Cardinal might have seemed the only means by which a forgotten poet might effectively resurrect his career.

THE ENVOYS

As has been suggested, Skelton's decision to write against Wolsey to further his own Court career was to prove a miscalculation. He had chosen to attack the Cardinal for pursuing policies which, despite the emphasis placed on

[85] Dr Dowling's assertion that 'Measure is an ingenious combination of Norfolk and Wolsey, since the figure's good qualities apply (in the poet's estimation) to the former, while the abuse showered on him by the minion figures and the deluded Magnificence recall Skelton's own vituperations against the Cardinal in the satirical poems' fails to convince. Measure is portrayed as an entirely laudable character throughout the play. The abuse which he receives from the 'Vice' characters, like all the insulting utterances of Sin and Vice figures in Morality Literature, reflects ill, not on him, but on the characters who speak it. It is an external manifestation of their internal corruption and folly. That the abuse of Measure in *Magnyfycence* resembles in some ways the abuse of Wolsey in the satires of the 1520s indicates only that Skelton's satiric invective was stereotyped. The language and phrasing in the relevant passages also recalls the abuse of Garnesh in *Agenst Garnesche*, and of the 'doltish' musician in *Agaynste a Comely Coystrowne*.

them in public and semi-public utterances, were not the main reason for the Calais mission. Furthermore the entire rationale behind the attacks was based on the mistaken assumption that Henry had developed a lasting distrust of Wolsey during their disagreements of September 1521. How Skelton coped with the gradual realisation of the scope of his miscalculation, and how he amended, explained and qualified his satire as a result, through the addition of supplementary verses, or envoys, over the following four months, will be considered below.

The major purpose of the political satire in the poem proper was, as we have seen, to suggest, by the use of biblical and classical exempla and by the creation of a complex web of *metaphora* which invested seemingly nonsensical remarks with a political significance, that Henry should trust his own judgement rather than Wolsey's, and that the latter ought to be relieved of his dominant position at Court, as, for all his apparent industry, his policies were wasteful and, ultimately, ruinous. The framework within which these criticisms were made was primarily that of foreign policy, and of the Turkish menace to Christendom, as this was perceived by Skelton to be the King's major concern at the time. What the succeeding envoys reveal is the gradual simplification of this obscure web of metaphor through the introduction of increasingly specific references to Wolsey and to Calais, which give the satire a greater immediacy. Clearly part of the justification for the continuation of the poem came from the apparent drift of Court opinion. As October progressed and Henry began, first to inquire after, and then to press for, Wolsey's return it must have seemed that Skelton's critical stance had been justified and that the Cardinal was indeed the target of royal displeasure. This both encouraged the poet to write further attacks, and provided him with a new charge to aim at Wolsey, that of the wastefulness of his continued dalliance in Calais and the desirability of his speedy return to England, the which charge appears in the first three envoys. Another factor seems to have been of equal importance in prompting these supplementary stanzas, however, and that was the reaction to the poem of Skelton's intended audience.

As has been suggested Skelton designed *Speke, Parott* to appeal to a learned, courtly audience. He intended his readers to be impressed by the complexity, the subtlety and the ingenuity of his work, but he also intended them to be able to tease out its inner significance and so fully appreciate his genius. Then, both as the result of what he hoped would be their sympathy with Parott's political comments, and as a result of their newly discovered respect for his poetic skills, he would be taken into favour once more by the King and Court. So much can be inferred from the continual references in the text to the allegorical and prophetic significance of Parott, and the metaphorical sense of his verses. Despite all such hints, however, it seems that the text was not understood at all by its readers and some even ventured criticism of it on the grounds that it was simply the wanton nonsense which it purported to be. Hence quite the reverse of Skelton's original intention had resulted, and, far from his being proclaimed a Master Poet, he was once more faced with allegations of folly and inconsequentiality. Thus, in order to rescue something from the ruins of his project, he began to make even more pointed reminders to his audience that they ought to read his texts carefully to seek out hidden meanings, whilst he simultaneously made those meanings even more obvious in the increasingly specific political stanzas of the envoys.

Skelton's decision to extend *Speke, Parott* into an indefinitely long series of pamphlets was, then, based on a number of factors, just as had been his decision to begin the project in the first instance. First, on the political level, the poet clearly began to feel that his criticisms were in tune with the mood of the Court. Hence Skelton seems to have been tempted to push his allusions closer to insolence and obvious political relevance in order to reap what he must have felt were the proper rewards due him. Additionally the lack of any official reaction against the work must have encouraged him, although it is unlikely that at this stage Wolsey was aware of what could only have been a small number of hand-written manuscripts circulated at Court and in the City, so retaliation was unlikely.[86]

Just as it became clear, however, that the chance remained for the successful completion of his project of self-advertisement, so it became equally evident that that chance was slipping away, for his audience were missing completely the very political implications of the satire on which the whole exercise relied. Certainly his remarks about the follies of humanist scholarship would have been understood, but the net result of this would only have been to sting his opponents into further invectives against him, whilst at the same time providing them with the ideal weapons with which to attack him. For his attack on the foolish and nonsensical methodology of the 'Greeks' appeared, to its readers, to be made within a text which was itself both extremely foolish and completely nonsensical.[87] Skelton had seemingly trodden too clumsily across the minefield between obscurity and provocation after all. Hence the need for him to return to *Speke, Parott* was central to his hopes for the future, and hence he sought, with increasingly obvious frustration at the results, to explain and justify the text to his critics, and to demonstrate Parott's sagacity to his courtly audience.

So much is evident from the remarkable amount of time that the poet took

[86] *Speke, Parott* was not printed until 1545, when it appeared in Richard Lant's edition of Skelton's works, *Here After Foloweth Certayne Bokes* (S.T.C. 22598). See the section below concerning the circulation of the satires.

[87] It is likely that it was Lily and the 'Greeks' who were the, unnamed, critics of *Speke, Parott* to whom Skelton refers.

to explain his text in each of the succeeding envoys. Each one, save for the last in which Parott resolves to 'sette asyde all sophysms, and speke now trewe and playne' (line 448), finishes with an indignant address to its readers which demonstrates how the text ought to have been approached. In the *Lenvoy Primere* of 30 October the reference is clearly to the reception which the poem itself had received.

> Yet some folys say ye arre furnysshed with knakkes,
> That hang togedyr as fethyrs in the wynde;
> But lewdlye ar they lettyrd that your lernyng lackys,
> Barkyng and whyning lyke churlysshe currys of kynde,
> For whoo lokythe wyselye in your warkys may fynde
> Muche frutefull mater. But now for your defence,
> Agayne all remordes arme yow with paciens. (292–8)

Here the attitude expressed is one of somewhat weary condescension. There have been critical 'remordes', but only from those too lacking in learning to aspire to Parott's sophistication, who suggest that the text is merely full of inconsequentialities ('knakkes'), with as much cohesion as wind-blown feathers. These Skelton dismisses as mere 'dumb dogs'. To the remainder of his readers he is more accommodating. Confident in his reading of Henry's mood, he had begun the envoy with the recommendation that Wolsey return home, which, although still carefully encoded within a complex metaphorical framework, was several steps away from the diffuse allegory of the poem proper. Now he points his readers back to the main text, indicating once more that they should read through the apparent nonsense and, by looking wisely, discover the 'frutefull mater' beyond.

By November, however, and the writing of the *Secunde Lenvoy*, the 'remordes' do not seem to have ceased. Indeed the plural form of the word 'poemys' in the text cited below suggests that the first envoy gained a similar reception to the main text, for all its explanatory final stanza. But by this time Skelton's reaction to this reception is rather less characterised by the 'paciens' which he had advised Parott to adopt. 'And thowe sum dysdayne yow', he remarks to his creation,

> . . . and sey how ye prate,
> And howe your poemys arre barayne of polyshed eloquens,
> There is none that your name woll abbrogate
> Then [i.e. but] nodypollys and gramatolys of smalle intellygens:
> To rude ys there reason to reche to your sentence;
> Suche malyncoly mastyvys and mangye curre dogges
> Ar mete for a swyne herde to hunte after hogges. (315–321)

It seems that Skelton's educated readers were still attacking his satire on purely literary grounds (because they felt that stylistically it was 'barayne of polyshed eloquens') and were ignoring its political implications. This continued failure draws a characteristically irascible response from the poet, who berates the intelligence of such short-sighted readers. Still confident, however, of the innate acceptability of his message, if only he could get them to see it, he uses this second envoy to make the political point of the text still more explicit with a further demand that the, as yet unnamed, target return home as his task was fruitless (lines 301–7). The identity of this 'passengere' is then further suggested by the more open and confident declaration of the second stanza,

> With porpose and graundepose he may fede hym fatte,
> Thowghe he pampyr not hys paunche with the grete seall;
> We have longyd and lokyd long tyme for that,
> Whyche cawsythe pore suters have many a hongry mele;
> As presydent and regent he rulythe every deall. (308–12)

Skelton could hardly have been more explicit without naming his target. His reference to the Great Seal could only have suggested one name to his readers. For Wolsey had taken the Seal with him to Calais, an action which, as Hall observes, 'had not been seen before' and had the consequences for the 'pore suters' which the poet asserted.[88] Thus Skelton's allusion was to an issue of great topical concern, not simply another circumlocutionary means of identifying Wolsey. Similarly the reference to a 'presydent and regente' seems unlikely to have been misinterpreted, as Wolsey was at that moment presiding over the Calais conference, and carried with him a royal commission, tantamount to a temporary regency, 'which had the Kynges power as if his grace had been present'.[89] The poet may well have felt that he had done sufficient in this envoy to remove any doubts in the minds of his readers about the applicability of Parott's 'pratyng'.

By the time that he came to write the *Dereyne Lenveoy* of 15 *Kalendis Decembris*, however, Wolsey was back in England. He had disembarked at Dover on 27 November and travelled from there 'to Blechyngly, where the Kyngis Grace welcomed hym gevying him also thankes for his great paines and travaill'.[90] Consequently Skelton's confidence seems to have taken a blow, and he appears to exhibit in his verses rather more than simple frustration. By this time, of course, the poet would have been fully aware of the political miscalculation that he had made. He would have discovered that Wolsey had returned, not in disgrace at having failed to secure a general

---

[88] Hall, *Union*, p. 625. Hall also notes (p. 627) 'Duryng the continuounce of the Cardinall in Calyce all writtes and patentes wer ther by hym sealed and no shyriffes chosen for lack of his presence'.

[89] *Ibid.*, p. 625. See also *St. P.* I 50, and B.L. Cotton MS Galba B VII 42 for Wolsey's confirmation that he was indeed, as he told his royal master, 'representing the rowme off your Lieutenaunt'.

[90] Hall, *Union*, p. 628.

peace in Europe, but in triumph. Indeed Henry, far from dismissing Wolsey, was evidently delighted with him, and granted him the Abbey of St Albans for his pains.[91] Skelton had taken a gamble and, presumably to his horror, had discovered not a responsive audience keen to pick up any jibes made at the expense of the suddenly unfashionable favourite but rather a disturbing mixture of stony, seemingly uncomprehending, silence and active criticism. The poet's response to this potentially hazardous political isolation was not to retract everything – he had pursued the point too far for that and submission was not in his character – but to clarify and reiterate his assertions for a final time, adding a direct plea to Henry to replace Wolsey, to suggest once more that there was method in his apparent madness, and to defuse any possible accusations of treachery with loyal declarations.

It is interesting to note that the Latin *Monosticon* to this third envoy shows a marked change from the previous two, seemingly in response to this new perception of danger. In the first the benediction to Parott had been merely that he should,[92]

Go as a wise or true speaking messenger of what is seemly.

The second benediction, reflecting the poet's loss of 'paciens' with his readers, runs,[93]

Parrot, go quickly to blunt the weapons of fools.

By the third, however, Skelton's critics are perceived as posing a definite threat, for that text is sent away with the dedication,[94]

Go hastening Parrot, reprove all *evil* tongues.

Those who had been simply fools before, when Skelton thought them out of step with his own genius and with Henry's wishes, have suddenly become evil, with the capacity to undo all that the poet had hoped to achieve with an accusation. Thus the third envoy finishes with an overt nod to the Crown,

Thow ye be tauntyd, Parotte, with tonges attayntyd,
Yet your problemes ar preignaunte *and with loyalte acquayntyd*. (343–4, my italics.)

That the poet should suddenly have felt it necessary to stress his own loyalty at this point suggests quite clearly that he felt himself, if not under threat, at least under possible scrutiny from above in a way which he had not been before. And the only event which could so rapidly have affected his outlook

---

[91] *L.P.* III (ii) 1759. Henry's public greeting for the returning Cardinal would have been sufficient to indicate to Skelton the scope of his miscalculation. It is not suggested here that the poet knew of Henry's satisfaction at Wolsey's fulfilling of his secret brief.
[92] *Speke, Parott*, line 299, trans. in Scattergood, p. 461.
[93] *Speke, Parott*, line 322, trans. in Scattergood, p. 462.
[94] *Speke, Parott*, line 345, trans. in Scattergood, p. 462, my italics.

was Wolsey's return to England. The sudden realisation on Skelton's part that he had not been following royal wishes at all (or more likely that he felt that Henry had changed his mind) forced him to offer a gesture of loyalty, in order to forestall any displeasure that Parott might have aroused.

The subsequent *Dysticon Miserabyll* follows this discernible shift to a defensive outlook. For there Parott is transformed into 'the royall popagay'; an aspect of his character hitherto mentioned only once (and that in passing, at line 217), who speaks the Latin exhortation to the 'King of Britain' to 'subdue the bull-calf' and rule himself. It is tempting to infer that the aged satirist, fearful for his future now that his target has returned and was thus more likely to become aware of his attacks, had temporarily lost his resolve to win favour by subtle means and was appealing to his former pupil directly for protection, whilst still attempting to justify his extravagant expenditure in time and effort in *Parrot* by further expounding his thesis. Otherwise it seems difficult to see why the poet should have issued this separate individually dated passage, which contains no new satirical material, save the Latin reference to the bull-calf's cruelty, and which merely strikes a humble and submissive pose, finishing with the contrite and pessimistic stanza,

> God amend all,
> That all amend may!
> Amen, quod Parott,
> The royall popagay. (353–6)

Certainly the next stanza, significantly another departure from the norm in that it is not the 'fourth' or 'fifth' envoy as one might expect, but the *Lenvoy Royall*, marks a further retreat from the aggressive satiric pose of the first two supplements, being almost entirely concerned with justifying the value of Parott's utterances and with begging for support and protection from all quarters against his unnamed critics.

> Go, propyr Parotte, my popagay,
> That lordes and ladies thys pamflett may behold,
> With notable clerkes; supply to them, I pray,
> Your rudeness to pardon and also that they wolde
> Vouchesafe to defend yow agayne the brawlyng scolde
> Callyd Detraxion, encankryd with envye,
> Whose tong ys attayntyd with slaundrys obliqui.
>
> For trowthe in parabyll ye wantonlye pronounce,
> Langagys divers; yet undyr that dothe reste
> Maters more precious than the ryche jacounce . . . (357–66)
>
> Wherfor your remorders ar madde or else starke blynde,
> Yow to remorde erste or they know your mynde.
> (369–70)

By this time Skelton seems to be desperate to stimulate a favourable response from his readership to justify his efforts, if not from Henry then from
his courtiers, or from the scholarly community. As the chances of success
diminish, so he widens the net and aims to appeal to more potential spon-
sors. Hence yet a further attempt to gloss and thus clarify the poem proper,
as he inserts a painfully obvious allusion back to the biblical *metaphora* of
the original text.

> Like aaron, and the people,
> So the ox's bull-calf,
> So the ox's bull-calf,
> So the ox's bull-calf.[95]
>
> Thus myche Parott hathe openlye expreste,
> Let se who dare make up the reste. (377–82)

Such passages as these deserve quotation at length to illustrate just how
imperative it seems to be to Skelton that his readers should appreciate his
intentions and offer him support. The above stanza is followed by yet
another self-justifying passage, prefixed with the somewhat overdue description 'The Parrot begins to explain' ('*Le Popagay sen va complayndre*'), in
which the poet laments of,

> . . . the dull abusyd brayne,
> The enfatuate fantasies, the wytles wylfulnes
> Of on and hothyr at me that have dysdayne.
> Some sey they cannot my parables expresse;
> Som sey I rayle att ryott recheles;
> Some say but lityll and thynke more in there thowghte,
> How thys prosses I prate of, hyt ys not all for nowghte. (383–9)

Could it be that after all this effort Skelton's audience still thought that his
poem was merely a pseudo-biblical nonsense? Such an assumption surely
underestimates the intelligence of a readership taught by tradition to see contemporary political comment in mock-biblical ballads and poetry.[96] What
the poet seems to be suggesting here is something rather different from his
earlier allegations of obtuseness amongst his readers. By this stage he no
longer claims that they cannot see beyond the 'ryche jacounce' to the weight-
ier matters beneath but rather that, having done so, they fail to respond,
offering instead various excuses – either claiming that the 'parables' are still
too enigmatic, that Skelton's attacks are unnecessary or are directed against
sins which do not exist. Failing that they merely pass no opinion at all. None
of which are the responses which the isolated poet–satirist would have

---

[95] Trans. in Scattergood, p. 462. The passage clearly echoes Isaiah, xxiv 2, 'As with the people,
so with the priest', and thus is a further indication that the villain of the piece, the 'bull-calf',
is a cleric.
[96] See Heiserman, chap. 4 (viii).

wished for. Thus he once again attempts to taunt his public into a reaction, this time quite clearly suggesting that it is fear of an official reaction that prevents them from acting.

> O causeles cowardes, O hartles hardynes,
> O manles manhod, enfayntyd all with fere,
> O connyng clergye, where ys your redynes
> To practice or postyll thys prosses here and there?
> For drede ye darre not medyll with suche gere,
> Or elles ye pynche curtesy, trulye as I trowe,
> Whyche of yow fyrste dare boldlye plucke the crowe. (390–6)

Exactly what it was that Skelton was expecting his readers to do to support him is unclear. Previously, when he felt he had King and Court with him, it had been patronage and acclaim that he desired, and clearly that is still a major factor here. But it also seems that now, once events had served to illustrate how inaccurate was his reading of the King's mind, he is trying to continue the project regardless and actually to convince both King and Court of the sense behind his utterances. Hence his continued attempts, first to get his readers to realise exactly what his allegations were, and then to gain their protection from criticism. Seemingly, having tried and failed with lords and ladies, he was now trying his luck with the clergy, trying to get them to take up his argument, whilst others 'boldlye plucke[d] the crowe' at Court. Having realised that he could not coast into favour on the crest of a wave of anti-Wolsey feeling, he now seems to be attempting to manufacture such a phenomenon by his own efforts rather than abandon the project in which he had invested so much of himself, and on which he had publicly staked his reputation. It is equally apparent, however, that such efforts as the poet was making in this direction were not meeting with success. Had the King been prepared to lead the criticism of Wolsey, there is no doubt that Skelton could have expected a favourable response to his satire from the Court, once he had simplified it sufficiently for it to be understood. But, as Wolsey had returned to even greater royal favour than he had left, it would have been a brave man indeed who would take up Skelton's promptings. Thus, far from creating a place for himself at Court, all that the poet's continued attacks achieved was to isolate him still further from the very people he hoped to attract. In such a situation it is not surprising that Skelton anxiously cast about him for support, initially from lords and ladies and notable clerks, then from the 'connynge clergye' too, and all the time from the King himself. This desperate search for favour culminated in the fulsome sycophancy of the succeeding Latin stanza, attributed to Parott, in which Henry, the King who 'rules this English realm', is compared to Jupiter, and declared to be a god himself, sitting on a golden throne.[97]

---

[97] *Speke, Parott*, lines 405–10, trans. in Scattergood, p. 463.

Just as the poet's mood seems to have been verging on desperation, however, during the December of 1521, when the stanzas cited above were written, a clear change is noticeable in his verse, which surely reflects a dramatic
rise in his personal morale. The last stanza of the contrite 'The Parrot begins
to explain' passage had clearly been an allegorical reference to Wolsey's
homecoming, which sought to portray its effects as disastrous for the realm,
the Church and, probably more immediately, for the poet himself.

There had been, the poet asserts, a period of bad weather, symbolic of the
Cardinal's return, but, rather than his being depressed by this, 'Lyacon'
(Wolsey),

> . . . lawgyth theratt and berythe hym more bolde;
> Racell, rulye ragged, she is like to cache colde;
> Moloc, that mawmett, there darre no man withsay;
> The reste of suche reconyng may make a fowle fraye. (400–404)

The Church (Rachel) is in jeopardy, but her plight can only worsen as
Wolsey (Moloc and Lyacon) exalts in his renewed power and domination,
and threatens to bring a foul reckoning down on everyone. This is probably
the most desperate moment in the life of the poem. Hereafter follows the
abject Jupiter hymn, then the final two envoys. These final supplements,
however, mark a sudden and obvious change of mood. After the Jupiter lines
all the apologetic material disappears to be replaced by the return of all
Parott's old confidence and vituperative bile, which is restored with re-
doubled force. All the alliterative jibes return. Wolsey is 'So bolde a
braggyng bocher' (line 485), 'So fatte a magott, bred of a flesshe-flye' (line
509), 'So mangye a mastyfe curre' (line 487). Skelton mocks his apparent as-
piration to become Pope and can paint a startling picture of the extent of the
Cardinal's ambitions, without circumspection,

> He tryhumfythe, he trumpythe, he turnythe all up and downe. (432)

> Hys wolvys hede, wanne, bloo as lede, gapythe over the crowne:
> Hyt ys to fere leste he wolde were the garland on hys pate, (434–5)[98]

He is even sufficiently enboldened to come within an ace (pun intended) of
naming his target in the line 'Of Pope Julius cardys, he ys chefe card-yn-all'
(line 431), and to subscribe his name to the final envoy with the proud
flourish '*Quod Skelton lawryat – Orator Regius*'.

---

[98] Scattergood's assertion (p. 463), and that of earlier commentators, that 'the garland' here
refers to the papal tiara seems odd. The context and whole drift of Skelton's allusions clearly
suggest that the poet means his readers 'to fere leste' Wolsey's ambitions should rise even to
the Crown.

Why the sudden change of approach? Is it not reasonable to infer an easing of the poet's material situation at this point which resulted in his freedom to take up the cudgels again with a vengeance? Clearly the fact that the Jupiter stanza stands between appeals for aid and ever-increasing self-justification on the one hand, and restored self-confidence and a renewed offensive on the other, suggests that it marks a watershed in the poet's career. Thereafter his appeals to his audience disappear and the satires increase in their hostility and clarity. What this watershed might have been is uncertain. It is unlikely to have been the poet's much-vaunted retreat into sanctuary, for he was living within the sanctuary confines at least as early as 1518.[99] Perhaps Henry stepped in to offer a word of protection for his old schoolmaster. Perhaps the fact that Wolsey did not notice, or did not choose to notice, the satire might have convinced Skelton that so long as he remained scrupulously loyal to the Crown in his writings, he could safely say more or less what he wished. It is true that Wolsey had imprisoned others on other occasions for criticising him in writing, but these had been cases of a different order. Polydore Vergil, for example, had been in communication with Cardinal Adrian in Rome, not circulating in manuscript form a series of verses which, by their own admission, were misunderstood or deliberately ignored by the politically important classes. Vergil had been spreading dangerous rumours in politically sensitive places and thus needed silencing: it seems that Wolsey simply ignored Skelton in the hope that he would go away.

Skelton did not, however, go away. Instead of abandoning his project now that it had demonstrably failed in its original intentions, he merely changed his approach. He dropped the scholarly games, the sophisms, the *metaphora* and *alegoria*, in favour of a more direct style. Why he persevered cannot be determined with certainty, but, again, the suggestion that his search for patronage provides the key cannot be ignored.

Clearly the poet did not win any royal favour as a result of Parott's appearance, as had been his original intention. Perhaps the Jupiter stanza marks the point at which Henry offered a token protection which removed Skelton's anxieties. Perhaps that stanza merely indicates where the poet conceded defeat. Having tried every means at his disposal to attract royal attention, he might finally have realised that the struggle was to be fruitless and directed his attention elewhere with more success. One cannot, however, infer from his renewed energies the arrival of a noble patron into the picture, for the very next envoy following the Jupiter stanza contains a thoroughgoing assault on the nobility for their servility in the face of Wolsey's domination of Court and Council (lines 425–31, see also 466–7). What seems

[99] The story that the poet was confined in the sanctuary, and even died there, because of the Cardinal's wrath, has no basis in fact.

more plausible, as the following section will suggest, is that Skelton turned his gaze, as the result of further events, further down the social scale, and found some measure of the support and acclaim that he sought from the London trading community, and from a minor courtier.

'WHY COME YE NAT TO COURTE?'

As was suggested in the previous section, the final stanzas of *Speke, Parott* mark a clear watershed in the progress of Skelton's anti-Wolsey satires. After the stanza in which Henry VIII was described as a British Jupiter the circumlocution and allegory which had marked the poem to that point disappear, and the classical and biblical 'parables' are replaced by simple, direct references to individuals, based on punning on their names, rather than indirect references to their political role or supposed qualities. Thus one sees not Moloc or Lyacon but simply 'He', the 'chefe Cardynall', orbited by such lesser luminaries as the unmistakable 'passe-a-Pase apase' (Richard Pace) and 'owur clerke Cleros' (Pace's assistant Thomas Clark). The poet seems intent on 'opening up' his work to a wider audience through greater clarity of style, through the delineation of his targets with greater succinctness, and through the laying of specific and understandable charges against Wolsey, which make a direct appeal to the reader's emotions. In the penultimate envoy, for example, Skelton portrays Wolsey's allegedly tyrannical treatment of the nobles at Court, who are made to 'droupe, to knele, to stowpe and to play / Cowche-quale' (lines 425–8). This is followed by a clear suggestion of Wolsey's, possibly regicidal, ambitions, as he 'gapythe over the crowne' with his predatory 'wolvys hede' (lines 434–5). These allusions are not supported by any evidence; rather they are simple, direct, caricatures designed to provoke an emotional response from the reader. This process of stylistic simplification is continued in the catalogue of complaints which constitute the final envoy in which Skelton bewails the state of things 'now-a-days' and mentions in the process such features of Wolsey's governance as his 'sanctuary breaking', his 'makyng of statutes of array' and his subsequently much-belaboured 'pollaxis and pyllers, [and] . . . mulys trapte with golde' (lines 503, 482 and 517).

It may have been that Skelton intended these envoys to continue in this more popularly accessible vein indefinitely now that Parott had begun to 'speke now trew and playne', but if this was the case no evidence survives of any subsequent additions. The next work which survives is the poet's second 'Wolsey-satire', *Collyn Clout*, which marks a shift from one traditional and popular form of versification, the complaint against the times,[100] to another, the anti-clerical satire, spoken, in the manner of *Piers Plowman*, by Collyn; a simple rustic *vox populi*, written in the short-lined 'Skeltonic' form which the poet had created himself and which had proved so useful a vehicle for vicious and ribald invective in the past.[101]

The reasons for the poet's change of mood and tone after the 'Jupiter stanza' of *Speke, Parott* have already been speculated on, but one also has to ask why this new stylistic change followed that earlier transformation. Skelton himself offers part of the answer in his introduction to *Collyn Clout*. There he suggests that it was precisely the poor reception of *Speke, Parott* which forced him to alter his approach. The task of trying to win favour and respect from a courtly audience with a subtle satire, he suggests, was a fruitless one, as he was forced to attempt to please all quarters at once and, as a result, succeeded in pleasing none of them.

> What can it avayle
> To dryve forth a snayle,
> Or to make a sayle
> Of a herynges tayle?
> To ryme or to rayle,
> To wryte or to indyte, (1–6)
>
> Or bokes to compyle
> Of dyvers maner style,
> Vyce to revyle
> And synne to exyle? (9–12)

The only result of attempting to find the optimum path between over-caution and over-simplicity had been that one half of his audience could not follow his subtleties and had reviled him for his apparent obscurantism. They 'say this and say that: / "His heed is so fat / He wottyth never what / Ne wherof he speketh"' (lines 15–18). But, had he attempted to adopt a more basic style, his scholarly critics would have reviled him for his baseness and lack of subtlety. For

> . . . yf he speke playne,
> Than he lacketh brayne:
> 'He is but a foole;
> Let hym go to scole!
> A thre-foted stole
> That he may downe sytte,
> For he lacketh wytte'. (26–32)

[100] For a helpful rehearsal of the 'now-a-days' tradition of Complaint literature, see Heiserman, pp. 181–9.

[101] The poet had used this form to castigate the blasphemous curate in *Ware the Hauke*, and to ridicule the licentious ale-wife in *The Tunnying of Elynour Rummynge*, to attack the Scots poet Dundas, and to complete the *flytyng* with Sir Christopher Garnesh.

Finally, if, as Skelton did, he managed eventually to impress upon his courtly readers the true nature of his satire, he merely discovered that they were unmoved by his exhortations.

> And yf that he hytte
> The nayle on the hede
> It standeth in no stede:
> 'The devyll,' they say, 'is dede,
> The devyll is dede.' (33–7)

The opening lines of *Collyn Clout* thus provide a succinct account of the history of *Speke, Parott* from its author's perspective. They reveal his painstaking efforts and anxieties over the choice of the vehicle in which to convey his satiric message and chart his increasing frustration at the apparent slow-wittedness of his audience, to the point at which he had glossed his original text sufficiently to make continued ignorance of its true subject matter impossible, only to find that his intended audience did not share his opinions and seemed to suggest that there was no sense in his attacks. He is told that he 'rayle[s] att ryott recheles', '"The devyll," they say, "is dede"'.

What follows then, in *Collyn Clout*, and more obviously in the succeeding *Why Come Ye Nat?*, is Skelton's response to this failure on the part of his courtly audience to appreciate his earlier work. This new simplicity of style, apparent in the final envoys of *Speke, Parott*, in the decision to complete that poem in the popular Complaint tradition and most obvious in *Collyn Clout* and *Why Come Ye Nat?*, suggests an attempt to woo a new audience. The changes in the subject matter of the later satires, particularly the last, help to define precisely who that intended new audience was.

Whereas *Speke, Parott* had been identifiably a Court poem in that it was written for a courtly audience, *Why Come Ye Nat?* is clearly a 'London' poem, written for an audience in the City.[102] Where *Speke, Parott* had attempted to mirror the mood and opinions of the King, *Why Come Ye Nat?* expands its purview and attempts, in addition, to match that of the literate, substantial men in London. In the former, the major issues touched on were those of foreign policy on the high diplomatic level; in the latter the issues are primarily domestic and concern the financial exactions imposed on the nation, and the City in particular, during 1522. The balance of subject matter in the first and last satires has completely altered, and serves as a valuable indication of the extent to which Skelton changed not only his poetic form but also its content, to suit his new audience. In *Speke, Parott* only 11 of the poem's 520 lines (91 of the *c.* 4,011 words, approximately 2.27 per

---

[102] *Collyn Clout* is also a popular satire aimed at a London audience but as its purview is primarily clerical it will be considered separately from the more secular satires, in chap. 4, following.

cent of the text) could be said to concern economic issues, and of these some 8 lines (65 words) occur in the final envoy in which the poet was already writing with his new audience in mind. In *Why Come Ye Nat?* 121 lines are concerned with taxation, government impositions and the consequent poverty of the populace, in a poem of 1,217 lines (532 words in *c.* 5,689, or *c.* 10 per cent of the poem). Such figures cannot be taken to be of any great significance but they do serve to underline the approximately five-fold increase in the amount of time spent by the poet on economic concerns between his first and last satire. Precisely why he chose to concentrate more on financial issues in order to appeal to his new audience can be ascertained from a brief examination of events in London at the time of the poem's conception, around November 1522.[103]

Wolsey returned from the conferences at Calais and Bruges with an Anglo-Imperial treaty in his possession which commited England to an aggressive campaign against the French, due to commence in early 1523. In addition, as the Imperial ambassadors repeatedly reminded both the King and Cardinal, the older Treaty of London of 1518 obliged England to declare war on France during 1522 if, as was to be the Anglo-Imperial argument, the French were seen to be the aggressors in the current confrontation with the Emperor.[104] If the realm was to be able to meet these obligations, and to support the campaign in France planned for the spring and summer of 1522 to be conducted by an army under the command of the Earl of Surrey, there was clearly an urgent need for the Crown to obtain large sums of money. Hence the ambitious scheme, forwarded by Wolsey, for a new and accurate assessment of the nation's capacity to raise and support an army and provide revenue which was put into practice during the spring and summer of 1522, and was intended to form the basis of future tax demands and to allow the raising of a general forced loan to cover the immediate costs of the war.

Both the assessment itself and the loans which followed it imposed novel and much-resented demands upon the populace at large, nowhere more so than in the City of London, which, as the readiest source of exploitable wealth, felt the demands most heavily. As J. J. Goring has shown,[105] the scope of the inquiries undertaken by the commissioners for this General Proscription excluded few potential sources of wealth that the beleaguered assessee might possess. The Essex commissioners' instructions to the Bailiff and Head Constable of Waltham are indicative of the scrutiny. These relate how the

---

[103] It may have been that the poem was issued in sections over a period of time (see Edwards, p. 219, but these can only have been a matter of weeks apart as the major topics under consideration all date the text *c.* October/November 1522.

[104] *Sp. Cal. Further Supplement to Volumes One and Two* (hereafter, *Sp. Cal. F. S.*) pp. 2, 33, 38, 46, 53, 56.

[105] J. J. Goring, 'The General Proscription of 1522', *E.H.R.*, 331 (1971), pp. 681–705.

latter should assemble all the men of the half-hundred in a muster, at which they should be interrogated under oath to ascertain,[106]

who is lord of every towne or hamlet . . . and who be stewardes . . . who be parsons of the same townes, and what the benefices be worth by yeere. Also who be owners of every parcell of land within the same townes, hamlets, parishes and villages. And every stocke and stockes of catell, or other things that be occupied upon every ferme . . . and who be owners of them . . . the value and substance of every person being of 16 yeares and above . . . as well spiritual as temporall.

In London this rigorous assessment came at a time of increasing financial strain. During August 1521 the citizens had been called on by royal command to contribute sufficient funds for the upkeep of one hundred archers in harness for service in Calais.[107] By April 1522, £945 13s 3/4d had been raised by the City, by means of a levy of one fifteenth and a half, in order to finance the civic celebrations for the visit of the Emperor Charles V, and a further hundred men had been prepared in harness for service in the navy, to protect the Channel during the visit.[108] Immediately following this imposition, and prior to the Emperor's arrival, the first commissioners for the General Proscription took their musters and made up their assessment books, not without some dissatisfaction in the capital at the nature of the assessment. For, as Hall observes,[109]

[at] this time commission was geven throughoute the realme, for general musters to be had, to knowe what power might be made with in thesame, and also men sworne of what substaunce and landes thei wer of. And the Cardinal advertised thesame not wythout grudging of ye people, & marveiling why thei shuld be sworne for their owne goodes.

In May, in the wake of this grudging and marvelling, Wolsey communicated to the City a demand for a forced loan of some £30,000, to meet the immediate costs of the army in France and for defensive measures to be taken against a possible French invasion.[110] In response to this demand the Court of Aldermen of the City offered the reduced sum of £14,400, provided that the loan be secured by bonds drawn on the wealth of a number of rich abbeys. Wolsey was evidently unimpressed with such scruples and stated 'with many mynatorye words' that the sum offered was insufficient, and that his own and the King's word should be sufficient surety for the loan.[111] The result, if Hall is to be relied on, seems to have been a compromise, with £20,000 being

---

[106] B.L. MS Stowe 570 fo. 165, cited in Goring, 'The General Proscription', p. 684.

[107] Rep(ertory of the Court of Aldermen) (henceforth, rep.) 4 fo. 88, rep. 5 fos. 216, 219, cited in J. Kennedy, 'The City of London and the Crown *c.* 1509–*c.* 1529', unpublished Manchester University M.A. thesis (1978), p. 166.

[108] For the levy see Kennedy, 'The City of London and the Crown', pp. 211–12; for the marines see Hall, *Union*, p. 630.

[109] Hall, *Union*, p. 630.

[110] *Ibid.*, pp. 642, 650. Hall places the date of the original demand in June rather than May, but this seems to have been the time of its collection.

[111] Rep. 5 fos. 296(v) and 297; cited in Kennedy, 'The City of London and the Crown', p. 148.

the sum eventually agreed. But even at this reduced figure there seems to have been some reluctance or inability to contribute amongst the City community. For, although the Common Council agreed to the loan on 24 May, there were still objections over the assessments in the following month; possibly an indication that the new, more detailed proscription books were being used as the basis for the loan. One Alderman Myrfyn, amongst others, had to be bound in a recognisance of £50 to accept the commissioners' decision. On 26 June, Sir Edmund Peckham, a commissioner, reported that only £9,000 of the total had been collected, and the majority of that had come in in penny pieces, whilst as late as August, after the loan had been substantially paid, a number of men were imprisoned on the orders of the Crown for refusing to pay their assessed contributions.[112]

This loan, which, unlike the Proscription loans to follow, seems to have been levied entirely in London, was repaid during September, but only after, as we shall see, further demands were made on the City. Indeed Wolsey took the opportunity provided by his formal offering of thanks to the citizens for the payment of the £20,000 loan to request a further 4,000 marks (or possibly £4,000) which was eventually paid on 7 October.[113]

Long before this, however, the Cardinal was expressing his dissatisfaction with the assessment books returned by the Proscription commissioners. As he informed the Bishop of Durham, Thomas Ruthall, it was felt by the Crown that the commissioners had been too lax in their enquiries, and had allowed many of those assessed to be 'not hooly but dyminytely estemed and certefied' through 'favour affeciion and other colourable driftes and practices'.[114] Hence a new assessment was determined on and conducted during the late summer and autumn of 1522, during the course of which Wolsey, who as the King's deputy acted as the personal commissioner for London, faced a truculent assembly of 'the maior, Aldermen, and the moste substanciallest commoners' of the City, on 20 August, in an attempt to assess their wealth. The Cardinal's efforts to persuade the Aldermen to act as commissioners for those citizens in their wards worth £100 or more, in order that they might be immediately assessed for a loan of one-tenth of their worth, met with some opposition, despite Wolsey's amiable assertion that such a sum was 'the least reasonable thyng that you can ayde your prince with'. It was the determination that the loan should be paid 'in convenient time' (i.e. swiftly) 'in money plate or juels' which caused the controversy. For, as the Aldermen protested,[115]

---

[112] Kennedy, 'The City of London and the Crown', p. 149.
[113] Ibid., p. 150. For the suggestion that the loan was for pounds rather than marks see Hall, Union, p. 650.
[114] B.L. Cotton MS Cleopatra F VI fos. 250–6, cited in Goring, 'The General Proscription', pp. 686–7.
[115] Hall, Union, p. 645.

it [was] . . . not two monethes sithe the Kyng had of the Citie, XX thousand pound in ready money in loane, whereby the Citie is very bare of money, for Goddes sake remembre this, that riche marchauntes in ware be bare of money.

Wolsey's uncompromising retort of 'this must be done, and therefore go about it' seems, however, to have been sufficient to have set them, albeit grudgingly, about the business of assessment.

According to Hall there were several factors contributing to this general dislike of the loan. First, the method of assessment was felt to be a novel imposition as each man was compelled to attest on oath to the accuracy of his assessment. This seems to have been no light matter for many of the contributors, as many seem to have doubted their ability to judge accurately their income and thus feared accidental perjury, or, perhaps more significantly, that their businesses would be adversely affected were it to be made public that their true wealth was markedly less than their reputed credit, as 'many honest mennes credence was better than his substance'. Thus, during the assessment, 'some avaunsed themselfes more than they were worth of pride not remembryng what was comyng'.[116]

A second reason for popular discontent at the loan was the covert manner of the assessment, which had, ostensibly and in the first instance, been made merely to assess the nation's capacity to raise a fighting force. Only once the musters had been taken was their true purpose made clear, which left those assessed with the feeling of having been deceived. Finally the 'great mournyng of the common people', which, as Hall observes, was 'as it is ever in suche cases of paymentes', was all the greater due to the rigour and accuracy of the assessment,[117] and to the fact that it followed so closely in the wake of the other demands indicated above, without those earlier contributions being taken into account in the later assessment.[118] The final rate of payment stood at ten per cent of their worth, for those assessed at between £20 and £300; thirteen and one-third per cent for those worth between £300 and £1,000; and at the discretion of the commissioners for anyone whose wealth exceeded £1,000. In total the two loans levied on the 1522 assessment during that and the following year brought in over £200,000 from laymen, and the first loan alone, levied in 1522, reaped approximately £100,000 from lay contributors in the period to 1 February 1523.[119] The sums raised were quite unprecedented, as Hall reports,[120]

---

[116] *Ibid.*, pp. 645, 650. See also W. Tyndale, *The Obedience of the Christian Man, Works*, I, pp. 187, 203, for a more general attack on the innovation.

[117] Goring, 'The General Proscription' p. 694.

[118] See Hall, *Union*, p. 646.

[119] Goring, 'The General Proscription' p. 700; G. W. Bernard, *War, Taxation and Rebellion in Early Tudor England* (Brighton, 1986), p. 119.

[120] Hall, *Union*, p. 650.

the commissioners did what they could to set the people to the uttermoste, whiche afterwards turned the people to much heavines; & by reason of this, greate summes of money were levied.

At the time that *Why Come Ye Nat?* was being written, then, the substantial citizens of London were facing almost unprecedented financial demands. A second major loan had been demanded before the first had been repaid and, as soon as the first was returned, a third was introduced. The effects for the commercial life of the City could have been of no small significance, particularly, as will be suggested, because of the demand that the impositions be paid in plate or ready money, those portions of a trader's wealth which marked his status, symbolised his self-esteem and facilitated the conduct of his trade. This temporary financial crisis, and the consequent 'heavines' of the people, is what is reflected in much of *Why Come Ye Nat?*. Excessive government expenditure, severe loans, and popular poverty, particularly poverty in coin and plate, are repeated motifs in the text. The survey of the realm which starts the poem proper makes much of these themes. It even returns to the Calais conference, the central event of *Speke, Parott*, to use it once more as a stick with which to beat Wolsey. But there, twelve months after the event, it is no longer the purely diplomatic consequences of the conference, but its economic effects which Skelton attacks. 'There hath ben moche excesse', he declares,

> With banketynge braynlesse,
> With ryotynge rechelesse
> With gambaudynge thryftlesse,
> With, 'spende', and wast witlesse,
> Treatinge of trewse restlesse,
> Pratynge for peace peaslesse.
> The countrynge at Cales
> Wrang us on the males!
> Chefe counselour was carlesse,
> Gronynge, grouchyng, gracelesse,
> And to none entente
> Our talwod is all brent,
> Our fagottes are all spent.
> We may blowe at the cole!
> Our mare hath cast her fole,
> And 'mocke hath lost her sho;
> What may she do therto?'
> An ende of an olde song:
> 'Do ryght and do no wronge',
> As ryght as a rammes horne!
> For thrifte is threde bare worn,
> Our shepe are shrewdly shorn. (70–92)

The conference has been transformed from a monument to Folly, an attempt to reconcile the irreconcilable, into a stratagem for defrauding the taxpayer. It is now a 'countrynge' not only in the sense of an 'encounter' between the three parties of England, France and the Empire, but also an 'accounting' and a manipulation of 'counters' in the Cardinal's counting-house, the only effect of which is to wring out the wallets and purses ('males') of the commonalty into Wolsey's collecting bowl.[121] The metaphor is a succinct one, but the remainder of the passage is largely general and conventional in its complaints. Expense and excess, waste and rich-living on the part of the governors, and especially Wolsey, are contrasted with the poverty and enforced thrift of the Commons in the same way in which they had been in political poetry throughout the previous three centuries.[122] But, as the poem progresses, the allegations and the arguments become more specific.

In the savage indictment of the government's policy towards the Scots which follows, the poet returns to the question of the 1522 loans, and asks what has happened to the money, raised on the pretext of supporting a two-front war against France and Scotland, now that the truce agreed by lord Dacre has brought about the cessation of hostilities along the northern border.[123] He bemoans,

> Our mony madly lent,
> And mor madly spent,
> From Croydon into Kent
> Wote ye whyther they went? (143–6)

Again the charge laid at Wolsey's door is one of wastefulness, as it was in *Speke, Parott*, but here the waste is of money (specifically the money 'madly lent' during the summer of 1522) not time and effort. And here again, as in the passage cited earlier, it is the grievances of the tax-paying community to which Skelton panders, rather than the imagined grander designs of the King and Court. The point is returned to frequently in the text, as Wolsey is referred to again and again as the creator of the excessive financial demands of the Crown, and as the main agent in the dissipation of the money thus collected.

---

[121] Dyce's suggestion (Dyce, II p. 352) that 'countryng' 'does not . . . mean encountering but is a musical term used here metaphorically' to indicate a song for many voices (at the conference table) does not seem helpful.

[122] See F. J. Furnivall and W. R. Morfill (eds.), *Ballads from Manuscripts*; T. Wright (ed.), *Political Poems And Songs Relating to English History, from the Accession of Edward III to that of Richard III*, Rolls Series, 14, 2 vols. (London, 1859–61); and chap. 4, below.

[123] For a detailed discussion of Skelton's treatment of this truce, and of his attitude towards English foreign policy in general, see, G. Walker, '"Baytyng The Bochers Dogge": A study of John Skelton's satires against Cardinal Wolsey as a source for the politics of the 1520's', University of Southampton Ph. D. thesis, 1985, chap. 5.

He bereth the Kyng on hand
That he must pyll his land
To make his cofers ryche;
But he laythe all in the dyche,
And useth suche abusyoun,
That in the conclusyoun
All commeth to confusyon. (452–8)

Such a prelate I trowe . . .
He wolde dry up the stremys
Of ix kinges realmys,
All ryvers and wellys,
All waters that swellys;
For with us he so mellys
That within England dwellys.
I wolde he were somwhere ellys;
For els by and by
He wyll drynke us so drye
And sucke us so nye,
That men shall scantly
Have peny or halpeny. (953, 957–68)

. . . the commune welth
Shall never have good helth;
But tatterd and tuggyd,
Raggyd and ruggyd,
Shavyn and shorne,
And all threde bare worne! (1024–9)

As the poem progresses these charges are made with increasing applicability to the poet's intended audience in the City, and that audience is singled out for his attention with corresponding clarity.

In *Speke, Parott* the narrator had been ostensibly a neutral reporter, making his cryptic observations concerning Wolsey's governance at the prompting of an uninvolved third party, and occasionally at the behest of Skelton in his guise as '*Laucture*' of the text. The dialogue had been internal, within the text, between the author and his creation, between Parott and Galatea, and between Parott and the other, unnamed, interlocutors. Where the subject treated required a more forceful mode of address the points were made in neutral generalities ('Let every man after his merit take his parte', 'some folys say ye arre furnysshyd with knakkes'). It was never assumed that the narrator directly addressed a real individual reader or group of readers. In *Why Come Ye Nat?* this is no longer the case. Throughout the text the poet, in keeping with his new-found directness of approach, isolates his intended audience and speaks to them directly, referring to issues which immediately concern them. And it is quite clear that this intended audience is primarily the literate Commons of London. Certainly the final Latin *apostrophe* to the text is addressed 'to the citizens of London' ('*Apostropha ad*

Londini cives'). But much of the text which precedes it is also spoken directly to the City, a noteworthy example being the passage to be cited below, in which the poet tells his audience 'A goldsmyth [is] *youre* mayre'. This has often been used by critics to date the text – Sir John Munday, a goldsmith, became Mayor on 28 October 1522 – but it is rarely mentioned as an indication of the text's prospective readership. Thus *Why Come Ye Nat?* has an immediacy to it beyond that created by its simplicity of style and content. It is a series of stanzas or segments of verse spoken by the poet directly to his audience which, unlike *Speke, Parott*, is unconcerned with literary merit or textual niceties, and is a poem for and of the moment.[124]

Once the immediate political context of the poem created by the imposition of the forced loans during the spring to autumn of 1522 is noted, the terms of the satire become far clearer. The references to popular poverty, for instance, no longer seem simply the generalised laments of the Complaint tradition, but can be recognised as specific statements concerning a specific financial crisis within the City. 'But howe comme to pas', the poet asks his audience,

> Your cupboard that was
> Is tourned to glasse,
> From sylver to brasse,
> From golde to pewter
> Or els to a newter,
> To copper, to tyn,
> To lede, or alcumyn?
> A goldsmyth youre mayre:
> But the chefe of youre fayre
> Myght stande now by potters,
> And such as sell trotters,
> Pytchars, potshordis.
> This shrewdly accordis
> To be a copborde for lordys!
>
> My lorde now and Syr knyght,
> Good evyn and good nyght!
> For now, Syr Trestram,
> Ye must weare bukram,
> Or canvas of Cane,
> For sylkes are wane,
> Our royals that shone,
> Our nobles are gone
> Amonge the Burgonyons
> And Spanyardes onyons,
> And the Flanderkyns.
> Gyll swetis and Cate spynnys!

---

[124] For a discussion of the forms in which the poems may have been made available to the public, see below concerning circulation of the satires.

> They are happy that wynnys,
> But Englande may well say
> Fye on this wynnyng allway:
> Now nothynge but 'pay, pay!'
> With 'laughe and lay downe,
> Borowgh, cyte and towne!' (900–32)

This is not simply the traditional description of a poor realm and an oppressed poor; it is, more specifically, a description of a usually affluent class reduced to penury by financial exactions. The references to the denuded cupboards of London are a specific reference to the impositions of 1522 which involved the City in the large-scale surrender of much of its available gold and silver, whether in plate or coin, in order to make good the sums for which it was assessed.[125]

> The Kyng about this very tyme sent to the Citie of London to borow xxM pou[n]des, which sore chafed the citizens but the somme was promised, and for the payment the mayer sent for none but for men of substaunce, *howbeit the craftes solde muche of their plate.*

What Skelton is referring to is the consequential conversion of the plate of the merchant class in the face of a marked shortage of coin caused by the loans of 1522, the most obvious burden of which fell on the citizens of London. For, after a period of relatively high food costs, during which wheat was sold in the capital for up to 20*s* per quarter,[126] there came the series of financial demands itemised above, each of which necessitated payment in either coin or plate. This placed great stress on that portion of an individual's wealth kept in liquid assets, a portion which, as the members of the 1523 Parliament informed Wolsey when asked for a subsidy of 4*s* in the pound, need not be commensurate with his total wealth, for[127]

> if the fifth part of substaunce of the realme, were but viii C M pound and if men shoulde paie to the Kyng, the fifth part of their goodes, in money or plate, it was proved, that there was not so much money out of the Kynges handes, in al the realme, for the fifth part of every mans goodes, is not in money nor plate: for although five men were well monied, v thousand were not so, the gentleman, hath not the fifth part of the value of coyne; the marchaunt that is ryche of sylke, wolle, Tynne, Clothe, and suche marchaundise, hath not the fifth part in money, the husbande man is ryche in corne and cattel, yet he lacketh of that some. Lykewyse viteilers and all other artificers, be ryche in householde stuffe, and not in money; And then consequently, if all the money were brought to the Kynges handes then men must barter clothe for vitaile, and breade for chese, and so one thyng for another.

Here then, was the nub of the difficulties of 1522. Although the loans exacted during that year were not, in theory, crippling – in that they were

---

[125] Hall, *Union*, p. 642, my italics.   [126] *Ibid.*, p. 632.   [127] *Ibid.*, p. 656.

aimed at the wealthier citizens only and individually amounted to only modest proportions of their total, notional, wealth – the practical, cumulative, effect of the demands was to create an unprecedented strain on a citizen's ready or quickly convertible assets. The demands for coin thus created both, in real terms, a shortage of the essential medium of trade (and thus further reduced a trader's wealth by reducing his means of conducting his living), and, in psychological terms, exaggerated the contributor's perception of his misfortune by necessitating the conversion of his plate and jewels, the most obvious measure of his prosperity. Both of these effects are, as has already been indicated, reflected and manipulated by Skelton in *Why Come Ye Nat?*. The potentially ruinous effects on trade and industry are suggested in the passage cited above, in which 'Gyll' and 'Cate', symbols of the nation's workforce, cease their industry as 'Englande may well say / Fye on this wynnyng allway', as the profits simply disappear in loans and taxes. The effects on the personal wealth and prestige of the merchants and substantial citizens are indicated in the extended and exaggerated exposition on the City's new-found poverty. The plate cupboards of the City which, as Skelton ironically points out, has only recently elected a goldsmith to the mayorality, are now to be found filled with brass, pewter, tin and lead, rather than silver and gold, and the knights and burgesses have had to sell their silks and now wear cheaper buckram and Caen canvas clothes instead, so that even the richest of them might now stand comparison with 'potters / And such as sell trotters'.

To emphasise the effects of these loans on even the richest of merchants, Skelton provides a protracted reference to a specific case in the lines devoted to 'Good Sprynge of Lanam' and his misfortunes. With a clarity and simplicity which would have been unthinkable in *Speke, Parott*, the poet cites the case of Thomas Spring of Lavenham in Suffolk as a man ruined by the exactions of the past year. This is no random choice of example, nor a convenient name on which to hang a generalised assertion, as had been the 'Syr Trestram' of the previous lines, but an unmistakable reference to an outstanding example of the Proscription commissioners' efficiency. For Spring, a leading clothier, widely accounted to be the wealthiest commoner in England, was, as Goring shows,[128] the victim of a particularly rigorous assessment at the time of the second Proscription.[129] After the first assessment,

[128] Goring, 'The General Proscription', p. 692.

[129] This assessment was to have far-reaching consequences. For it was the actions of the Suffolk clothiers (Stowe, in his *Annales* (1615 edition, p. 525) specifically mentions Spring's son) in laying off large numbers of workers in the face of the demand for the, so called, Amicable Grant of 1525, which prompted the rising of the cloth towns against the imposition. It seems that the memory of the, never to be repaid, loans of 1522 (often cited as a reason for the inability to contribute to the 1525 assessment) was sufficient to prompt this reaction to the new demands. See Hall, *Union*, p. 699; Bernard, *War, Taxation and Rebellion*, pp. 117–21 and D. MacCulloch, *Suffolk and The Tudors* (Oxford, 1986), pp. 291–2.

which Wolsey dismissed as too lenient, the commissioners were informed by the Crown that henceforth an individual's assessable wealth was to include not only his coin and plate, jewels, ornaments and 'merchaundises of all maner sorts and qualities', but also his household stuff and utensils and a proportion of the debts which he might theoretically be able to call in. Hence Spring was reassessed at the second muster as possessing the remarkable sum of £3,200 in goods, which was taken to include £1,400 in realisable debts. This, as Goring states, was the highest figure for wealth in goods recorded in any of the extant Proscription records,[130] and would have placed the clothier at the mercy of the commissioners as to the exact percentage at which he would be asked to contribute.

No doubt the fate of so eminent a man as Spring was notorious amongst the City community. Thus Skelton, by referring to it, can evoke all the worst aspects of the loans. The clothier's ready money, the poet asserts, is exhausted ('his purs wax dull') and his trade is thus in jeopardy. He,

> Muste counte what became
> Of his clothe makynge.
> He is at suche takynge,
> Though his purs wax dull,
> He must tax for his wull. (934–8)

Though he has no coin he is assessed for the full value of his goods and assets. Even the fleeces on the backs of his sheep and in the houses of his outworkers is taken into account ('He must tax for his wull'). The course of Skelton's argument, rudimentary though it is, follows closely the course of the 1522 impositions. Spring has already been assessed for a large payment (of 'an hunderd pounde and more'), at the first forced loan. Yet Wolsey was, as we have seen, dissatisfied with the level of this assessment and imposed a second more exacting demand, which threatened to ruin even a man of Spring's affluence.

> By nature of a new writ. [the second assessment]
> My lordys grace [Wolsey] nameth it
> A 'quia non satisfacit'.[131]
> In the spyght of his tethe
> He [Spring] must pay agayn
> A thousande or twayne
> Of his golde in store.
> And yet he payde before
> An hunderd pounde and more,
> Whiche pyncheth him sore!

---

[130] Ipswich Public Library MS 942.64 fo. 75, cited in Goring, 'The General Proscription', p. 692.
[131] Scattergood, p. 490, gives 'because it is not enough'. The reference is clearly to the first assessment.

> My lordis grace wyll brynge
> Downe this hye sprynge,
> And brynge it so lowe
> It shall nat ever flowe. (939–52)

Even in the simple and direct *Why Come Ye Nat?* such a passage is remarkable for its specificity and for the clarity of its argument.

It is not the purpose of this chapter, however, to offer a detailed exposition of the text of the last of Skelton's anti-Wolsey satires. All that is attempted here is a consideration of why that text, and *Collyn Clout* which preceded it, may have appeared. To summarise what has gone before: the two satires which followed *Speke, Parott* (and particularly the second, *Why Come Ye Nat?*) mark a definite and observable change of direction for Skelton. Having failed to win the patronage and respect which he so obviously craved from an audience at Court, and from the King in particular, he moved his gaze outwards, towards the substantial men of the City, and tailored his verse to suit this new audience by concentrating his satirical attention on the articulation of their frustration at the loans of 1521.

Clearly there is much in *Why Come Ye Nat?* which is not primarily concerned with the economic grievances of the City, just as there was much in *Speke, Parott* which was not primarily concerned with the specific case of Wolsey's arbitration of the Calais conference. But, equally obviously, the loans of 1522 form the core of the text's satirical concern, just as Calais formed the core of the political sections of *Speke, Parott*. Again, as in *Speke, Parott*, Skelton's motivation in this last satire, like his logic, is *ad hoc*. The loans form the basis of the text purely because they were what he perceived to be the preoccupation of his intended audience. It is the prospective readership which determines the subject matter, not vice-versa. And he pursues the new lines of reasoning, the new satiric goals, regardless of their contradictory effect on his earlier arguments. Hence, because he is now writing for a notably pro-Imperial audience amongst the traders whose livelihoods depend on uninterrupted access to the markets of the Low Countries and thus on good relations between England and the Empire, and because Crown policy is now in favour of the Imperial alliance and war with France he rediscovers his old hatred of the French and Scots, which had been muted in *Speke, Parott*, and begins vociferously to demand an aggressive campaign against both enemies. And yet, because the forced loans are the major objection of his audience, the poet can at the same time criticise the policy of spending money abroad,

> Amonge the Burgonyons
> And Spanyardis onyons,
> And the Flanderkyns. (924–6)

The fact that it is the very war which he advocates which necessitates the expenditure abroad (as the draft speech, prepared for the 1523 Parliament and attributed to Thomas Cromwell so graphically argued[132]) is overlooked, in order that the maximum capital could be gained from the various self-contradictory arguments which Skelton advances. The Londoners' distrust of all foreigners and 'strangers', who were felt to be stealing their trade and evading their taxes,[133] can thus be appealed to in the lines cited above, whilst the poet simultaneously advocates the war and criticises its finance. The unifying factor in the series of assertions is not any consistent logical argument, but the poet's desire to reflect as many aspects of the Londoners' grievances and prejudices in his verse as is possible. What unifies the remainder of the text is its attack on and ridiculing of Wolsey.

That the Cardinal should have been the focus of the Londoners' discontent at that moment in 1522 is a natural consequence of his activities in that period. The General Proscription and the loans were clearly Wolsey's schemes, if not in conception, at least from their earliest stages.[134] Indeed this identification of the loans with Wolsey would have been closer in the capital than elsewhere, for in London it was he who communicated the financial demands directly to the civic authorities, and who acted himself as sole commissioner for the City for the second, stricter, assessment of August and September. Hence, for this brief period, whilst the difficulties created by the loans were at their height, criticism of Wolsey and criticism of the loans would have been almost synonymous. Hence the populace would have been in an ideal mood to appreciate the contemporary allusions to the Cardinal which Skelton scattered in his text, among the more conventional allegations and the commonplaces of the Complaint tradition which, as the following chapters will show, he chose to revitalise and include there. Indeed these very commonplaces are likely to have been as influential in attracting the popular audience which the poet sought as the contemporary references. For the aggrieved citizen was likely to listen to any commentary which purported to identify the cause of his woes and offer him a strong voice of protest; all the more so if that commentary carried with it the authenticity imparted by tradition, and the plausibility of the general truth.

Why Skelton decided to appeal to this new source of patronage, once he became convinced that the Court had failed him, can never be ascertained with final certainty from the sparse amount of non-subjective evidence which survives. It may have been that the popular discontent at the exactions of 1522 was alone sufficient to convince him that a ready audience existed

[132] R. B. Merriman, *The Life and Letters of Thomas Cromwell* (Oxford, 1902), I pp. 30–44, (*L.P.* III (ii) 2958).

[133] See the account in Hall, *Union*, p. 645, of the citizens' protest to Wolsey during the meeting of 20 August that 'the citie is sore appaired by the great occupying of straungers'.

[134] Goring, 'The General Proscription', p. 702.

for an anti-Wolsey satire slanted to emphasise popular grievances and that patronage from the City community was thus a more readily achievable goal than patronage from the Court. This may have been enough to prompt him to continue the project which he had begun with *Speke, Parott*, and which he had proved so loth to abandon. This might adequately explain the appearance of *Why Come Ye Nat?*, but it does not account for the poem which preceded it, *Collyn Clout*. This seems to have been conceived and produced only slightly earlier, but in it the poet chose, apart from a brief allusion to 'prests and lonys, / Lent and never payde, / But from daye to daye delayde' (lines 350–2), to concentrate on religious rather than economic subjects. In any attempt to provide a narrative account of the circumstances of *Collyn Clout*'s appearance one needs to return to the small handful of surviving biographical facts concerning Skelton. For it may well have been that direct prompting by a prospective patron, albeit perhaps an unexpected one, lay behind his decision to write that text.

From the internal evidence considered elsewhere in this chapter, it seems clear that the vast majority of Skelton's courtly readers either openly criticised or simply ignored *Speke, Parott* and its increasingly specific envoys. But there is external evidence to suggest that one individual was sufficiently impressed with that work to take up Skelton's promptings. For, in his *Animadversions Upon . . . Chaucer's Works*, Francis Thynne states that his father, William, a minor official in the King's kitchen, 'furthered Skelton to write his Collyn Clout against the Cardinal' at his house in Erith.[135] The statement is bald and unsupported, but, if true, sheds some small amount of light on the poet's fate immediately following the completion of *Speke, Parott*. It may have been that Thynne contacted him and persuaded him to simplify his satirical approach in the final envoy in order to seek a wider audience. It may have been that it was the poet's own decision to do so which attracted Thynne's attention to his work. Whichever was the case, it seems that something of a temporary satirical alliance was forged between these two literary men (Thynne was an avid student of Chaucer's writings and produced an edition of his works in 1531), the net result of which was *Collyn Clout*, which was written at some time during the late summer of 1522.

Thynne's motives for favouring such an attack on Wolsey do not seem difficult to follow, for he seems to have been a long-time critic of the Cardinal and of the ecclesiastical establishment. His son observes that Wolsey was 'his olde enemye for manye causes', only the chief of which was his decision to

---

[135] F. J. Furnivall (ed.), *Francis Thynne's Animadversions Upon Speghtes First (1598) Edition of Chaucer's Works*, E.E.T.S. 9 (London, 1865), pp. 9–10. Thynne became second Clerk of the Kitchen in 1524, and Chief Clerk in 1526, before becoming one of Anne Boleyn's cofferers in 1533, Clerk Comptroller of the household by 1536, and Clerk of the Green Cloth by 1542 (*D.N.B.*, Thynne, William (?–1546)). Thus it is reasonable to assume that he held some lesser post in the kitchen, or the household generally, prior to 1524.

aid Skelton.[136] At the root of his objections seems to have been his religious sympathies which, if not at this time reformist or actively evangelical, were certainly anti-papal. As his son relates, Thynne had, during his researches for his edition of Chaucer's works, come across a text which was a candidate for inclusion in *The Canterbury Tales*, possibly the apocryphal, pseudo-Chaucerian *The Plowman's Tale* which was in essence a Lollard attack on the abuses of the Roman Church. This he was determined to include in his edition, despite his certain knowledge that the 'byshoppes [would] call [him] ... in questione for yt'.

In support of his son's reminiscences of his father's radicalism one might cite the evidence of Thynne's will, proved in 1546, in which he bequeathed[137]

My soule to my swete savior Jhesus Christe, my only Redemer and savyor, And to the hole holly company of heven of the which, in faiethe I believe to be one of them, throwghe the merytes of Christs Passion, and no otherwyse.

Clearly a will professing Justification by Faith alone written *c.* 1546 is no indication of evangelical sympathies as early as 1522. But, when taken with his son's statements cited above, the suggestion that Thynne was of, at least, reformist sympathies in the 1520s seems a plausible one. Particularly convincing seems Francis' assertion, concerning *Collyn Clout*, that '*the moste parte* of the whiche booke', rather than the whole of it, 'was compiled in my father's howse at Erithe in Kent',[138] which seems an overpedantic distinction to draw if the anecdote were simply fictional. There are objections to the total authenticity of the account,[139] but these do not invalidate the general picture which it provides. What may well have happened (again one is forced to speculate for want of concrete evidence) is that Thynne, sympathising with the anti-Wolsey sentiments expressed in *Speke, Parott*, convinced Skelton that a popularist anti-clerical satire in the manner of *The Plowman's Tale*, or *Piers Plowman* and its many (often Lollard) imitations, would be a more effective means of pursuing his satirical campaign, and offered him some of the patronage and appreciation which he sought. This offer Skelton seems to have accepted. The end result, an anti-clerical satire based firmly on doctrinal orthodoxy, might not have been quite what Thynne had been hoping for, but it seems to have been virulent and reformist enough in its attack on abuses to win the sympathy of those contempory reformers and a succeeding generation of Protestants who read it. For, as chapter 1 suggested, the reformist member of the Grocer's Company, John Collins, took the

---

[136] Furnivall, *Animadversions*, p. 9.
[137] Printed in *ibid.*, p. 11.
[138] *Ibid.*, pp. 9–10.
[139] Thynne's fifty-four-year lease on the house at Erith was not obtained from the Prior and Convent of Christchurch near Aldgate until 1531, so another house must have been Skelton's base for the project. Francis error is, however, understandable as Erith was where Thynne 'passed much of his life' (*D.N.B.*).

trouble to copy the text, along with the more populist sections of *Speke, Parott*, into his commonplace book, along with other snippets of literary works and anti-clerical texts, and *Collyn Clout* seems to have been the basis of the short-lived reputation which Skelton enjoyed among the early Protestants.[140]

Whether Skelton won the popular audience which he sought through the circulation of *Collyn Clout* cannot be judged with any certainty, but the subsequent popularity of the text and the fact that Wolsey should have taken a disliking to Thynne partly as a result of his involvement in its production make that suggestion seem plausible. What is more certain is that, by the time of the completion of his final satire against Wolsey, *Why Come Ye Nat?*, he had gained some measure of a popular following. For in that text the poet who had openly bewailed the indifference of his audience in the envoys of *Speke, Parott*, and who had painted a graphic description of his inability to please the public in the opening lines of *Collyn Clout*, can be found grandly describing himself as 'the famous bard whom thousands quote', or 'of whom a thousand speaks'.[141] This may in part be merely bombast on the poet's part, but his honesty in recognising his popular failures in the earlier texts gives one cause to allow some grounds for his confidence in the later. And if that was indeed the case, a significant transformation in the poet's stance and fortunes can be traced during 1521–2. From the misguided and unheeded author of courtly crypticisms of 1521, the poet has become, within fourteen months, the strident articulator of popular grievances. His motivation had not changed. He was still writing with the intention of attracting patronage and acclaim, but clearly he had become more successful, more important and perhaps more dangerous, and this last was not to be without significance, as chapter 6 will suggest, for the course of his future career.

---

[140] Witness William Barlowe's *Burial of The Mass* (1528) (*S.T.C.* 1462.7) (which borrows many of Skelton's arguments to attack Wolsey in the course of lampooning the Catholic sacraments), and the subsequent use of the 'Skeltonic' verse-form for anti-Catholic works such as the anonymous *Image of Ypocrysy* (printed in Furnivall and Morfill, *Ballads from Manuscripts*, I pp. 167–274), and parts of Luke Shepherd's *The Upcheringe of the Messe* (*c.* 1548) (*S.T.C.* 17630). This reformist reputation, centred on the stance adopted in *Collyn Clout*, would also explain the text's popularity after 1530, as was suggested in chap. 1. It was printed in 1531, by Thomas Godfrey (*S.T.C.* 22600.5); in 1545 by William Copeland (*S.T.C.* 22601); *c.* 1553, again by Copeland (*S.T.C.* 22602); in *c.* 1560 by John Day (*S.T.C.* 22603); and in 1568 as part of Stowe's edition of Skelton's *Pithy, Plesaunt and Profitable Workes* (*S.T.C.* 22608). Note also Bale's assertion that the poet 'continually waged war on certain babbling friars, especially the Dominicans', opposed Bishop Nix of Norwich and denied the immorality of clerical marriage: all myths perpetuated by the *Merie Tales*, and seemingly based on extrapolation from passages from *Collyn Clout* (John Bale, *Scriptorum illustrium maioris Brytannie, quam nunc Angliam & Scotiam vocant: Catalogue* (Basel, 1557–9), p. 651. For Collins' commonplace book, see B.L. MS Harley 2252 fos. 133v–140r.

[141] '*Hec vates ille / De quo loquntur mille*', *Why Come Ye Nat?*, lines 29–30 and postscript.

FOOTNOTE: THE CIRCULATION OF THE SATIRES

Hitherto this chapter has been somewhat lax in its references to the specific form in which Skelton's poems were made available to his public. The terms 'audience', implying a spoken performance, and 'readership', implying a circulated manuscript or printed volume, have been used rather indiscriminately and may have led to some confusion. Were the satires designed for performance, perhaps accompanied by music, or were they intended to be distributed in written form? Again, as has so often been the case in this study, the only available evidence is either internal or purely negative and consequently problematic. There are always dangers inherent in accepting the testimony of a work of fiction, particularly verse fiction, as the basis for judgements about its historical context. The choice of a given word, which one might consider particularly significant or revealing, may have been determined as much by the rhythm of the line which contains it, or by the rhyme-scheme, as by any desire on the part of the poet to transmit precisely the ideas implied by that one word and no other. And yet, with such reservations in mind, it must be observed that there are a number of seemingly suggestive remarks within the anti-Wolsey satires which tempt some general inferences about the methods of publication which Skelton employed.

Speke, Parott seems the easiest text about which to comment in this context, for its very complexity and crypticism mean that it must surely, as Edwards asserts, have been intended for 'a mere handful of educated readers'.[142] Such readers were evidently based in the Court and the royal household, for it was the attitude of the King and the personal relationship between Henry and his chief minister from which the text drew its inspiration and only a courtly audience could be expected to appreciate such allusions. The form in which the text was circulated amongst these readers seems equally evident.

Thus far the words 'readers' and 'readership' have been used, and not 'audience', when referring to this first satire and the text seems to confirm that such are the correct terms to employ. In this poem there are no references to a performance or recitation, and the text is always described as being just that, a text. In *Lenvoy Primere* it is twice referred to as a 'litelle quayre' (lines 278 and 290), and its public are described as 'them that yowe beholde' (line 290). In the *Lenvoy Royall* the poet expresses the wish that 'lordes and ladies *thys pamflett* may behold (line 358, my italics), and in the Latin *Disticon*, he tells his creation that,

> *Vix tua percipient, qui tua teque legent* (372)

(They shall scarcely understand your poem, who read you and your poem)[143]

---

142 Edwards, p. 210.   143 Trans. in Scattergood, p. 462.

In addition to these clear descriptions of a written text, the very nature of the poem is evidence of its textual circulation. For the crypticisms of Parott's 'ryche jacounce' seem singularly ill-suited to the rapid declamation of a public performance. This was a poem not only to be read but to be read many times over if it was to be even partially appreciated. It thus seems safe to assume the circulation of a written text and also of a manuscript rather than a printed volume, for there is no record of a printed version of 1521; the first printed version being the mutilated text printed in Richard Lant's *Certayne Bokes* of 1545. Skelton's method of writing also argues for a handwritten manuscript, as the various envoys seem likely to have been prepared in some haste and circulated whilst they were still topical news.

Thus one has a manuscript, or series of manuscripts, written in or around the poet's Westminster home and circulated among a small number of educated courtiers, clerics and scholars. Beyond that, however, little can be stated with any certainty. How many copies the poet prepared, whether he copied them himself or used the services of a scribe, as he had used the services of a Cambridge University copyist, the anonymous vicar of Trumpington, to provide the final versions of his mock-epitaphs for two of his parishioners at Diss, is not known.[144] Similarly whether he attempted to sell the finished texts through a bookseller, displayed copies publicly in Westminster or elsewhere, or merely gave them to courtiers of his acquaintance to circulate, is unclear. It seems obvious, if the arguments advanced in the first section of this chapter are correct, that the poet would have made efforts to present a copy to Henry VIII, but whether he succeeded and whether the King ever read the text can only be guessed at. Evidently Skelton's humanist critics saw a copy, for the poet testifies himself to stylistic criticism from such quarters. Indeed he is likely to have publicly displayed the text at St Paul's or elsewhere in order that they should see it. But who else, save William Thynne and Collins, saw the poem is unknown and too little precise information is available about the circulation of manuscripts at Court during this period for any informed speculation to be attempted. Until more is known, Edwards's 'mere handful of educated readers' must remain virtually the sum of our knowledge on the subject.

If anything, one is even less well-informed about *Collyn Clout* and *Why Come Ye Nat?*. For the same problems remain, whilst new questions arise concerning these texts which did not exist for the former. Given Skelton's dramatic change of poetic style and satirical content after his first satire, is it possible that he altered his method of presentation also? Clearly if *Collyn Clout* did mark a serious attempt to gain a wider popular following, it would no longer be entirely practical to distribute the text in the form of a 'mere

---

[144] *Colophon* to the *Epitaphe* for 'Adam Uddersall', printed in Scattergood, p. 110

handful' of carefully copied manuscripts. One obvious means of surmounting this difficulty would have been to have the text printed as a broadsheet or pamphlet. The problem would have been to find the money to finance such a scheme, and to find a printer willing to publish so contentious a work. This may well have been the difficulty which prevented the poem from reaching the presses – for, again, no record of an exactly contemporary printed version exists. The first edition seems to have been that of Thomas Godfray of around 1531. The poet himself seems to have been mindful of such difficulties even as he wrote, for one finds him complaining in the text of the 'saducees',

> Whiche hate for to be corrected
> Whan they be infected,
> Nor wyll suffre this boke
> By hoke ne by croke
> Prynted for to be. (1235–9)

Yet, if the avenue of printed circulation was apparently sealed off, is there any evidence to suggest that the poet may have tried to perform his works from the pulpit or in the manner of the balladeer, in order to gain them a wider hearing? Of the former possibility there is no concrete suggestion in the text beyond the possibility that the rhythm of the poem is based on plain-song.[145] A hint of the latter possibility appears, however, in the Latin *Epilogue* to the text, in which Skelton considers the reception which *Collyn Clout* will receive.[146]

Although to the multitude my songs are foolishly contemptible, yet they are rare inspirations to the cultivated ... it concerns me much less, although the envious tongue is prepared to injure me, because, although I sing rustic songs, nevertheless I shall be sung and celebrated everywhere while the famous English race still remains.

This use of the terms '*carmina*' and '*canto*' to denote *Collyn Clout* may be simply conventional here, but one cannot entirely discount the possibility that the poem was indeed intended to be 'sung and celebrated'.

The evidence that this may have been the case with *Why Come Ye Nat?* is somewhat stronger. In that poem one finds a curious allusion to the poet's motivation, and to how he intended his work to be received. When taxed by an anonymous interlocutor over whether a patron had prompted him to write, Skelton observes that he was,

> ... forcebly constrayned
> At Juvynals request
> To wryght of this glorious gest,

[145] A. F. Kinney, 'John Skelton: the poet as priest', paper read to the History Graduate Seminar, University of Southampton, 31 May 1984.
[146] *Collyn Clout, Epilogue*, lines 1–7, trans. in Scattergood, p. 481.

> Of this vayne gloryous best, [beast, i.e. Wolsey]
> His fame to be encrest
> At every solempne feest. (1210–15)

Elsewhere *Why Come Ye Nat?* is referred to as a creation of 'pen [and] ... inke' (line 684), as a 'memoryall' (line 824), a 'byl' (*Epilogue*, line 33), and a 'wanton scrowle' of blotted paper (lines 826 and 831), but here the poet clearly suggests that it will be performed 'at every solempne feest'. This observation, disregarding Skelton's optimism regarding the frequency of performance, need not be as fanciful as it seems. For the type of entertainment suggested here is clearly the interlude and, as Paula Neuss confirms, the poet was not entirely without experience of this genre; his *Magnyfycence*, she asserts, had been performed in a merchants' hall in the City, such as that of the Merchant Tailors' Company.[147] It is not difficult to imagine such works as *Collyn Clout* and *Why Come Ye Nat?* being performed in such a setting. Again this is purely speculative, but there is much internal evidence within the Skeltonic canon to suggest that the poet did write poetic works for performance, apparently by himself, earlier in his career. In the Latin invective accompanying *Agaynste a Comely Coystrowne*, for example, (which Scattergood dates *c.* 1495, but which could well hail from as late as 1502–4) the poet describes the text as[148]

A sarcastic poem against *another singer* and doltish musician who criticised the muse-like Skelton. The tunes you play on your lute are not to be preferred to *my songs, nor is your pipe as clear as ours* . . . our pipe is more pleasing to Phoebus.

Seemingly Skelton not only wrote for performance but for musical performance also.

By the various estimates of the poet's age and of the date of *Agaynste a Comely Coystrowne*, Skelton would have been somewhere between thirty-five- and forty-five-years old when he was making such grand claims for the clarity of his 'pipe'. That he sang his own verses at that time is clearly a different proposition from the suggestion that he was intending to perform *Why Come Ye Nat?* in 1522, when he would have been, by most accounts, approximately sixty-two. And yet in 1514 he was writing the series of *flytyngs, Agenst Garnesche*, when only nine years younger, and these were clearly designed for performance at Court by the poet, whether as a purely spoken tirade or accompanied by the lute. It is also noteworthy that the later verses in this *flytyng* series were written in exactly the same style as the last two satires against Wolsey, utilising specific charges of personal vice interspersed with long rhyme-chains of coarse invective and name-calling in the Skeltonic line-form, which were ideally suited to public performance. Per-

[147] P. Neuss (ed.), *Magnificence* (Manchester, 1980), pp. 42–3.
[148] *Contra alium Cantitantum*, trans. in Scattergood, p. 392, my italics.

haps the similarity of form and style of the satires to these earlier works implies that the poet was envisaging a similar method of presentation, if only to supplement the written circulation of the verses, or to draw attention to copies which may have been displayed at the Cross at Cheap or some other public gathering-place.[149]

[149] This last was the manner in which many of the verses against Empson were displayed in 1509; see A. H. Thomas and I. D. Thornley, eds., *Great Chronicle of London* (London, 1938), p. 236.

4

'Lyke Mahounde in a Play': conventional elements in Skelton's portrait of Wolsey

Any analysis of the Wolsey satires which ignores the influence exerted on them by literary convention will result in a misleading account of their historical value. Both contemporary politics and literary tradition contributed to the overall effect of the satires, not only in terms of form and style (that is, of how the poet arranged his material) but in terms of content also. Much of what appears to be purely political or biographical commentary in the texts proves on closer examination to be a subtle utilisation of conventional models, arguments or assumptions for deliberate effect. Hence, for example, the choice of the personal vices of which Wolsey is accused. He is proud ('borne up on every side / with pomp and with Pryde'). He is lecherous ('He foynes and he frygges / Spareth neither made ne wyfe') and gluttonous ('In lent, for a repast, / He eateth capons stewed, / Fesaunt and partriche mewed / Hennes, checkynges and pygges'). He is charged with greed and avarice ('Dame philargerya / Hathe so his herte in holde: / He loveth nothyng but golde'); with envy ('Hyt ys to fere lest he wold were the Garland on hys pate'); with sloth ('... he falleth into *Acidiam*, / Whiche, truly to expresse, / Is a forgetfulnesse, / Or wylfull blyndnesse'); and with wrath (lords of noble blood, 'He plucks them by the hode / And shakes them by the ear').[1] In short, all seven of the Deadly Sins are ascribed to the Cardinal. Is this pure coincidence? Later in *Why Come Ye Nat?* they are all brought together to reinforce the point. Wolsey is, the poet states, full of the following 'lewde condicyons',

> Presumcyon and vayne glory,
> Envy wrath and lechery,
> Covetys and gloteny,
> Slouthful to do good
> Now frantick, now starke wode! (574–8)

Skelton does not seek to illustrate or substantiate these claims here, they are in themselves sufficient for his purpose. For he is simply portraying Wolsey as a villain in a manner which his audience would recognise, by associating

---

[1] *Why Come Ye Nat?*, lines 203–4, 224–5, 220–3, 206–8, 466–9; *Speke, Parott*, line 438; *Why Come Ye Nat?*, lines 304–5.

him with the sins which homiletic writings and Morality Drama indicated marked out the enemy of the virtuous man.[2] Here and elsewhere the poet draws on his readers' experience of moralising literature, drama and homily to gain his desired effects. That the Cardinal may not actually exhibit any particular one of these sins is irrelevant. The convention provided by the Deadly Sins determines that they should all be there, for the more sins that Skelton is able to accuse Wolsey of, the more damning will be his condemnation of his target. It is precisely this sort of literary influence on the texts which historians must be aware of if they are not to misuse the satires as historical evidence.

Far from being the vivid sketch-from-the-life which many scholars have assumed, Skelton's picture of Wolsey is actually remarkably allusive. Wolsey is rarely seen as himself, except in the moments of specific vilification such as the attacks on his alleged tyranny in the Star Chamber, and even there the picture created relies for much of its effectiveness on cross-reference, proverb and literary allusion. Wolsey is 'Lyke Mahounde in a play', 'Lyke to a mamelek' and 'Lyke Pharao, voyde of grace', all references to characters and types from the Morality plays. He is compared to Robin Hood, to Naaman the Syrian, to Antiochus and to Amalek, to Polyphemus, to Pandulph, to Asaph and to Datan, to Zalmunna, Zeeb and the Scourge of Jeremy, all within the lines of the most specific of the satires, *Why Come Ye Nat?*. Very often Skelton is referring not to Wolsey but simply to villains with whom his audience was familiar, with the intention of adding weight to his allegations by analogy rather than analysis. So much is this so that at times Wolsey the man disappears entirely beneath the over-piled *topoi* which create the satirical figure: Wolsey the Skeltonic villain.

Often convention can be seen not only to have influenced *how* Skelton wrote, but also *what* he wrote. From the point of view of the historian it is of only limited interest that literary conventions influenced the *form* of Skelton's satires. That the poet was following tradition in listing Wolsey's vices in a certain manner, or in using the persona of a rustic orator to protest against the Cardinal's failings as a cleric, is not a grave concern in the present context. An analysis of the conventional elements of Skelton's poetry is beyond the scope of this study.[3] The purpose of this chapter is more modest. It is simply to make the reader aware of when and how such literary conventions may have directly influenced *the substance* of Skelton's satires: when, for example, conventional approaches to writing may have prompted the poet to fabricate or contrive an allegation in order to give his text a satisfying conformity to the norms of the genre in which he was writing, or to achieve a

---

[2] See M. W. Bloomfield, *The Seven Deadly Sins* (Michigan, 1952).
[3] Such a study is provided by Heiserman's *Skelton And Satire*, to which the present chapter is indebted, despite my disagreements with some of Professor Heiserman's conclusions.

specific rhetorical effect. For in such cases conventions of writing are directly relevant to the value of the poems as historical source material. That the Deadly Sins tradition influenced Skelton to list Wolsey's alleged vices together, for example, is less significant for the historian than that it prompted him to contrive a spurious charge of sloth against a minister whose evident industry had previously induced the poet to complain of his continued 'besynes', in order to provide a full complement of the traditional sins. What follows is an attempt to suggest which of Skelton's assertions concerning Wolsey cannot be seen to stem from a genuine attempt at political analysis but from other less politically illuminating sources.

Perhaps nowhere is Skelton more reliant for his criticism of Wolsey on his literary antecedents than in *Collyn Clout*. This text has often been taken as evidence of popular criticism of Wolsey's personal life and of his policies as head of the Church. Yet, as what follows will demonstrate, more than the other anti-Wolsey poems, it borrows extensively from centuries of anti-clerical literary tradition. A brief summary of the arguments and assertions contained in the text will serve to illustrate the scope and nature of this borrowing.

The text begins with the ironic analysis of the stylistic dilemma facing the satirist cited in chapter 3 above concerning *Why Come Ye Nat?* ('What can it avayle / To dryve forth a snayle'). It then identifies its narrator as 'Collyn Clout', the simple rustic soul who will tell of the disruptive 'hoder moder' brought about by the division between the laity and the clergy. Like Parott's, his style will not be exactly what polite society might expect – this time it will be the 'Tattered and jagged / Rudely rayne-beaten' ragged rhymes of the 'Skeltonic' verse-form (lines 53–5), well suited to the honest, unsophisticated, countryman, rather than the elaborate biblical metaphors of the learned and enigmatic bird. But, as with Parott's 'ryche jacounce', Collyn's commentary will contain 'matters more precious' for those readers wise enough to pursue them. For, as Collyn assures them, 'Yff ye take well therwith / It hath in it some pyth' (lines 57–8).

In *Collyn Clout*, however, the effort required of the reader is far less than that demanded by *Speke, Parott*. Here the only satiric stratagem to be negotiated is the inconsistently sustained fiction that the narrator is merely reporting with horror the calumnies of the clerical estate which he has overheard in the streets, and with which he heartily disagrees. Once one has read beyond the ironic distaste with which Collyn repeats the charges which he has heard 'laye men say', the critical broadside against clerical abuses and their consequences requires little further exposition. And, as A. R. Heiserman has demonstrated, the failings of the churchmen which Collyn attacks are the conventional sins and follies ascribed to their estate by authors from the twelfth century and earlier.[4]

[4] Heiserman, pp. 190–243.

The poet's assertions concerning the nature and provenance of his satire clearly cannot be taken at face value. Skelton was neither simply using Collyn as a spokesman for public opinion, nor reflecting in the text a genuine personal concern at an increasing rupture of Church and laity. Collyn's claim that he was merely repeating 'what men say' was a thoroughly conventional method of proceeding in a satire, particularly one with anti-clerical overtones, as it gave the narrator's voice a semi-divine authority, similar to that of Langland's Piers, as that *vox populi* which is also *vox Dei*.[5] Gower had made precisely the same defence of his *Vox Clemantis*, in which he had declared that,[6]

Nothing I write is my own opinion. Rather I shall try to speak what the voices of the people have reported to me.

[And] I am not speaking of these things on my own part: rather the voice of the people has reported it to me, and it complains of their adverse fate at every hand. I speak as the masses speak, and even as I write I lament over what I say . . .

Gower had also employed the guise of the innocent bystander, horrified at the growing rift between Church and people. 'The Clergy now blame the people', he declared, 'and the people blame the clergy. But both persevere in their guiltiness. Envious of one another, each man blames the other, and no group mends its own course.'[7] Such sentiments are directly echoed in Collyn's complaint that,

> . . . as farre as I can se,
> It is wrong with eche degre;
> For the temporalte
> Accuseth the spiritualte :
> The Spiritualte agayne
> Doth grudge and complayne
> Upon the temporall men.
> Thus eche of other blother
> The tone against the tother. (59–67)

Such passages as these should not be taken as evidence of a rising tide of popular anti-clericalism in the early 1520s. They are simply conventional rhetorical devices designed to indicate the character and motivation of the persona through which Skelton will launch the satire. The poet deliberately distances his attack on Wolsey from the charge of personal vindictiveness by placing it in the mouth of one who is ostensibly a supporter of the clergy, and

---

[5] See R. S. Kinsman, 'Skelton's "Colyn Cloute": the mask of "Vox Populi"', in *Essays Critical and Historical Dedicated to Lily B. Campbell* (California, 1950), pp. 12–23, 260–61.

[6] J. Gower, *Vox Clemantis*, in E. W. Stockton (ed.), *The Major Latin Works of John Gower* (Seattle, 1962), IV chaps. 1 and 3, Prologue.

[7] *Ibid.*, VI, chap. 7.

gives it a veneer of authenticity by setting that narrator in a long tradition of honest Christian witnesses. Only slowly will that ironic pose be lifted, in order that the most capital may be made from the humour and rhetorical advantage which it provides.

The 'hoder moder' which Collyn reports, and the ruinous condition of Church and realm which he witnesses are also, as Heiserman has shown, the stock complaints of centuries of anti-clerical satire. That senior clerics were gluttonous, lecherous, simoniacal absentees, that they failed to preach as they should and so left the laity open prey to foolish junior clergy and drunken heretics, that they sought secular preferment above spiritual advancement, 'And assay[ed] to crepe / Within the noble walles / Of the Kynges halles, / To fatt theyr bodyes full' (lines 125–8), all of this had been said many times before. Langland had condemned in *The Vision of Piers Plowman* those clergy who petitioned their bishops,[8]

> To have a licence and leve at London to dwelle,
> And syngen ther for symonie, for silver is swete . . .

and those 'Bisshopes and bachelers, both mastres and doctours', who

> Liggen at Londoun in Lenten and ellis.
> Some serven the King and his silver tellen
> In Cheker and in Chauncerie chalangen his dettes
> Of wardes and of wardemotes, weyves and streyves,
> And somme serven as servaunts lordes and ladies,
> And in stede of stywardes sitten and demen.

Walter Map had made the same point at the end of the twelfth century in observing that,[9]

when pastors run after kings' courts, their pastoral guidance and duty are abandoned. The flocks are scattered by the shepherd's absence, and, once scattered, are wounded with a fatal bite [of sin or heresy].

Skelton's plea that bishops should offer a lead to their erring juniors and straying flock by preaching (a plea which Kinsman suggests may have been taken up from the preaching of Colet[10]), also had a long history. When the poet stated that,

> Ye bysshoppes of estates
> Shulde open the brode gates

[8] A. V. C. Schmidt (ed.), *The Vision of Piers Plowman* (London, 1978) (hereafter *Vision*), Prologue, lines 85–7, 91–6.
[9] W. Map, '*Cum Sint Plures Ordines*', cited and trans. in J. Mann, *Chaucer and Medieval Estates Literature* (Cambridge, 1973), p. 57.
[10] R. S. Kinsman, 'The voices of dissonance: pattern in Skelton's *Colyn Cloute*', *H.L.Q.*, 26 (1963), pp. 291–313.

> For your spirytuall charge,
> And com forthe at large,
> Lyke lanternes of lyght,
> In the peoples syght,
> In pulpyttes autentyke,
> For the wele publyke. (690–7)

he was doing no more, in substance, than repeating the claims of Gower and
the anonymous author of 'A Good Makynge of Lour Delaye' that, without
proper guidance from the 'ligte of lanterns to lede the way', the poor flock
would inevitably roam astray.[11] Similarly Skelton's condemnation of those
uneducated priests who although hardly 'As wyse as Waltom's calfe', must
'preche a Goddes halfe / In the pulpyt solempnely' (lines 809–11), is an echo
of conventional attacks on the stupidity of clerics, and their capacity either
wilfully or through ignorance to misinterpret the gospel. For his personification of Sloth, for example, Langland chose a cleric who had[12]

> . . . be[en] prest and parsoun passynge thretti wynter
> Yet [could] . . . neither solfe ne synge ne seyntes lyves rede.

In the Lollard *Plowman's Tale* the anonymous poet asserted that[13]

> Such that cannot say her crede,
> With praier shull be made prelates
> Nother can the gospell rede
> Such shull now wield high estates.

And in *Pierce The Ploughman's Crede* a Carmelite is made to criticise the
lack of learning of the Dominicans who,[14]

> Ben digne as dich water – that dogges in bayteth
> Loke a rihaut of hem – that can nougt wel reden
> His rewle ne his respondes – but be pure rote.

There is thus little which is either new or specific in Skelton's vision of a corrupt and crumbling Church. Even the poet's measured and cynical concession that 'almost two or three' senior clerics might be performing their
duties correctly (line 148),[15] which has prompted speculation as to precisely
which clerics Skelton may have wished to exempt from his criticism,[16] is a

[11] Gower, *Vox Clementis*, III, chap. 29; 'A Good Makynge of Lour Delaye', in J. Kail (ed.),
   Twenty Six Political and Other Pieces, E.E.T.S., O.S. 124 (1904), no.8.
[12] *Vision*, V 422–3.
[13] *Plowman's Tale*, in T. Wright (ed.), *Political Poems and Songs Relating to English History*,
   Rolls Series, 14, 2 vols. (London, 1859–61), I pp. 304–346, 316.
[14] W. W. Skeat (ed.), *Pierce The Ploughman's Crede*, E.E.T.S., 30 (1867), lines 375–7.
[15] Similar observations are made at lines 244–54 and 1095–1106.
[16] P. E. McLane, 'Prince Lucifer and the fitful "Lanternes of Lyght": Wolsey and the Bishops in
   Skelton's *Colyn Cloute*', *H.L.Q.*, 43 (1980), pp. 159–79.

conventional rhetorical device. The anonymous author of a poem attacking nuns, preserved in B.L. Cotton MS Vespasian D IX, was careful to observe that, although 'the most part' of their number were sinful,

> ... I say not alle,
> God forbede, for than hyt were harde
> For sum bene devowte, holy and towarde,
> And holden the rygt way to blysse.

Similarly Hoccleve in *The Regiment of Princes*, in condemning the behaviour of lords' retainers was swift to point out that 'I seye nat all lordes men thus do / That sue unto oure Courte', and that, although the clergy were also culpable as a class, 'many of hem gye hem as hem oghte'.[17] All that Skelton has done in *Collyn Clout* is to limit the concession to virtuous clergy still further by implying that only 'two or three' are innocent of all crimes, an observation which gives further weight to his conventional denunciation of a failing priesthood and a doomed laity.

And yet within this generalised conventional critique of the clergy there appear increasingly specific allusions to Wolsey and his policies of the sort which littered the final complaint of *Speke, Parott*. The references to the clergy who 'hauke on hobby larkes / And other wanton warkes / Whan the nyght darkes' (lincs 193–5) may well be an allusion to the Cardinal's mistress, Joan Lark, whilst the charge that 'some of you dothe eate / In lenton season flesshe meate' (lines 205–5) might be prompted by his licence to eat meat during Lent, obtained from Pope Leo X in February 1520.[18] There also seems to be a continuation of Parott's condemnation of Wolsey's adoption of the 'pollaxis and pyllars' symbolic of his Legatine authority in the passage describing how,

> ... the pope may
> An holy anker call
> Out of the stony wall
> And hym a bysshop make
> Yf he on hym dare take
> To kepe so hawe a role,
> To ryde upon a mule
> With golde all betrapped,
> In purple and paule belapped; (302–10)

Sixty-four lines later the monastic dissolutions of 1521–2 are reintroduced in the lines alleging how,

---

[17] Thomas Hoccleve, *The Regiment Of Princes*, in *Works*, ed. F. J. Furnivall, E.E.T.S., 72, 3 vols. (London, 1897), I 541–2, 444.

[18] *L.P.*, III (i) 634, 647. For a summary of these assertions, see Scattergood, p. 467 n. 193 and nn. 204–19.

> Relygous men are fayne
> For to tourne agayne
> *In secula seculorum*,
> And to forsake theyr *corum* . . . (374–7)

> And to synge from place to place,
> Lyke apostataas,
> And the self same game
> Began, and now with shame,
> Amongest the sely nonnes. (385–9)

There are also caricatures of Wolsey's political dominance combined with allegations of other personal vices, and mockery of his low birth.

What is one to make of this combination of the universal with the particular? It has been suggested that the conventional nature of many of the charges in *Collyn Clout* indicates that Skelton's intention was thus to attack general abuses; social ills and spiritual disorder *per se* rather than Wolsey as an individual.[19] But this view of Skelton's motivation is too self-consciously literary, too divorced from contemporary political reality to be of assistance to the historian. It is A. R. Heiserman's contention that neither of the first two Wolsey satires had a specific application. In *Speke, Parott*, he asserts, 'Parrot attacks not particular evildoers but the folly of his times' and 'the eternal excesses of politics'.[20] Yet, although such general criticism might have been a by-product of the texts, the main stimulus for Parott's appearance was clearly, as the previous chapters have shown, a desire to attack Wolsey in particular. The conventional elements of both *Speke, Parott* and *Collyn Clout* do not indicate that Skelton was trying to assert general philosophical truths about the nature of political management: such immediate and ribald satires as the latter were hardly the ideal medium for such statements. Nor does the existence of a tradition of political complaint and satire imply that such texts were in some way self-replicating. Men did not write political complaint solely because other men had done so in the past. Each individual example of the complaint tradition was written for a specific, contemporary, and essentially political purpose. Convention determined how and what the poet wrote, it did not provide the particular stimulus for writing.

Collyn Clout like *Why Come Ye Nat?* is a text forged as a weapon with which to attack Wolsey; it is not a general complaint which happens to utilise the Cardinal as an exemplar of some of its themes. Had the poet been writing a general satire the finished article would have been different, and what he chose to exclude is as informative as what he includes in this context. The criticism of the noble class in both *Collyn Clout* and *Why Come Ye Nat?* is, for example, extremely circumscribed, as Skelton has no wish to

---

[19] Heiserman, pp. 196–208.   [20] *Ibid.*, pp. 141, 127.

antagonise the nobility. Thus there are none of the attacks on noble pride or foppishness, none of the criticism of their retainers, or of the decline of charity and hospitality which characterised other appearances of the aristocracy in satires and complaints.[21] Significantly there is also no criticism of the merchant class ('one of the few secular estates regularly treated in estates satire'[22]) to be found in either text: no allegations of usury, venality or fraud, or of avarice and exploitation of the poor, of the sort which one might have expected to find in a satire with a general rather than a specific object. But once the specific, political, purpose of the satires is taken into account, this omission becomes readily understandable. For Skelton was writing for a City audience largely comprised of merchants and traders, and his intention was not to improve their morals by castigating their sins in homiletic fashion, but to appeal to their prejudices and grievances. Hence the merchant class is portrayed, in passing in *Collyn Clout* and more fully in *Why Come Ye Nat?*, simply as the victims of Wolsey's impositions. Similarly there is no criticism of the legal estate in any of the satires. The conventional charges concerning the corrupt practices of lawyers and the expensive, convoluted and pettifogging procedures of the law courts are omitted precisely because the texts are directed at a specific object: Wolsey. Thus again it is as the innocent victims of Wolsey's policies, this time his tyrannous misuse of the Court of Star Chamber, that the judges and lawyers of the Common Law are of most use to the poet. Any widening of the satiric perspective, any generalisation of the attack which might indicate that the lawyers or the traders were themselves villains, would have detracted from the attack on Wolsey as both the epitome and the cause of society's ills. Thus the focus of the satires is kept narrow, and remains focused upon the Cardinal.

Where Heiserman's analysis of the satires is particularly useful in the present context, however, is in his identification of the amount of conventional material to be found within a satire which, as this study demonstrates, has both a specific occasion *and* a specific object.[23] When Skelton came to write the text which would open out his attack on Wolsey to a wider audience he clearly had to be more direct in his allegations. Yet before the forced loans became the predominant focus of controversy he had little more political information at hand from which to fashion the specific charges which a more open satire required. Hence the poet fell back on, and adapted for his own ends, the logical framework and stock allegations provided by literary conventions. The anti-clerical tradition provided him with a model from which to work. As Heiserman observes, such conventions gave the poet 'scope', 'he

---

[21] Compare, for example, *The Simonie*, lines 258–64.
[22] Mann, *Medieval Estates Literature*, p. 99.
[23] For Heiserman's distinction between what was, in his opinion, the specific occasion and the universal object of the text, see Heiserman, p. 197.

need not begin each poem in a vacuum, because he [could] . . . count on certain images, structures, [and] characters having certain effects'.[24]

In *Speke, Parott* Skelton had simply abused and criticised Wolsey for opportunist reasons. In *Collyn Clout* the need to appeal to a wider audience necessitated a more 'rational' approach. Thus the poet attempts to demonstrate why Wolsey deserved such denigration through what appears to be an analysis of the social and spiritual consequences of his rule, and of his practice and acceptance of the sins of the clergy. A specious picture of a church and state fallen into corruption is painted, using the commonplace allegations of anti-clerical satire and polemic illustrated above. Into this picture the poet then introduces what specific charges he is able to lay at Wolsey's door, or which he is able to fabricate, in order to suggest that it is the Cardinal who is the cause of all this corruption. It is gradually implied that it is his example which has prompted and condoned the lordly, luxurious lives of the higher clergy, his lack of enthusiasm for preaching which has resulted in an ignorant and benighted laity, his stranglehold on political power which has emasculated secular government. Thus it is only at the end of the satire that the individual prelate, the poet's caricature of Wolsey, steps out from the general corruption to rage in his own voice and condemn himself in his own words,

> For, be it good, be it yll,
> As it is, it shall be styll. (1217–18)

> Renne god, renne devyll,
> Renne who may renne best,
> And let take all the rest!
> We set nat a nutte shell
> The way to heven or to hell! (1222–6)

And yet, although the *intention* of the satire is entirely specific and political, the actual content, even when apparently at its most specific, is far less valuable to the historian interested in contemporary attitudes to Wolsey and his administration. It should not be imagined, for example, that the attacks on the Cardinal's personal vices and excesses were included in *Collyn Clout* and in *Why Come Ye Nat?* because they were the cause of public scandal and protest. Skelton includes them because the anti-clerical literary tradition suggested that they should be included, and that they should be included in a particular form.

The lines in both the later satires which attack the magnificence of Wolsey's buildings at Hampton Court and York Place, and the ostentation of his large retinue, have often been cited by historians and commentators as evidence of the Cardinal's corruption and pride. In such passages as the following, the poet speaks generally of the clerical estate, but aims specifically

[24] *Ibid.*, p. 3.

at Wolsey's building programme at Hampton Court. He attacks those clerics who pretend,

> . . . gravyte
> And seygnyoryte,
> With all solempnyte, (924–6)

> Buyldyng royally
> Theyr mancyons curyously,
> With turrettes and with toures,
> With halles and with boures,
> Stretchynge to the sterres,
> With glasse wyndowes and barres;
> Hangynge about the walles
> Clothes of golde and paules,
> Arayse of ryche aray,
> Fresshe as flours in May; (934–43)

The tapestries which the poet proceeds to describe can be identified with those known to have been owned by Wolsey and used at Hampton Court. Thus the reference seems to have a specific and purely contemporary significance. Yet the buildings of the senior clergy and of the monastic orders had been a conventional focus of abuse and criticism for satirists and polemicists for centuries.

A vernacular sermon of the late fourteenth century complained that[25]

prelates, that ben now-adaies, hav many dyverse castellis and maners, as rial as the kynge him selfe, to chaunge whanne so evere hem likith for to take divers eiris, wythynne araied as realli with costli clothes of gold and selk and in multitude of other jewellis bothe of selver and of gold: in al maner housis office as thou[gh] it were in Salaman's temple . . .

Walter Map had complained of parsons who spent the money gained from the poor man's tithe in the purchase of manors, and Gower had condemned the sumptuous buildings of the mendicant friars.[26] In *The Plowman's Tale* the Christ-like pelican had denounced those clergy who robbed the laity and[27]

> Therwith . . . purchase hem lay fee,
> In londe there hem liketh best;
> And builde also as brod as a citie,
> Both in the east, and eke in the west.

Similarly, when Lady Mede attempts to bribe the Friar in *Piers Plowman*, it is with the prospect of magnificent new buildings which she tempts him;[28]

---

[25] B.L. Add. MS 41321 fos. 17–17B, cited in G. R. Owst, *Literature and Pulpit in Medieval England*, 2nd edn (Oxford, 1961), p. 283.

[26] *Latin Poems Attributed to Walter Mapes*, pp. 125–6, 253; Gower, *Vox Clementis*, IV.

[27] Wright, *Political Poems and Songs*, I p. 326.

[28] *Vision*, III, lines 60–3.

> . . . I shal cover youre Kirk, youre cloustre do maken,
> Wowes do whiten and wyndowes glazen
> Do peynten and portraye [who paied] for the makynge,
> That every segge shall see I am sustor of youre house.

And the avaricious Dominican Friar in *Pierce the Ploughman's Crede* is found begging for money in order to pay for new building work, despite the luxury of his minster church, chapter house and refectory,[29]

> For we buldeth a burwah a-brod and a large,
> A Chirch and a chapaile with Chambers alofte,
> With wide windowes y-wrought and walles well heye,
> That mote ben portreid and paynt and pulched ful clene,
> With gaie glittering glas glowing as the sonne.

What Skelton is doing, then, in illustrating the luxury of Wolsey's palaces, is not necessarily reflecting popular resentment at the Cardinal's lifestyle, but reflecting a literary convention which indicated that the buildings of religious figures were a suitable target for abuse. When one wished to portray an erring cleric in literature, conventions dictated the manner in which one did so. Traditional approaches, traceable back through the satirists and homilists of the past four centuries to classical and biblical sources, indicated which errors, sins and vices it was appropriate to ascribe to an individual and which others it was not. Had Skelton wished to eulogise Wolsey he might have cited the role of such palaces as centres of alms-giving and hospitality, since he wished to portray him as a villain it was their material luxury which he stressed. Thus on closer examination the 'men' whose allegations concerning Hampton Court Collyn was repeating can be seen to be not citizens of the London of 1522, but rather satirists like Langland, Gower and Walter Map.

The descriptions of Wolsey's retinue have a similar lineage. In *Collyn Clout* the poet attacked the low-born bishop who,

> . . . dare take
> To kepe so harde a rule,
> To ryde upon a mule
> With golde all betrapped,
> In purple and paule belapped;
> Some hatted and some capped,
> Rychly bewrapped,
> God wote, to theyr great paynes,
> In rotchettes of fyne raynes,
> Whyte as mares mylke;
> Theyr tabertes of fyne sylke;
> Theyr styrops of myxt golde begared,

[29] *Crede*, II, lines 169–73.

> There may no cost be spared,
> Theyr moyles golde dothe eate,
> Theyr neyghbours dye for mete. (306–20)

Had Wolsey been the first prelate to be abused for his magnificence in such a manner those commentators who have used such lines to indicate how unacceptable was Wolsey's ceremonial grandeur to his contemporaries would clearly have a strong case. Under those circumstances it would be possible to argue that Skelton's texts provide *prima facie* evidence of the unpopularity of Wolsey's retinue amongst the general populace. The conventional nature of such a portrait of the luxuriously appointed wordly prelate amidst his retainers inevitably compromises such arguments.

Thomas of Wimbledon, in a sermon written in the late fourteenth century, had made essentially the same assertions concerning the wordly clergy as Skelton produced almost one hundred and fifty years later. They attempted, he claimed, to rival the laity[30]

in the magnificence of their steeds and [saddlery], in the pompous throng of their servants, each according to his ability, some like squires, others like knights, others like barons, others like earls and dukes. Nay rather do they strive to appear more stately then kings in secular pomp and wordly vanities.

Such allegations of wordly ambition are also clearly taken up in Skelton's hint of Wolsey's aspirations to 'were the garland on hys patc', to 'rule kynge and kayser', and to outdo the royal Court with the magnificence of Hampton.

An identical description of a worldly prelate in procession can be found in *The Plowman's Tale*, which attacks those clergymen,[31]

> That high on horse willeth ride
> In glitterande gold of great array
> Ipainted and portred all in pride,
>
> And miters mo than one or two
> Ipearled as the queenes head;
> A staff of gold, and perrle, lo,
> As heavy as it were made of lead,
> With cloth of gold as green as gall.
>
> They riden with her royall route
> On a courser, as it were a king;
> With saddle of gold glittering
> With curious harneis quaintly crallit
> Stirrops gay of gold mastling.

Such repetition of charges, even of language and simile, does not indicate a

[30] MS Cambridge Univ. Libri I i III 8 fos. 129ff. cited and trans. in Owst, I p. 281.
[31] Wright, *Political Poems and Songs*, I pp. 307–8.

lack of imagination on the part of each individual writer, a willingness simply to adopt the technique and images of others in the absence of inspiration of their own. It reveals the existence of a vital and potent satiric convention. By using certain key words, phrases and comparisons, writers were able to condition the response of their readers or audience. For reference to such lordliness in apparel and retinue had been developed into a means of indicating the psychological and spiritual failings of the clergy. As Lydgate, following Boccaccio, observed, the 'waste of cloth and superfluite' in garments indicated more than simple extravagance: it was itself both cause and effect of deeper failings, for[32]

> It causeth pride and ambicioun
> Ageyn the vertu of humylite;
> To lecherie it yiveth occasioun,
> Which is contrarie unto chastite
> Wast of array sett folke in poverte,
> Causeth also such costage spent in veyn
> Off othir porere to have ful gret disdayn
>
> Wher superfluite is usid of aray
> Riot folweth, proud port and idilnesse.

More specifically such excesses in clerics were traditionally used as a metaphoric representation of Pride. As the author of the vernacular sermon cited above observed,[33]

Pride thanne schal be ful hi[gh] in prelatis. For hir pride shal passe alle temporalle lordes in all thynges that longet to lordes estaat, as in stronge castellis an ryall maneris . . . Also in proude araye of here owne persones, bothe in costtew cloth and pelure as fyn as emperour, kyng or quene. Also in gret multituds of fatte horses and proude, with gai gult sadeles and schynyng brideles, with miche waste and proude merynge more niseli disgysid thanne any temporal lordes meynye . . . whan he schal onwer ride oute, [y]ea, thouh it be to visite his pore scheep, he must ride with foure or fyve score hors proudeli apareilid at all poyntes, his owne palfrai for his bodi worth a 20 or 30 pound, al bihangid with gliterynge gold as thou[gh] it were an hooli hors, himself above in fyne scarlet or other cloth as good, and withynne as good pelure as the quene hath any in her gowne: hir persones and hir clerkis rydynge aboute hem, al in gult harneise, with bastard swerdis overgild bi hire sides hangynge, as though it were Centurio and his kny[gh]tes ridynge towardes Cristes deth . . .

The similarities of such a passage to Skelton's portrait of Wolsey with his golden-trapped mule, his pole-axes and his pillars is striking. It is also informative as it allows one to see the uses to which such conventional portraits were put. They are, as the sermon–writer implies, descriptions which work on both the literal and the symbolic level. They may contain specific allus-

---

[32] H. Bergen (ed.), *Lydgate's Fall of Princes*, E.E.T.S., Extra Series, 121 (1924 for 1918), bk IV 2682–90.
[33] Owst, I pp. 282–3.

ions to particular clergy but they are also metaphorical representations of wordly pride.

Such conventions could be utilised in a number of ways by writers. Chaucer, in *The General Prologue*, is able to allude to it in order subtly to suggest that his Friar is a sinner, whilst seeming only to praise his attractive appearance,[34]

> For ther he was nat lyke a cloysterer
> With a thredbare cope, as is a poure scoler
> But he was lyk a maister or a pope.

The possible irony of this assertion only becomes apparent once one is aware of the anti-clerical traditions which insisted that friars and priests should *not* look like a master or a pope, and that such an appearance betokened an abandonment of their pastoral duties and a fall into the sin of pride. Conversely the convention could be used, as it is by Skelton, to associate a specific individual with a villainous stereotype. By describing Wolsey in a manner which associated him with the stock clerical sinner of estates and homiletic literature, the poet need not prove any specific charges against him: the association was sufficient to carry with it all the failings of the stereotype. Again, it is the way in which Skelton chose to portray Wolsey which is crucial, and which governed the specific details of the portrait, not the vices of the Cardinal himself. For *all* clergymen beyond the 'poure scoler' and the simple parish priest could be criticised for their wordliness and their finery. All bishops lived in palaces and all the higher clergy sullied their hands to some degree in the impure waters of secular politics, whether it be at the centre as members of the Council or the House of Lords, in their dioceses as representatives of the Crown in tax-collection and local administration, or in the more worldly aspects of ecclesiastical court jurisdiction. Skelton's decision to portray that worldliness, and to portray it in the ways which have been outlined above, as magnificent retinues, clothes and buildings, was a conscious decision to set Wolsey in the tradition of anti-clerical complaint, and to do so in order to indicate to his readers that the Cardinal suffered from the sin of pride. His purpose is didactic; he is not simply reflecting public opinion.

The influence of convention on the composition of the text did not end there, however. It is not sufficient to say that Skelton felt that Wolsey was a sinfully proud man and chose a conventional means of conveying that feeling to his audience. For the allegation of pride itself was not simply a literal assertion; rather it was the symbol and focus of a whole tradition of satiric and homiletic literature. Indeed for Skelton to say that Wolsey was proud was, in essence, merely to state that he was a thorough villain, since pride, as the

---

[34] Chaucer, *The General Prologue*, lines 259–61.

satanic sin, was seen to be the chief root and first cause of all wordly sin and evil. As More wrote in *The Four Last Things*, pride was 'the very hed and rote of al sinnes . . . the mischievous mother of al maner vice'.[35] This point had been made throughout the medieval period. As Lydgate advised, 'Ye that be wise, considreth how the roote / Off vicis alle is pride.'[36] Pride was thus a heavily loaded word for the late medieval and early Renaissance writer. It indicated not simply personal vanity but a multitude of personal corruptions, and author and readers alike were attuned to such nuances. It was a sin particularly associated with the Royal Court, with the powerful and the elegant.[37] More significantly still, it was also linked with clerics in whom it indicated a betrayal of Christian values for wordly gain and with the upstart, the character of low social origins who rose to high eminence through the favour of his betters. It is then, easy to see how an allegation of pride suited Wolsey's circumstances: he was a low-born, magnificent cleric, who was a centre of courtly and political activity. Thus when Skelton came in search of charges of villainy with which to attack him, it is not surprising that the allegation of pride was one of the first which he found.

It would be useful at this point briefly to examine a number of these other traditions which contributed to Skelton's portrayal of Wolsey as a proud prelate, in order that a better understanding might be gained of its literary origins. Perhaps the most potent of those traditions mentioned above was that which condemned the upstart, the man of ambition who rose in wordly affairs beyond his 'natural' station. Such a man opposed both the religious imperatives which forbad too great a devotion to material goals, and the conservative social values favouring government by the nobility which were a commonplace in literature. Hence he was the target for much satirical and didactic writing.

Gower reviled such men thus in the *Vox Clemantis*,[38]

Nothing is more troublesome than a lowly person who has risen to the top, at least when he was born a serf. His thinking continues along the old way of the serf, let fate confer upon him whatever high rank he will . . . Fame will ultimately establish who he is.

The Scots poet Dunbar similarly, if more colourfully, condemned the elevation to high clerical honour of the 'ruffie' better suited to cleaning stables,[39]

---

[35] *The Four Last Things*, in W. E. Campbell and A. W. Reed (ed.), *The English Works of Sir Thomas More*, 2 vols. (London, 1931), I, p. 82.

[36] Bergen, *Fall of Princes*, I, lines 1338–41.

[37] Heiserman, p. 59.

[38] Gower, *Vox Clemantis*, v, chap. 15.

[39] 'To the King', lines 53–61 (*c.* 1513), in J. Kingsley (ed.), *The Poems of William Dunbar* (Oxford, 1979).

> Ane pykthank in a prelottis clais,
> With his wavill feit and wirrok tais,
> With hoppir hippis and henches narrow,
> And bausy hondis to beir a barrow;
> With lut schulderis and luttard bak,
> Quhilk natur maid to beir a pak
> With gredy mynd and glaschane gane,
> Mell-hedit lyk ane mortar-stane,
> Fenyeing the feris off ane lord.

Probably the most strident voice denouncing the upstart was Lydgate's. His *Fall of Princes*, which was widely admired and copied through the fifteenth and early sixteenth centuries,[40] was little more than an exercise in condemning upward social mobility. The story of Saul, King of Jerusalem, who forgot his debt to God 'Which had hym reised onto estat royall / Fro pore degre',[41] prompted the following digression from the poet,[42]

> What thyng in herte mor frowad mai be thouht
> Than is the sodeyn fals presumpcion
> Off a wreche that cam up off nouht,
> To yeve hym lordshepe and dominacioun?
> And fer to make a pleyn comparisoun
> Men sholde off resoun dreede a leoun lesse
> Than the reudnesse off a crownyd asse
>
> What thyng to God is mor abhomynable
> Than pride upreised out off poverte?
> And nothyn gladli is founde more vengable
> Than ar wrechis set in hih degre:
> For from his stok kynde may not fle:
> Ech thyng resortith, how ferr ever it go,
> To the nature which that it came fro.

The moral was considered so crucial to the didactic purpose of the text that Lydgate repeated it, using the same metaphors, two books later.[43] The reasoning used to justify such assertions was simple and gave rise to a number of further claims. Those ministers or rulers who rose from low estate were, it was argued, inevitably ambitious. How else would they have overcome the difficulties in the way of their rise thus far? Thus they would be covetous, and would soon prove dissatisfied with their present circumstances and extort more from their subjects or from their masters, which would result in the ruin of the commonweal. They would also, whether sooner or later, fall from grace, although Lydgate does not finally declare whether this is the inevitable result of divine justice, of Fortune's caprice, or of ruinous tendencies inherent in the very act of rising to high office ('Hih clymbyng

---

[40] D. Pearsall, *John Lydgate* (London, 1970), p. 250.
[41] *Fall of Princes*, ii, lines 229–30.
[42] *Ibid.*, II, lines 232–45.
[43] *Ibid.*, IV, lines 2675–88.

up, off resoun who can see, / Dulleth of braynes the memoriall, / Blureth the sihte, in hih and low degre, / Which from a-lofte makith hem have a fall'[44]).

Such a conventional model is the basis of Skelton's portrayal of Wolsey. Hence the number of predictions and warnings of the Cardinal's impending doom to be found within the satires, of 'a fatall fall for one / That shall sytte on a trone / And rule all thinges alone' from whom 'Fortune may chaunce to flytte' (*Collyn Clout*, lines 473–5, 994). Clearly when writing *Speke, Parott* the poet may have expected such a fall actually to occur, but by the time that *Collyn Clout* came to be written it has a less specific significance. Wolsey is portrayed in the later satires as in imminent danger of a fall from power in order to demonstrate to the readers of the poem that he was at the mercy of Fortune's wheel, and that he was thus an over-ambitious and villainous upstart governed not by reason but by passion and wilfulness. For as Lydgate observed, 'Fortune hath no domynacioun / Wher noble pryncis be governed by resoun'.[45] Such predictions are thus allegorical and emblematic rather than specific, and are used to further delineate the nature of Wolsey's villainous character as defined by the poet. They should not be mistaken for evidence of Wolsey's unpopularity or as estimates of the likelihood of success of political opposition to his regime.

A further conventional element in Skelton's portrayal of Wolsey has already been touched on. As Lydgate makes clear, the upstart courtier or governor was held to be particularly prone to the sin of pride and all its attendant evils.[46]

> . . . when a wrech is set in hih estat
> Or a begger brouht up to dignite
> Ther is non so proud, pompous nor elat,
> Non so vengable nor ful of cruelte.
> Void of discrecioun, mercy and pite:
> For cherlish blood seelde doth recure
> To be gentil be weie of his nature.

The pride, arrogance and wilfulness of the upstart was a common theme in medieval social or estates writings. Lydgate was simply making the same claims for the secular tyrant as Walter Map for the young monk newly elevated to the office of Keeper of the Cell, or Giles Li Muissis for the ambitious brother who would soon become a petty tyrant in his house.[47] Once the upstart became elevated, his pride conventionally led him to 'forget himself' and to exult over and humiliate his social superiors.

---

[44] *Ibid.*, III, lines 141–4.
[45] *Ibid.*, II, lines 55–6.
[46] *Ibid.*, II, lines 55–62.
[47] For Map and Li Miussis' complaints, see Mann, *Medieval Estates Literature*, p. 32. For other examples of this model, see Wright, *Political Poems and Songs*, I p. 230, and Barclay, *Eclogue I*, lines 851–64.

The author of *Pierce The Ploughman's Crede* prefigured much of Skelton's later criticism of Wolsey's domination of the nobility ('This is a pyteous case: / To you that over the whele / Lordes must crouche and knele, / And breke theyre hose at the kne' (*Collyn Clout*, lines 626–9)) in his attack upon the low-born men who would,[48]

> . . . wi[th] a lorde dwell . . .
> So of [th]at beggers brol – a byshop schal wor[th]en,
> Among [th]e peres of [th]e land – prese to sitten,
> And lordes sones lowly – to [th]o losells aloute,
> Kny[gh]tes crouke[th] hem to – and cruche[th] full lowe; . . .
> Alaas! [th]at lordes of [th]e londe – leve[th] swiche wrechen . . .
> For her kynde were more – to y-clense diches
> [Th]an ben to sapers y-set first – and served wi[th] silver.

Dunbar's 'pykthank in a prelottis clais' was also possessed of an *animus* against the nobility, for,[49]

> Nobles of bluid he dois dispys,
> And helpis for to hald thame downe
> That thay rys nevere to his renowne.

And Langland had criticised those 'false prophetes fele, flateris and gloseris' who,[50]

> Shullen come and be curatours over kynges and erles.
> And thenne shal Pride be Pope and prynce of Holy Chirche,
> Coveitise and unkyndenesse Cardinals hym to lede.

The self-same problem of explaining the failure of the lay lords to act against the upstart which troubled Skelton had also prompted the author of *The Plowman's Tale* to ponder,[51]

> Wonder is, that the parliament
> And all the lordes of this lond
> Here-to taken so litell entent
> To helpe the people out of hir hond . . .
> But lordes be ware and hem defend;
> For now these folk be wonder stout.

Again the charges made in this context in the Wolsey satires are not new. They reflected a number of conventions of anti-clerical and anti-court literature which Skelton utilised for his specific critical purpose. His caricature of Wolsey is reliant on stereotypical satirical and polemical attacks on wordly clerics, on criticisms of social upstarts, and on generalised homiletic maxims

[48] *Crede*, lines 746, 748–51, 753, 759–60.
[49] Dunbar, 'To the King', lines 64–6.
[50] *Vision*, XIX 222–5. See also Wright, *Political Poems and Songs*, I pp. 309, 317, 334.
[51] Wright, *Political Poems and Songs*, I p. 324.

such as that a king should never give exclusive executive power into the hands of 'oon singuler man'.[52] It is thus not a representation of the real Wolsey – even a biased one; it is a confection, decorated with details of the Cardinal's life and set in a conventional mould.

Even in those passages in which one is ostensibly offered the Cardinal speaking directly to the reader in his own words, it is a conventional stereotype rather than an historical individual which one hears. Wolsey's rages, his abuse of honest preachers (*Collyn Clout*, lines 1154–6), his dismissal of the lay lords as 'javells' (line 600) and his tyrannical judgements in the law courts ('Take him, wardeyn of the Flete / Set hym fast by the fete! / I say, lieutenaunt of the Towre, / Make this lurdeyne for to lowre? (lines 1165–8)), are all modelled upon the speeches of the Morality play tyrants, Herod, Satan and their kin. All that Skelton has done is add a gloss of contemporary relevance to the model in the form of the names of the principal London prisons. The poet admits as much in his direct allusion to such dramatic scenes in *Why Come Ye Nat?*, when he observes of Wolsey that

> His servauntes menyall
> He dothe revyle and bralle
> *Lyke Mahounde in a play.*
> No man dare him withsay.
> He hath dispyght and scorne
> At them that be well borne;
> He rebukes them and rayles.
> 'He horsons, ye vassayles,
> Ye knaves, ye churles sonnys,
> Ye rebads nat worth two plummis'. (595–604, my italics)

Again Skelton is deliberately associating Wolsey with a villainous stereotype with a view to visiting the sins of the latter on the former by analogy. The scenes which he is recreating are not those of Wolsey in the Star Chamber, or amongst his household, of which the poet would know little or nothing, but those in which Herod abused his household knights on the public stage as,[53]

> . . . losels and liars! Lurdons ilkone!
> Traitors and well worse!
> Knaves, but knightes none!

Similarly Wolsey's proud boasts in *Collyn Clout* ' . . . we wyll rule and rayne, / And our matters mayntayne, / Or who dare dysdayne, / At our pleasure and wyll' (lines 1212–16). 'We set nat a nutte shell / The way to

[52] For this last, see R. Steele (ed.), *Three Prose Versions of The Secreta Secretorum*, E.E.T.S., (1898), p. 210; and R. Steele (ed.), *Lydgate and Burgh's 'Secrees of Old Phillisoffres'*, E.E.T.S., 66 (1894), lines 2196–2200.

[53] *The Wakefield Pageant of Herod The Great* (from the Towneley Cycle), lines 163–4, in A. Cawley (ed.), *Everyman and Medieval Miracle Plays* (London, 1970).

heven or to hell!' (lines 1225–6) are not evidence of Wolsey's behaviour noted down by a poet eavesdropping in the halls of the mighty, they are conscious allusions to such self-damning declarations of medieval theatre as Herod's,[54]

> I am King of all mankinde
> I byd, I beat, I loose, I bynde,
> I master the moone . . .
> I am the greatest above degree,
> That is or was or ever shall be.
>
> Of bewte and of boldnesse I bere ever-more the belle
> Of mayn and of myght I master every man
> I dynge with my dowtynes the devyl down to helle
> For both of hevyn and of herth I am Kyng Sertayn.

The poet's intention in such passages is thus allegorical and allusive, not biographical. His pictures of Wolsey is didactic rather than literal, it seeks to suggest that the Cardinal is a villain by associating him with known villainous types rather than by holding up examples of his actual behaviour for close scrutiny.

Even at its apparently most specific and most personal, when Skelton presents what appears to be Wolsey speaking in his own voice, the satire often proves to be stylised and stereotyped. Hence one must be wary of even the most innocuous looking details of habit, lifestyle and temperament referred to in the poems, for it is as likely that they are the details of sins required by traditional models or the allegorical apparatus associated with a conventional argument as they are biographical flashes of 'the real Wolsey'.

Yet Skelton has had a profound effect on the way in which one sees the historical Wolsey. That the poet cites fair examples of the Cardinal's behaviour and policies, examples which can be verified from other sources, has blinded one to *how* he uses such examples, and to what he brings in with them. Often the commonplace nature of the arguments which he employs against Wolsey in *Collyn Clout* and elsewhere can give an appearance of validity to assertions which are, if taken literally, at best misleading and at worst completely false.

Skelton's allegations of Wolsey's taking of bribes, of his 'parcyall promotynge / Of those that stande in [his]. . . grace', and his chasing out of the incumbents of offices to make way for his protégées (*Collyn Clout*, lines 1073–8), have found favour with historians, despite the fact that they have little relevance to the Cardinal's use of what practical clerical patronage he enjoyed. The work of M. J. Kelly has shown that Wolsey certainly used his legatine right of prevention extensively and made a handsome profit as a

[54] H. Deimling (ed.), *The Chester Plays*, E.E.T.S., 62 (1892), p. 167; and K. S. Block (ed.), *The Ludus Coventriae*, E.E.T.S., 120 (1922), p. 151.

result, but, as Peter Gwyn has argued, to prove as much is not to demonstrate that the Cardinal used that right in favour of his own creatures and allies. The gifts which he received from aspirant nominees were, like the pensions which he received from France and the Emperor, simply the perquisites of office, the universal lubricants of the early Tudor bureaucracy. Although clearly theoretically sinful, they were, in practice, an accepted fact of life. There is little basis for the allegation that Wolsey 'parcyally promoted' his protégées. Of those clergy obtaining high office in the period between 1515 and 1523, only John Longland, promoted to the bishopric of Lincoln in 1521, and John Clerk (Bishop of Bath and Wells after 1523) can be definitely identified as 'Wolsey's men', and both were of sufficient learning to have merited their promotions without assistance from the Cardinal. In the vast majority of other cases, including the notorious instance of the Wilton election, Wolsey's nominees were, as Kelly accepts, the strongest candidates.[55]

Wolsey's provision for his illegimate son Thomas Winter seems the exception to this rule, but such nepotism was hardly unique. Indeed, contrary to received wisdom, Wolsey's was far from the most obvious case. A comparison with Archbishop Warham, the nearest equivalent figure, is instructive. Not only was the Archbishop's 'nephew' William given the archdeaconry of Canterbury as a sinecure, but further livings were heaped upon him under dispensations for pluralism from four successive popes. These livings included the rectories of both Harrow and Wrotham, worth respectively £88 and £42 yearly at a time when the average yield of livings in Warham's gift was only £25. Similarly the Archbishop's brothers and their families and his New College associates were the recipients of his metropolitan largess on a scale which Wolsey, for all his legatine powers, did not match.[56]

Another charge laid at Wolsey's door is that his use of his legatine powers to gain control of probate administration was novel and rapacious. This too overlooks the context in which that action took place. It may have been that Wolsey's steadily expanding probate jurisdiction excited resentment among the ordinaries and other patrons who found themselves deprived of their privileges, but such procedures always created administrative friction. For from being outrageously rapacious, Wolsey's legatine jurisdiction seems to have created less problems in practice than the Canterbury archiepiscopal prerogative which it superseded. Wolsey was always prepared to come to a composition with the ordinaries and archdeacons concerned, whereby the

---

[55] M. J. Kelly, 'Canterbury jurisdiction and influence during the episcopate of William Warham, 1503–1532', unpublished Cambridge University Ph.D. thesis, 1963, pp. 195–8 and 198, n. 1. Concerning the more positive view of Wolsey's clerical patronage I am grateful to Mr P. J. Gwyn for the opportunity to read, discuss and cite from his as yet unpublished paper 'Wolsey as Church reformer', read at the History Faculty Library, Oxford, 18 February 1985.

[56] Kelly, 'Canterbury jurisdiction and influence', pp. 8 and 27–30.

fruits of the administration were shared. Under first Morton and then Warham the archiepiscopal jurisdiction had been forcibly imposed on the unwilling suffragans by an unsubtle mixture of intimidation, citation in the Roman and archiepiscopal courts and excommunication.[57]

The whole thrust of Skelton's argument, that Wolsey's vicious lifestyle and personal sloth were the major stumbling blocks to ecclesiastical reform, is grossly misleading, as the Cardinal had taken determined strides in the direction of a rationalisation and revitalisation of the Church in the years immediately prior to the composition of *Collyn Clout*. In 1519 at a specially summoned conference of bishops, and in 1520 and 1521 in the introduction of new legatine constitutions for the secular clergy and the Benedictine and Augustinian orders, Wolsey had advanced the case for reform and provided the administrative machinery for its practical implementation rather than hindered it.[58] It is difficult to agree with David Knowles that these reforms lacked conviction. They began where any serious reforming initiative would be expected to begin, with the Austin canons, widely recognised as the weakest and laxest of the orders in England, who were the recipients of a new legatine constitution in March 1519. Thereafter Wolsey berated the provincial chapter held in Westminster in 1522 over the laxness of contemporary practice and issued his own book of statutes. No lack of conviction in these initiatives was detected by the regular religious themselves, who pleaded with the Cardinal not to jeopardise the future of monasticism by demanding too rigorous a return to the austerity of their rules, nor by Wolsey's agent, Doctor Allen, who when visiting Much Wenlock in 1523 showed every sign of wanting to bring the new constitutions into immediate practice.[59]

Wolsey was, then, far from the indolent and apathetic head of a fallen Church which Skelton suggests. Indeed the very monastic visitations, dissolutions and attacks on sanctuary rights cited by the poet as evidence of a corrupt Church demonstrate clearly that Wolsey was serious in his commitment to reform. That such policies were not taken further does not, given the other calls on his energies, prove that Wolsey was not a genuine seeker after reform. That Skelton should have complained that they took place at all is a further indication of the inconsistent and essentially *ad hoc* nature of his arguments.

How meaningful is it, then, to judge a man in Wolsey's position by the idealised standards of satiric and didactic literature employed by Skelton and later poets, chroniclers and writers? The one epithet which modern historians consistently apply to the Cardinal is 'proud', and their reasons for this ascription are evidently those applied by Skelton, for Wolsey's flamboy-

[57] *Ibid.*, pp. 43–66.
[58] Gwyn, 'Wolsey as Church reformer'.
[59] D. Knowles, *The Religious Orders in England*, 3 vols. (Cambridge, 1959), III pp. 14, 158–60.

ant retinues, buildings and lifestyle, and his idiosyncratic conduct of business are often cited in support of this assertion.[60] But in a society in which symbol, ceremony and display were a prominent and fundamental part of political activity, how sensible is it to equate such display with personal qualities such as pride? It was conventional for medieval writers to condemn the upstart courtier who proudly flaunted himself at Court in his new-found finery, but how relevant is such a judgement to someone who, like Wolsey, was called on to wield the politically eloquent symbolism of dress, ornament and retine for purposes of state? How valid are criticisms designed to ridicule the foolish pretensions of lowly priests and ostentatious prelates who acted as if they were princes of the state when they are applied to a prelate who, as Lord Chancellor and the King's lieutenant, *was* a prince of the state? Where do the necessary trappings of public office end and where does self-indulgence begin?

Clearly much selectivity of judgement has been exercised by historians in their descriptions of Wolsey, and it seems that Skelton's adoption of the standards of didactic literature to describe him has influenced such judgements. Does, for example, the Field of Cloth of Gold demonstrate Henry VIII and Francis I's sinful pride? Historians have largely kept silent on this point, preferring, instead, to praise the magnificent demonstration of Tudor Court pageantry which the occasion provided. Yet Wolsey's ceremonial processions have been roundly condemned as the outward manifestations of rampant and dangerous megalomania. Wolsey's replacing of Warham's single silver cross with two of his own is taken for the unbearable pride of the upstart. Yet the non-noble Warham's wearing of vestments and silks, his bearing of ceremonial ornaments and his building of the palace at Otford have never been taken to be morally illuminating behaviour.[61] Such selectivity of criticism suggests rather more than the simple empirical decision that use of one cross is a normal and healthy exercise of prerogative but use of two is excessive.

Even the language of the didactic moral exemplar has been adopted by modern historians in their treatment of Wolsey in a way which has not affected their consideration of other individuals.[62] Yet it is far from clear that

---

[60] Pollard demonstrates the connection most clearly in his index entry under 'Wolsey, characteristics: pomp and pride', Pollard, p. 392.

[61] For the Field of Cloth of Gold, see P. Williams, *The Tudor Regime* (Oxford, 1979), p. 364; J. A. Guy, 'The Tudor age', in W. O. Harris (ed.), *The Oxford Illustrated History of Britain* (Oxford, 1984), p. 252; M. M. Reese, *The Royal Office of Master of the Horse* (Bradford, 1976), p. 120; R. J. Knecht, *French Renaissance Monarchy; Francis I and Henry II* (London, 1984), p. 36. For Wolsey's crosses, see Pollard, p. 57. For the work on Otford, see J. Newman, *The Buildings of England: West Kent and the Weald* (London, 1969), pp. 60, 446–7.

[62] See, for example, Professor G. R. Elton's description of Wolsey 'flaunting his scarlet, his maces and tapers, his canopies, the trappings of his mule, in the faces of men who thought themselves good Christians but socially superior to one whose upstart origins showed

what Skelton and subsequent writers chose to portray as the Cardinal's pride was not in fact his effective use of theatricality and ceremony in the service of the Crown. The pomp and magnificence evident in his retinue, far from diminishing by contrast the esteem in which the Crown was held by the populace and by foreign diplomats, seems to have been calculated to enhance it. For Wolsey took pains to demonstrate that he was simply Henry's lieutenant, and that his own grandeur was merely a pale reflection of that of his master. As Cavendish noted of his mission to Charles V, Wolsey's flamboyant entourage was consciously fashioned to demonstrate the power, honour and influence of Henry VIII, not the personal wealth of the Cardinal.[63] When,[64]

for dyvers urgent causys touching the Kynges ma[jesty] yt was thought good that in so waytie a matter / And to so noble a prince that the Cardinall was most meate to be sent on so worthy an Ambassett / wherfore he beyng redy to take uppon hym the charge thereof / was ffurnysshed in all degrees and purposys most lykest A great prynce w[hich] was myche to the highe honour of the Kynges ma[jesty] and of this realme.

Apparently Henry was quite content with Wolsey's use of ceremonial ostentation during the mission for, as Cavendish further observed, the Cardinal 'retourned home agayn in to England wt great tryhumphe beyng no lesse in estymacion wt the Kyng than he was byforc but rather myche more'.

Evidently Wolsey's magnificence and plenitude of temporal and ecclesiastical attendants was less of an obvious and clearly defined evil than literary tradition would suggest. Even Edward Hall, usually a consistent advocate of the conventional post-1529 attitude to the Cardinal who was 'of a great sto-

through the pomp bestowed by Pope and King', (*Reform and Reformation* (London, 1977), p. 64). Is it clear that Wolsey 'flaunted' his finery in a manner in which other Cardinal-Legates did not? Contemporary theory and practice suggest not. See F. Wasner, 'Fifteenth-century texts on the ceremonial of the papal *legatus a latere*', Traditio, 14, (1958), pp. 295–358. Wolsey's use of his legatine powers was in fact restrained. He could, for example, have gone further in restricting Warham's use of his Court of Audience by legatine prevention, and could have insisted on even greater ceremonial respect for his papal office, but he chose not to do so. For the Court of Audience, see Kelly, 'Canterbury jurisdiction and influence', pp. 166 and 177, for the ceremonial, see Wasner, 'Fifteenth-century texts', pp. 302–12.

63 This point was explicitly stated by Wolsey himself when defending his vestments and ornaments against the criticisms of the reformist friar, Robert Barnes. In reply to Barnes' attack Wolsey is reported to have asked 'Whether do you think it more necessary that I should have all this royalty, because I represent the King's Majesty's person in all the high courts of this realm, to the terror and keeping down of all rebellious treasons, traitors [and] the wicked and corrupt members of this commonwealth: or to be as simple as you would have us? To sell all these aforesaid things, and to give it to the poor, who shortly will caste it against the wall? And to pull away this majesty of a princely dignity, which is a terror to all the wicked, and to follow your counsel in this behalf?' See G. Townsend (ed.), *The Acts and Monuments of John Foxe* (8 vols., London, 1837–1841), V p. 416.

64 G. Cavendish, *The Life and Death of Cardinal Wolsey*, ed. R. S. Sylvester, E.E.T.S. 243 (1959), p.21.

mack, for he compted himselfe egall with princes',[65] can be found attesting elsewhere to the benefits to the realm and to the Crown manifest in Wolsey's eminence. In a long and laudatory account of the magnificence of the English preparations for the meeting at the Field of Cloth of Gold, and of how such splendour reflected honour on Henry and the nation, Hall describes Wolsey's role in the preliminary niceties. Here, in a passage worthy of lengthy quotation, one sees a completely different perspective upon Wolsey's 'proud' displays.[66]

In this tyme the reverent father lorde Thomas Wolsey Cardinall & legate a Latere as the Kynges high ambassador rode with noble repair of lordes, gentlemen & prelates to the toune of Arde, to ye French courte where of the frenche kyng, thesame lord cardinall was highly entertained. Of the noblenes of this Cardinall, the frenchemen made bokes, shewyng the triumphant doynges of the Cardinalles royalte. The nomber of the gentlmen, knightes and lordes al in crimosyn velvet, with the marveilous nomber of chaines of golde, the great horse, Mules, Coursers, & cariages, that there were which went before the Cardinalles commynge unto Arde with sumters & cofers. Of his great Crosses and pillers borne, the pillowe bere or cace broudered, the two mentelles, with other the Ceremoniall offices, with greate & honourable nomber of bishoppes gevyng their attendaunce, the mightie and great number of servauntes, as yomen gromes, all clothed in Scarlet who so redeth of the french boke, shall find wonder fully set furthe . . .
When the lord Cardinall . . . toke his leave of the french kyng . . . [he] repaired unto the Castle of Guysnes, where he founde the kyng of England his sovereigne lorde. And the same kyng by his letters patentes, had geven full power and aucthoritie to thesame lord Cardinall, concernyng all matters to bee debated, touchyng the Kyng and the realme, and also gave unto thesame Cardinall, full strenght, power, and aucthoritie, to affirme & confirme, bynde, and unbynde, whatsoever shoulde be in question, betwene hym and the french kyng, as though the Kyng in proper person had been there presently.
When the lordes of the frenche counsaill, sawe the high and greate aucthoritie that the Cardinall had, thei shewed it unto ye french kyng, who incontine[n]t commaunded his commission to be made of like power and aucthoritie . . . then hastely was sent to the Kyng of Englande the frenche Kynges patent, for the lorde Cardinall saied humbly to the frenche kyng, that he would no suche power receive, without the consent of the kynge of England his sovereigne Lord: but when the Kyng of Englande and his counsaill, had seen and viewed the french kynges patent and well considered, then he sent thesame patent of power to the lorde Cardinall with full assent: then the lorde Cardinall the power received with much gladnes. It was highly estemed & taken for great love that the frenche kyng had geven so greate power to the kynge of Englandes subject.

Here one finds no references to Wolsey's pride; indeed it is his humility in refusing further honours without Henry's consent which the chronicler

---

[65] Edward Hall, *The Union of the Two Noble Families of Lancaster and York*, ed. Henry Ellis (London, 1809), p. 774.
[66] *Ibid.*, p. 607.

chooses to emphasise. Nor does Hall mention the sinful nature or socially disruptive effects of his large and eminent retinue. Evidently the offensiveness of such display was purely relative. As soon as Henry is added to the equation the sins of the proud prelate become the honourable trappings of the loyal Crown servant. In the province of political reality, where honour was a virtue, and personal magnificence a reflection of honour, such sins as marked out Wolsey the sinful cleric had no meaning.

It seems clear that both Henry and Wolsey were of one mind in approving the latter's adoption of the trappings befitting his offices and titles as Lord Chancellor, Cardinal-legate and Archbishop, and his role as Henry's lieutenant. The crucial phrase in Hall's account of the Anglo-French meeting is that which noted Wolsey's role as Henry's representative, 'as though the Kyng in proper person had been there presently'. This function as an extension of Henry's own magnificence was one which the Cardinal cultivated carefully. What might be misinterpreted as personal pride by the commentator influenced by the conventional 'black legend' of Wolsey the upstart, on closer examination often proves to have been an entirely proper concern for his status as the King's surrogate, and thus for Henry's honour.[67]

This role as Henry's lieutenant was, of course, as important and necessary at home as it was abroad. There also, in the administration of the King's laws in the courts, and in taking the King's place at the Council table and in the receipt of suitors and ambassadors, such display as Wolsey employed can more reasonably be interpreted as an attempt to invest the Crown with an aura of formal majesty than as mere self-indulgence on the part of an over-confident minister, or as the flaunting of the symbols of papal authority in the face of royal jurisdiction. In practice, as the following chapter will demonstrate, Wolsey was Henry's man, not the Pope's.

Skelton's picture of Wolsey is not a complete fiction. The poet did not invent the poleaxes and pillars, the palaces and the political authority which he describes. But the standards of anti-clerical and homiletic literature which he used to judge these phenomena are clearly not those by which Wolsey may properly be judged by the historian. Nor were they those by which contemporaries judged political reality on the immediate level. Only reformers like Colet (who, significantly, seems to have had a good relationship with Wolsey)[68], theorists like Erasmus, and the early Protestants would attempt to adopt the moral messages of anti-clerical satire as a political programme, and these last only as far as suited their doctrinal aims. For the vast majority of the community, including the political elite, such standards seem to have existed on the level of the notional ideal rather than that of actual political conduct. Christ may have preached pacificism and poverty, but this did not

---

[67] See, for example, B.L. Cotton MS Galba B VII fos. 42 and 113 (*St. P.*, I 24 and 28).
[68] Gwyn, 'Wolsey as Church reformer'.

mean that the governments of expressly Christian nations such as England, administered by such clerics as Warham and Fox as well as Wolsey, and by such saintly laymen as More, would not devote the majority of their political energies to the preparation and conduct of wars and the collection of taxes. Thus even where works such as Skelton's might blur the lines between literary and political comment, one must remain aware of their distinct frames of reference. Satirical literature might condemn the Court as 'in earth an ymage infernall. / Without fayre paynted, within uggly and vile',[69] but such statements reveal little about the real Court, to which the readers, and often the writers, of such works petitioned and flocked to gain advancement.

It is neither wise nor accurate to judge Wolsey by the standards employed by Skelton in the satires. Such standards were adopted, along with the conventions which they support, for specific purposes by a poet intent on the production of a satirical text to further his own ends. They only superficially resemble a political judgement. And in other works the poet can be found passing judgements based on clearly quite different sets of assumptions and standards. In *Howe The Douty Duke of Albany*, for example, Wolsey is not condemned, but praised without irony for his contribution of troops to the army sent to oppose the Scots in 1523. This is a tacit acceptance of political necessity, of the need for the large retinues and lay following of a leading churchman (the troops came from Wolsey's archdiocese of York), rather than the conventionalised criticism of such followings to be found in *Collyn Clout*.

Less obviously, the conclusion that many of the allegations advanced in *Collyn Clout* were prompted by conventional models rather than the heartfelt concern of the poet for specific political grievances is also supported by reference to Skelton's own circumstances and conduct. For it is amusing to note that the poet who so violently condemned the absentee, pluralist clergy for their worldliness, vanity, pride, lack of celibacy and desire for secular promotion was the same man who had deserted his parish church in order to seek favour at Court in 1512, who was to petition Wolsey for a second living in 1523, who had launched the anti-Wolsey satires in an attempt to secure worldly favour and esteem, whose professional pride led him to proclaim himself 'England's Homer' and who, if Bale and the *Merry Tales* tradition are to be believed, kept a mistress at Diss who bore him at least one child. In such circumstances it is surely impossible to see *Collyn Clout* and *Why Come Ye Nat?* as cries from the heart of an enraged observer of the failings of the clergy in general and Wolsey in particular.

Yet Skelton's legacy is persistent. His fictionalised Wolsey still influences subconscious judgements about the historical original. This has created in

[69] Barclay, *Eclogue I*, lines 1260–1.

even the best work on the Cardinal a kind of schizophrenia of approach.[70] On the one hand a historian's own research suggests that Wolsey was a devoted Crown servant who did much that was good for conciliar justice, or ecclesiastical administration, yet on the other the author feels obliged to conclude none the less that, although the evidence does not necessarily suggest it, he was no doubt also proud, over-ambitious, arrogant and domineering: in short, precisely the tyrannical upstart which Skelton portrayed him.

That is not to argue that Skelton's poetry has provided the major source of inspiration for modern historians studying Wolsey and his regime; that would, of course, be foolish. But it is not entirely fanciful to suggest that Skelton's influence, both direct and mediated through other works, has been considerable in the moulding of Wolsey's historical reputation. In a direct way the stridency of poet's testimony, and the lurid and eminently quotable allegations which he provides, have ensured him a place in most studies of the Cardinal, where his invective acts as a persuasive counter to any more specific and more positive findings which the authors might reach. Indirectly Skelton can be seen to have influenced subsequent writers of both didactic and polemical representations of the Cardinal. It is not possible to prove that Hall, Foxe, Tyndale, Fish or Vergil read Skelton (although the fact that, as we have seen, Hall quotes a couplet of the poet's suggests that he was familiar with his work), but it is possible to suggest that the poet helped to set the agenda for later discussions of Wolsey and his career.

When those hoping to gain from his fall were searching for charges with which to attack the Cardinal in 1529, for example, Skelton's poetry seems to have provided them with some inspiration. John Palsgrave's use of the phrase the 'countering at Calais' in his list of indictments, for example, suggests either direct borrowing from *Why Come Ye Nat?* or that the phrase had entered into common parlance after Skelton's coining of it in 1522[71] More obviously the satirists who berated Wolsey at his fall also leant on Skelton's work. Roy and Barlowe's *Burial of The Masse* and the anonymous *Impeachment of Wolsey* drew heavily on *Collyn Clout* and *Why Come Ye Nat?* in their arguments, choice of language and images.[72] Skelton was the first writer purposefully to link the Cardinal with the conventional model of the upstart. Unlike later writers who were able to view not only the spectactular rise but also the equally spectacular fall, and thus appreciate how Wolsey's career exemplified the conventional pattern, Skelton had to manufacture such a didactic caricature from the raw materials of a still-successful career. This provided the poet's work with an aura of prophecy once Wolsey's disgrace

---

[70] I owe this diagnosis to Peter Gwyn.
[71] *L.P.*, IV (ii) 5750 (p. 2560).
[72] See P. L. Wiley, 'Wolsey's career in Renaissance English literature', Stanford University Ph.D. thesis, 1943, pp. 131–40.

seemingly vindicated his assertions and added to the renewed popularity of the satires (particularly *Collyn Clout*) during the 1530s.[73] Thereafter his innovations became the orthodoxies of later writers for whom Wolsey became the prime example of the over-mighty upstart.[74]

[73] Indeed the passage from *Collyn Clout* predicting Wolsey's 'fatal fall' (lines 462–80) seems to have been redistributed separately during 1529 as 'The Prophecy of Skelton' (B.L. MS Lansdowne 762 fo. 75 (71)).

[74] See Wiley, 'Wolsey's career', pp. 131–2, and *passim*.

5

'So mangye a mastyfe curre, the grete greyhoundes pere': Skelton's account of Wolsey's relations with King and Court during his ascendancy

We have seen in how many ways the picture of Wolsey which Skelton presents needs to be qualified and now possess good reasons to mistrust the way in which the poet's verses have been utilised in the past. What remains to be done is with such doubts in mind to provide a clearer view of Skelton's Wolsey and of the relevance of that portrait to the historical original, through a close study of certain of the satires' central assertions.

The first and most obvious comment which must be made about the portrayal of Wolsey in the satires is that Skelton does not provide simply one Wolsey, he provides several. As political circumstances changed, and as his strategies evolved and matured, the aspects of his Wolsey which he sought to portray and to emphasise changed, and his techniques and resources changed with them. Certainly Wolsey is always portrayed as a dangerous force in the realm; but the way in which that danger is described changes from poem to poem in *Speke, Parott* from envoy to envoy. Hence, as Skelton ceased to tailor his satire primarily for a royal audience and turned towards those who were not Wolsey's master but his subordinates, his portrayal evolved from that of the untrustworthy servant of the early sections of *Speke, Parott* to that of the tyrannical ruler of *Why Come Ye Nat?*.

The Wolsey of *Speke, Parott* is perhaps the simplest portrait and also that with the least relevance to the Cardinal himself. Partly, of course, this was a product of the poet's strategy of employing *metaphora* and *alegoria*, and to his misreading of Wolsey's true role in Calais. But there is more here than simply obfuscation born of caution and error. As has been suggested, the poet's intention was for *Speke, Parott* to appeal to the King and to the most sophisticated readers at Court. Thus he pitched his wit and irony at their level, played the word-games and allegorical manipulations with a very deft hand, and, as we have seen, confused most of his readers in the process. In *Speke, Parott*, consequently, the object was not, at least until the final envoys, to reveal Wolsey in vivid detail but to conceal him, to hide him amongst the plethora of biblical and classical exempla as the lure to draw the

154

reader into the allegory, and as the prize which awaited him or her when they had successfully unravelled the puzzle. The only political points which Skelton wished to make were those concerning Wolsey's handling of the Calais conference and his general inability to make sound judgements; the remainder of the text serves simply to magnify the ridicule. All one sees is a parade of tyrants with vague and often extremely tenuous links with Wolsey, which lead one to the general conclusion that he, like these infamous forebears, is a villain who will bring ruin to King, realm and commonweal.

Even when Skelton does get down to cases and produces an allusion to a policy, event, or personality trait which may be recognised as Wolsey's, his strategy often prevents his making any more specific use of it than as a simple reference. The allusions to the Cardinal's dissolutions, during 1521, of certain small monastic houses are a case in point. For historical purposes the poet's critique of the policy behind these dissolutions is almost non-existent. He alludes to its outward manifestations and suggests that they are harmful, but makes no attempt to say why or to suggest any administrative motive behind them. There is a cryptic reference to the intended dissolution of the priory at Bromhall, near Whetstone, in the lines,

> Esebon, Marybon, Wheston next Barnet;
> A trym-tram for an horse-myll it were a nyse thyng,
> Deyntes for dammoysels, chaffer far-fet.
> (127–9)

But nothing is extrapolated from this. The implication seems to be that Wolsey might turn the priory into a commercial mill and use the profits to support a succession of mistresses ('Deyntes for dammoysels, chaffer far-fet'). But Skelton's lack of accurate knowldge of the situation is revealed by the fact that Bromhall had a watermill, not a horse-mill.[1] And there seems to be no understanding of the Cardinal's professed desire to rationalise the network of religious houses and reform some of their more obvious abuses.[2] Thus, although one needs a knowledge both of Wolsey's monastic dissolutions and of local geography (in order to link Bromhall with 'Weston next Barnet') before one can have any idea to what Skelton is referring in this passage, having established the nature of the allusion one is not rewarded with any more illuminating insight into the dissolution policy than the general impression that the poet does not approve of it. Such references as these are simply clues to help the reader to the conclusion that it is Wolsey who is the poem's mysterious central figure; they are keys to the cypher of the text, not specific political comments. Beyond the basic allegations concerning

---

[1] *L.P.*, III (ii) 2080.
[2] Note Henry VIII's letter to Edmund Audley, Bishop of Salisbury, of 13 December 1521, in which he thanked the latter for the suppression of the priory 'for such enormities as was by them used'. *L.P.*, III (ii) 1863.

Wolsey's untrustworthiness and the futility of the Calais conference the poet really has no political points to make.

The remainder of the 'political' parts of *Speke, Parott* are thus not a critique, nor even truly a statement, but simply a complex and dazzlingly executed series of insults. Even in the passages explicitly concerned with Calais, the majority of the satiric material relies on name-calling rather than political argument. Rather than expose his lack of knowledge concerning the details of the conference, and rather than risk losing the royal approval which he sought by producing arguments of his own which might run contrary to the King's feelings, Skelton confined himself to advancing the few simple assertions which he felt it safe to make, supported by sophisticated but general mockery and ridicule. Hence Wolsey is referred to throughout the envoys, not by his name or titles but by a series of enigmatic allusions to characters from the Bible or from legend. He is mocked as Jerobesethe (line 279) and 'Lyacon of Libyk' (line 289, a pun upon his name, as Lycaon of Arcadia was transformed into a wolf by Zeus, and Wolf-see, as we have seen, was a favourite perversion of 'Wolsey'), as 'owur soleyne seigneour Sadoke' (line 304)[3] and 'owur solen syr Sydrake' (line 326).[4] Even in the final envoy with its catalogue of woes and abuses, in which Parott is asked to 'sette asyde all sophysms and speke now trew and playne', many of the details are merely peripheral to the poet's intentions, despite their greater clarity, and thus add little to one's knowledge of Wolsey.

It is clear that much of what Parott declares is wrong in the Commonwealth is attributable to Wolsey. He is said to dominate a foolish and cowed nobility,

> So many bolde barons, there hertes as dull as lede;
> So many nobyll bodyes, undyr on dawys hedd.
> (466–7)

He acts far above his station;

> So mangye a mastyfe curre, the grete greyhoundes pere.

And he makes too great a display of his power and wealth,

> Suche pollaxis and pyllers, suche mulys trapte with gold –
> Sens Dewcalyons flodde, in no cronycle ys told. (517–18)

There is also much play made with details of Wolsey's administration of the

---

[3] The reference is to Wolsey's impending return to England, as Zadok was a priest summoned home to Jerusalem by David. II Samuel, xv, 27. In Nehemiah, x, 21, a second Zadok was one of the 'chiefs of the people' of Israel who sealed the Covenant. Skelton may well be playing with both biblical characters here.

[4] Sydrake was the King's adviser in *The Historie of Kyng Boccus and Sydrake*, printed in England in 1510, trans. from the French version of Hugh of Caumpeden. See Dyce, II p. 346, n. 326.

law and justice. But here again little is made of each reference save to give a general impression of Skelton's disapproval. Skelton's purpose is still primarily to identify Wolsey as the target of the poem proper. This he inserts well-known examples of Wolsey's legislation into the list of conventional complaints, in order to prompt his readers finally to make the connection between the contemporary minister and the troupe of antique tyrants which the poet has portrayed, whilst he simultaneously introduces new economic complaints into the text in the hope of attracting new readers in the City. 'So many thevys hangyd', he laments,

> ... and thevys neverthelesse;
> So myche presonment, for matyrs not worth a hawe;
> So myche papers weryng for ryghte a smalle exesse;
> So myche pelory pajauntes undyr colowur of good lawe ...
>
> So myche mokkyshe makyng of statues of array ...
>
> Suche statutes apon diettes, suche pyllyng and pollyng ...
>
> Syns Dewcalyons flodde the world was never so yll. (477–80, 482, 495, 497)

That these items refer to Wolsey's governance seems clear. The 'statutes apon diettes' and 'statutes of array' are evidently the Act of Apparel of 1515, and the Proclamation on the same subject of 19 February 1517, and the Sumptuary Regulations of 31 May 1517,[5] the instigation or at least the enforcement of which were attributed to Wolsey: thus John Palsgrave in his articles against the Cardinal puts into the latter's mouth the phrases 'we have begun to punish forfaictours against the Statute of Apparel', and 'we have begun an ordinance for the reforming of our diet'.[6] The references to stricter enforcement of the laws, often for trivial matters, the 'so myche presonment', 'so myche papers weryng', and 'so myche pelory pajauntes', also suggest Wolsey's new broom in the Courts of Law, and his attempt to bring the 'new law of Star Chamber' to bear on wrongdoers.[7] Yet despite the obvious relevance of these references, the poet makes little or no further capital from them. He has identified the Cardinal through allusions to some of his more notorious policies, and indicated a dissatisfaction with them through the disparaging tone of such references. But no more is said. The poet's strategy here is still designed to clarify the target of his satires, not to introduce new

---

[5] P. L. Hughes and J. F. Larkin (eds.), *Tudor Royal Proclamations*, 3 vols. (New Haven, 1964–9) I, nos. 80 and 81 pp. 127–9; *L.P.*, II (i) 1223.

[6] *L.P.*, IV (ii) 5750. See also Edward Hall, *The Union of the Two Noble Families of Lancaster and York*, ed. Henry Ellis (London, 1809) p. 583, 'And assone as he [Wolsey] was Chancellour, he directed Commissions into all Shires, for to put the Statute of apparell and the Statute of labour in execucion'.

[7] Hall notes that Wolsey 'so punyshed perjurye with open punyshment and open papers werynge that in his time it was less used', Hall, p. 585. See also *L.P.*, IV (ii) p. 2561. Perjury was also punished by use of the pillory. See also J. A. Guy, *The Cardinal's Court* (Brighton, 1977), *passim*.

arguments. Only in the later poems is there anything new or specific, and only there is any attempt made to produce anything approaching a critical analysis of the Cardinal's personality and regime.

In *Collyn Clout* and particularly in *Why Come Ye Nat?* Skelton carried this simplification of his satire and the more detailed exposition of his subject matter several stages further. The suggestions concerning Wolsey's domination of the nobility and of the Court, of his personal arrogance and of his unnatural influence over the King, all tentatively advanced in *Speke, Parott* are here expanded considerably and proposed with far greater vigour and confidence. 'Ye are so puffed with pryde', the poet declares of Wolsey,

> That no man may abyde
> Your hygh and lordely lokes.
> Ye caste up then your bokes
> And vertue is forgotten,
> For then ye wyll be wroken
> Of every lyght quarell
> And call a lorde a javell.
> A knyght a knave ye make.
> Ye boost, ye face, ye crake,
> And upon you take
> To rule Kynge and Kayser.
> And yf ye may have layser,
> Ye wyll brynge all to nought.
> And that is all your thought. (593–607)

This is the definitive exposition of Wolsey as tyrant: over-proud, violent tempered and domineering, envying the high birth of his rivals for power and influence, and intent on ruling the realm for his own glorification at everyone else's expense. The Cardinal is attacked for his low birth, for his dictatorial behaviour in the royal Court and the Court of Star Chamber, for his poisoning of the King's mind against the counsels of others, for lechery and for secret necromancy. These are just some of the allegations. Rather than simply examining what Skelton said about Wolsey, however, it would repay the effort to also consider how the satiric assertions in *Collyn Clout* and *Why Come Ye Nat?* are constructed. What are the major allegations which the text conveys? How are the charges constructed, and what effects do they produce? The answers to such questions are central to any understanding of the value of the satires as historical documents.

Let us begin, however, by looking in detail at just two of Skelton's major allegations, with the intention of discovering just how accurate a picture of the Cardinal they present, and how far they may thus foster an appreciation of the true nature of Wolsey's personality and administration.

The poet's allegations concerning Wolsey's arrogance and pride are central to the satire, for it is these alleged character defects in the Cardinal which, Skelton suggests, are the root cause of all the nation's ills. A major product of these failings is, he asserts, Wolsey's haughty and contemptuous treatment of personal suitors.

The most often quoted passage from *Why Come Ye Nat?* is that in which Skelton's unnamed inquisitor asks him for the second time the question which gives the poem its title:

> Ones yet agayne
> Of you I wolde frayne
> Why come ye nat to Court? (399–401)

Skelton's answer is well known to most historians of the period, even those unfamiliar with the remainder of the poet's canon. It voices a central premise of the text. He does not go to Court, he asserts, because in effect there are two courts, and he cannot choose which to attend. There is the royal Court, debased by Wolsey's injustices and denuded of its courtiers by a potent mixture of his overbearing hegemony and the political elite's own ignorance. And there is the upstart Cardinal's rival court, luxuriously appointed with the spoils of his acquisitive policies, and attracting all the traffic which ought to flow towards the King. Thus Skelton answers his questioner with a question of his own.

> To whyche court?
> To the kynges courte?
> Or to Hampton Court?
>
> Nay, to the Kynges Court!
> The Kynges courte
> Shulde have the excellence;
> But Hampton Court
> Hath the preemynence!
> And Yorkes Place,
> With, 'my lordes grace',
> To whose magnyfycence
> Is all the conflewence,
> Sutys, and supplycacyons,
> Embassades of all nacyons. (402–15)

Much is usually made of this passage by commentators wishing to illustrate the accuracy of Skelton's picture of the two courts. The magnificence of Hampton Court and York Place can be detailed, and the facts about their fine furniture, carpets, tapestries and art treasures listed.[8] Comments from the royal correspondence can be found, in the hands of the royal secretaries, Ruthal, Pace and Sampson, speaking of the denuded state of the royal Court, and informing Wolsey that surplus courtiers from his own entourage should

---

[8] See Edwards, p. 215; E. Law, *A Short History of Hampton Court* (London, 1906), p. 28; Rawdon Brown, *Four Years at the Court of Henry VIII*, 2 vols. (London, 1854), II p. 314.

be despatched to the King at once in order that visitors should not find him entirely 'bare, without noble and wise personages about him'.[9] The reports of foreign ambassadors can be used to illustrate the fact that their traffic was indeed far heavier in the direction of the Cardinal's hat than towards the Crown, and examples can be found of visiting envoys remarking on the need to visit York Place or Hampton Court prior to their arrival at Court in order to retain the Cardinal's good faith. As Giustiniani informed the Doge on 11 May 1519,[10]

The fact is, as I have informed the Signory at least a thousand times, that . . . were it a question of neglecting his Majesty, or his right reverend . . . lordship, the least injurious course would be to pass over the former. I shall therefore impart [my news] . . . to both, but first to the Cardinal, lest he resent the precedence conceded to his Majesty.

All of this can be used to suggest the usefulness of Skelton's vignette of political life during Wolsey's ascendency as an historical source, and to indicate how perceptive a contemporary critic of the Cardinal's regime the poet was.

Yet such apparent honesty is deceptive. It is worth noting how his argument develops as he moves on to describe the sort of reception which a prospective suitor might expect upon arrival at the Cardinal's anti-court,

> No man dare come to the speche
> Of this gentell Jacke Breche,
> Of what estate he be
> Of spirituall dygnyte;
> Nor duke of hye degre,
> Nor marques, erle nor lorde;
> Whiche shrewdly doth accorde!
>
> Thus he, borne so base,
> All noble men shulde outface,
> His countynaunce lyke a kayser.
> 'My lorde is nat at layser.
> Sir, ye must tary a stounde,
> Tyll better layser be founde;
> And syr, ye must daunce attendaunce,
> And take pacient sufferaunce,
> For my lordes grace
> Hath nowe no tyme nor space
> To speke with you as yet'
>
> And thus they shall syt –
> Chose them syt or flyt
> Stande, walke or ryde –
> And his layser abyde,
> Parchaunce halfe a yere;
> And yet never the nere! (615–38)

[9] *L.P.*, III (ii) 2317. See also II (i) 2018; (ii) 3487; III (i) 1597.
[10] Rawdon Brown, *Four Years*, II p. 269 (*L.P.*, III (i) 217).

Again, this elaboration of the original assertion seems to refer to real events, for Wolsey's tardiness in the reception of suitors was notorious. The Venetian ambassador Giustiniani seems to confirm much of what Skelton alleges. 'No one', he informed the Doge during July 1519,[11]

obtains an audience from him unless at the third or fourth attempt. As he adopts this fashion with all the lords and barons of England . . . [I] made light of it and at length had recourse to the expedient of making an appointment through [my] . . . secretary, who sometimes went six or seven times to York House before he could speak to the Cardinal.

An even more graphic example of the problem is provided in a letter written to the Earl of Shrewsbury by his agent in London, Thomas Alen, *c.* November 1517.[12]

Pleaseth your Lordshyp to understande upon Monday was sennight last past I delivered your letter with the examinacyon to my Lord Cardynall at Guilford, whence he commanded me to wait on him to the Court. I followed him and there gave attendance and could have no Answer. Upon ffriday last he came from thence to Hampton Court, where he lyeth. The morrow after I besought his Grace I might know his plesure; I could have no Answer. Upon Mondaye last as he walked in the parke at Hampton Court, I besought his Grace I might knowe if he wolde command me anye servyce. He was not content with me that I spoke to hym. So that who shall be a suitour to him may have no other busynesse but give attendance upon his plesure. He that shall so doe, it is needfull shuld be a wyser man then I am. I sawe no remedy, but came without Answere, except I wolde have done as my Lord Dacre's servaunt doth, who came with Letters for the Kynges servyce five moneths since and yet hath no Answere. And another Servaunt of the Deputy of Calais likewyse who came before the other to Walsyngham, I heard, when he aunswered them, 'If ye be not contente to tary my leysure, departe when ye wille'. This is truthe, I had rather your Lordshyp commaunded me to Rome then deliver him Letters, and bring Aunswers to the same.

Even Skelton's 'parchaunce halfe a yere' no longer seems simply poetic fancy! If such examples as these are anything like typical, it is no surprise that Skelton's charge to that effect should be so accurate. The easy availability of sources of first-hand information, in the form of frustrated would-be suitors cooling their heels in the corridors and ante-rooms of the Court and Westminster, prepared to air their grievances to the first available sympathetic ear, must have aided the poet greatly in his gathering of material.[13] Simply because Skelton has got his facts right, however, need not mean that his interpretation of them must be similarly flawless. His astuteness in the gathering of valuable material is not always matched by his treatment of that material once it is assimilated into his satires. Here, for instance, he seems to

---

[11] Rawdon Brown, *Four Years*, II p. 315 (*L.P.*, III (i) 402).
[12] E. Lodge, *Illustrations of British History*, 3 vols. (London, 1791), I p. 34.
[13] The specific reference to delays of 'parchaunce half a yere' certainly suggests that Skelton had spoken to, or was familiar with the fate of, lord Dacre's hapless messenger.

attribute the delays in granting audiences to simple haughtiness and contrariness on the Cardinal's part, as he imperiously commands his suppliants 'ye must daunce attendaunce'. Yet a far more plausible reason for such delays would seem to be the vast amount of work which Wolsey had to conduct in a day. Skelton himself testifies to it elsewhere. We have already seen his suggestion that 'all the conflewence' of Court traffic ran to his door. But the suitors, the suppliants and ambassadors of all nations which the poet notes were merely part of the log-jam which funnelled into York Place, Westminster and Hampton Court. As Lord Chancellor, Cardinal-Legate and the King's most trusted minister Wolsey attracted not only the flood waters of state business, both foreign and domestic, but also all matters of Church administration, whilst his delving into the minutiae of legal cases in order to involve himself in the finding of 'straighter and speedier ways of justice' attracted a third stream of litigants and lawyers. Parott's cry of 'Besy, besy, besy and besynes agayne! / . . . what meneth this besynes?' (lines 57–8) can have been but a faint echo of the Cardinal's own thoughts when confronted with each new day's burdens.

Wolsey was not, of course, the first minister to acquire a multiplicity of offices, preferments and responsibilities. Nor was he the last. But his unprecedented combination of clerical and lay offices gave him more than most. And, unlike most other bureaucratic pluralists, he did not frequently seek recourse to the safety-valve of delegation. All the major responsibilities, and a large proportion of the minor ones, he kept in his own hands. Despite the fact that, as J. A. Guy has shown, Wolsey's period as Lord Chancellor was marked by a steady increase in the number of legal cases delegated to *ad hoc* committees of Councillors and individual judges for resolution,[14] his continued involvement in the detailed investigation of the cases before him and in the search for equitable solutions to them is quite remarkable.[15] Add to these commitments the facts that his acquisitive nature led to what George Cavendish, his Gentleman Usher and first biographer, referred to with nice tautology as 'the increase of his gains', and that his zeal for reform and his lack of trust in others to perform it led him continually to increase the purview of those offices he already held, and one has a recipe for complete administrative paralysis, were it not for Wolsey's huge reserves of personal energy. As Giustiniani noted,[16]

He is . . . of vast ability and indefatigable. He alone transacts the same business as that which occupies all the magistracies, offices and councils of Venice, both civil and criminal, and all state affairs are likewise handled by him let their nature be what it may.

14 Guy, *Cardinal's Court*, pp. 35, 38, 40.
15 *Ibid.*, pp. 68–9.
16 Rawdon Brown, *Four Years*, II p. 314 (July 1519) (*L.P.*, III (i) 402).

Support for this impression can be found in Bishop Fox's suggestion to Wolsey that 'I consider well that ye have as much labour of body and business of mind as ever had any in your room, and more, and never none had less help'.[17]

Wolsey's unwillingness to delegate responsibility was also readily apparent to those who had to deal with him. As de Mesa and De Caestres, the Imperial ambassadors, noted on 6 November 1522,[18]

Henry leads his usual life, leaving all the cares of state to Wolsey, who is so very ill that he is in danger of losing an eye, and the rest of his body seems almost equally affected. There seems little hope of his immediate recovery, especially as he will not abandon the affairs of the Kingdom to others, and must see many people daily.

Hence the backlog of suitors which prompted Skelton's charge was more a sign of the Cardinal's willingness to admit people than of his refusal so to do. His was a virtual open-house which, because of the limits upon his resources, soon became a virtually closed one to all but the most crucial of callers: a fact which, to their credit, some of his suitors appreciated. As de Mesa and De Caestres informed the Emperor on 23 March 1522, 'we shall do our best to see Wolsey frequently and write [to] your Majesty at least twice a week, but we cannot always do as well as we would, since the Cardinal is always busy, and our own affairs sometimes compel delay'.[19]

When Wolsey wished to see someone, however, there was rarely any problem in arranging an audience. On such occasions the Cardinal was at his most willing and affable. When, for instance, Crown policy favoured a strong line against the French and required detailed negotiations with the Imperial envoys to co-ordinate a war strategy Wolsey always made himself available to the Spanish ambassadors, as their correspondence shows.[20] On 4 January 1522 De Caestres informed his master that he had just arrived in London and 'was met at once by the Cardinal who had just disembarked and was on his way to see the King'.[21] 'The following day . . . we presented your letters to the Cardinal and asked for an audience, which he granted for the next day, before dinner'; and on 24 January, 'having read your letters we immediately asked for an interview with the Cardinal, and he, although the King was a guest at his house at the time, granted one for the following Tuesday'.[22] Wolsey's availability continued into February, for on the fourth of that month the ambassadors reported that 'we immediately obtained audience with the Cardinal, to whom we communicated the contents of your let-

---

[17] *L.P.*, II (i) 1814, 23 April 1516.
[18] *Sp. Cal.* Further Supplement (hereafter *F.S.*) p. 164.
[19] *Ibid.*, p. 103.   [20] *Ibid.*, p. 38.
[21] *Ibid.*, pp. 14–15.   [22] *Ibid.*, p. 38.

ters'.[23] Conversely, when in 1523 King and minister had begun to lose faith in Imperial goodwill and begun to favour a new truce, Wolsey's diary suddenly became too crowded to find room for such easy access for the Imperial envoys. As the ambassador noted ruefully on 8 May, 'I notified Wolsey immediately on the arrival of the couriers but, since it was Holy Week, I was unable to have an audience with him until Easter Sunday, after dinner'.[24] Indeed Wolsey's attitude towards the Spanish mission had entirely changed. 'Le Sauch will inform you', wrote de Mesa on 20 January 1523,[25]

of Wolsey's constant complaining [and] of the very strange manner in which he has treated us daily of late, often making us wait two or three hours at his door, and then sending us away without an audience, [and] insisting on seeing all our correspondence, or at least copies . . . we find these fashions very strange, and quite contrary to the ordinary custom of treating ambassadors.

It is quite evident that Wolsey could make life exceptionally difficult for ambassadors and other suitors, no matter how eminent their status, should he so wish. In detail if not in interpretation Skelton was perhaps only slightly overstating the case, as the papal Nuncio Chieragato was to discover, when he suggested that,

> Ye [Wolsey] are so puffed with pryde,
> That no man may abyde
> Your hygh and lordely lokes. (*Collyn Clout*, 593–5)

The Venetian ambassador, Giustiniani, writing to the Signory and the Council of Ten on 7 December 1516 is our source for the information that,[26]

a few days ago, the nuncio was sent for by the right Reverend Cardinal who, when he reached his presence, took him into a private chamber, where he laid hands upon him, telling him in fierce and rude language that he chose to know what he had written to the King of France, and what intercourse he held with me . . . and that he should not quit the spot until he had confessed everything, and unless he told him by fair means, that he would put him to the rack.

At times such as this it might appear that Wolsey's impatience for results had produced in him a condition very close to the 'ierarchy of frantycke frenesy' which Skelton describes. Yet to dismiss the Cardinal as simply a blustering tyrant as Skelton, borrowing from the Morality Plays, seeks to do is to try to impose too simple a framework, too neatly manageable and too obviously conventional a role, on a particularly complex and enigmatic individual. Unsurprisingly Wolsey the man very often confounds the expectations raised by Skelton's portrait of him. Occasionally Wolsey may

---

[23] *Ibid.*, p. 42.   [24] *Ibid.*, p. 208.   [25] *Ibid.*, pp. 186–7.
[26] Rawdon Brown, *Four Years*, II p. 17.

have appeared to some to be the braggart whom Skelton portrays. He was cast in this role in June 1520 when, in conversation with the papal auditor de la Camera, he informed him that he, Wolsey,[27]

would do or undo whatever he liked and conclude or not conclude an alliance between the King of England, [Charles V] ... and the King of France ... [and] boast[ing] that it was in his power to bring about an interview with all three of them.

At such a moment Wolsey may well have seemed to merit Skelton's scorn as, for all his words, he could only instil in his hearer, and in Juan Manuel to whom the conversation was reported, the feeling that he 'would do well to be more careful in the words he uses when he speaks of what he can do'.

Yet like the more-than-capable servant of a demanding master that he was, Wolsey could be relied on to play more roles than simply the braggart or the willing and amiable receiver of embassies when it was demanded of him. Much of his histrionic behaviour, his chewing of his cane and his rages, which Skelton portrays as merely 'frantycke frenesy and folysshe fantasy', seem more like conscious theatricality designed to secure political objectives to the less partial observer. The Imperial ambassadors' account of 28 February 1522 describes how, in their last interview with Wolsey,[28]

the Cardinal, for what reason we do not know, before we had said anything of the contents of your letters, said to us with great emotion, his face deadly pale, 'Ambassadors, say to the Emperor from me that I, with a profusion of sighs, and as his good servant, beg him to act sincerely with this King, who is the faithful, useful and good friend of his Majesty. If he does so he will find here true and sincere friends, ready to do their utmost in his service. But he should remember that we are friends, not subjects.' We sought to discover what was troubling him, but he changed the subject abruptly and would say nothing further.

Such a performance, with white face and 'profusion of sighs' included, was clearly motivated by a shrewd political calculation and seems to have had its effect on the surprised ambassadors. 'It may be guessed', they surmised, 'that he was disturbed by a suspicion . . . that your Majesty has suggested that, unless Henry increases the loan to 200,000 crowns, you will negotiate in another quarter.' Wolsey had thus seized the diplomatic initiative from the ambassadors before they could put the Emperor's case to him and suggested to them that he knew of their potentially duplicitous designs without revealing the extent of what, if any, knowledge he possessed, simply by a piece of forceful character acting.

This ability to appear in many roles according to the dictates of a situation was to benefit the Cardinal greatly in his service as the Crown's leading diplomatic agent. Moreover he was not averse to using it to his own private

---

[27] *Sp. Cal. 1509–25*, p. 281.   [28] *Sp. Cal. F.S.*, p. 67.

advantage either. Some days prior to the interview of 28 February the Imperial ambassadors were similarly exposed to Wolsey the tragedian, once more in the role of the outraged innocent, this time promoting his own ends. 'Several days ago', de Mesa informed Charles V,[29]

when I . . . was talking to the Cardinal about his pension . . . and speaking of your Majesty's feeling for him, he replied to me with a very disturbed expression, 'I can see that these are all words, and I may properly suspect that I am being played with. It was not thus that I risked many thousand crowns in going to Calais for the sake of his Imperial Majesty. Indeed I have already lost what I used to draw from France, both my pensions, and the money due on account of the treaty for the surrender of Tournai; and other sources of income which I had in France. I may well complain, therefore, of this conduct toward me which pays me with words only. I have letters patent from the Emperor, for 1,000 angels which have been long unpaid. If I do not see another sought of behaviour, I will send his Majesty back his letters and bulls, and he may do what he likes with them.'

De Mesa's response to this declaration was not, as a reading of Skelton might suggest, to express contempt for the Cardinal's erratic behaviour, but hastily to despatch a report to his Emperor to inform him that 'it is of the utmost importance, not only to send such letters promptly, but to add something more'. Thus what Skelton chose to portray as simply irrational behaviour had its very obvious uses in the day-to-day handling of diplomacy. In a state such as Henrician England in which power and responsibility, both creative and executive, were concentrated in a very few hands, the role of the foreign ambassador at Court became, increasingly, simply to observe and interpret the actions and motives of the men at the helm, in order to pre-empt future policy and so choose the correct moment and manner in which to advance his own cause. If the helmsman, like Wolsey, was adept at switching his roles, at appearing as different things to different men, then he would inevitably hold higher and stronger cards than the perplexed ambassadors in their diplomatic game. Hence what Skelton decried as wilfulness could in actuality have been Wolsey's greatest asset in his pursuit of the interests of the Crown.

That Wolsey could assume different roles before different audiences is undeniable. In addition to those which we have already touched on there was also Wolsey the faithful ally, working against all the odds, sometimes swimming alone against the current of Court opinion, in pursuit of his correspondent's interests.[30]

The mask of the embattled ally was one which the Cardinal adopted in

[29] *Ibid.*, p. 67.
[30] See the Cardinal's attempts to coax the Earl of Shrewsbury back to Court from his self-imposed exile on his estates during 1516. 'Wolsey is a great friend to [you]', Thomas Alen informed the Earl on 31 May 1516 (*L.P.*, II (i) 1959). Wolsey's actual intentions may well, however, have been to proceed against the Earl for illegal retaining once he was back at Court. See G. W. Bernard, *The Power of the Early Tudor Nobility: A Study of the Fourth and Fifth Earls of Shrewsbury* (Brighton, 1985) Part I, for a full account of this incident. Note

many of his dealings with the various ambassadors resident at the Court, often regardless of which party in the Franco-Imperial feud was favoured by the prevailing policy of the moment. On 31 March 1522, for example, the Imperial ambassadors were induced to inform Charles V that they found Wolsey 'constant in his devotion to your Majesty', despite the fact that he was at the same time secretly receiving envoys from France.[31] Similarly on 12 August following, the Cardinal could convince the credulous diplomats, despite such covert negotiations, that 'he had already been accused in the King's presence of serving the Emperor, rather than his master, and to calm Henry he had been obliged to make a gift of 20,000 angels to the war chest'.[32] Similarly Wolsey was not averse to adopting the same tactic with the French, whose representatives at the Calais conference of 1521 he had informed of the great love which Henry and he held for Francis I and the French, and the envy and malice which he had incurred in England because of that love, despite the fact that he already had the aggressive Anglo-Imperial alliance secured at Bruges signed and sealed in his baggage.[33]

The Cardinal was, then, far more than the simple tyrannical braggart which Skelton painted him. Yet before we replace one simplistic model, that of the tyrant, with another, the Machiavell (perhaps more suited to modern literary tastes), it must be stated that not all of Wolsey's amicability can easily be dismissed as play-acting for political gain. He seems at times, and in specific circumstances, to have been capable of great conviviality and natural generosity. George Cavendish's account of the Cardinal's dismissal of his household retainers prior to his journey to York in 1530, although perhaps questionable in some of its details, seems none the less a trustworthy demonstration of the Cardinal's genuine affection for his faithful servants.[34] Similarly his personal loyalty to and friendship with his royal master, although

also Wolsey's dealings with the Princess Mary during her unhappy sojourn in France during 1514 (B.L. Cotton MS Caligula D VI fo. 253 (H. Ellis (ed.), *Letters Illustrative of English History*, 3 vols. (London, 1824, 1827, 1846), First Series, I p. 115)), and with Charles Brandon, duke of Suffolk during the same period. *L.P.*, II (i) Introduction, pp. xii–xiii; *L.P.*, II (i) 113; B.L. Cotton MS Caligula D VI fo. 186 (*L.P.*, II (i) 145). See also *L.P.*, II (i) 187, 132, 222; and Ellis, *Letters* third series, I p. 214.

[31] *Sp. Cal. F.S.*, p. 107.
[32] *Ibid.*, p. 144.
[33] *L.P.*, III (ii) 1513. See also *L.P.*, III (ii) 1602. That this was a deliberate deception of the French on Wolsey's part is made clear by his description of his use of a 'colour' to justify his visit to Charles V (*L.P.*, III (i) 1480, 1493).
[34] R. S. Sylvester (ed.), *The Life and Death of Cardinal Wolsey, by George Cavendish*, E.E.T.S., 243 (1959) pp. 107–8. Sylvester's suggestion (here and in 'Cavendish's *Life of Wolsey*: the artistry of a Tudor biographer', *Studies in Philology*, 1960) that the biography is too evidently based on literary convention to be of any help to the historian cannot be seen as an objection here. For, were this scene a deliberate invention of Cavendish's, one would expect it to be placed at the end of the narrative where the *Fall of Princes* dictated that such 'repentence' scenes should be located. That it appears in the 'wrong' place, well before the most dramatic phase of the Cardinal's fall from power, is thus strong evidence for the broad authenticity of the biographer's narrative of the incident.

qualified by the caution and humility born of dependence, seem to have been entirely sincere.[35]

In the majority of his dealings Wolsey seems to display the undeniable ability to handle the men with whom he had to work, a faculty which at times required the use of theatricality and occasionally of duplicity, but which at others could be accomplished by simple good humour. Yet whatever the manner in which he performed his duties, duties they surely were. His activities were, in by far the greater part, necessitated by his pursuit of the Crown's interests and not the personal appetites and desires which Skelton alleges. His stern handling of certain noblemen in the Star Chamber, which the poet chose to portray as raging tirades, was the result of the King's determination to uphold the dignity of the Crown and the integrity of the law against what he saw as the presumptuous misuse of liveried retainers by those individuals, not by any *animus* of the Cardinal's against the nobility in general or those men in particular.[36] And Wolsey's unwillingness to grant audiences to suitors was not motivated by the haughtiness apparent in Skelton's account, but by the former's desire to conduct as much as possible of the most pressing Crown business himself.

Yet even if Wolsey's methods of handling public business were determined by his pursuit of his master's wishes, Skelton's assertions still would deserve further attention. For one cannot ignore the suggestion that the overall impression created by the Cardinal's zealous monopoly of Crown business was that, to all intents and purposes, Wolsey was the centre of real power in the state and Henry simply the figurehead. As this study has shown, this point was repeatedly stressed, with ever-increasing clarity, in the anti-Wolsey satires.

In *Speke, Parott* there were the veiled allusions to the ensnared 'estrych fether', to Melchisedek, Aaron, Moloc and the domineering bull-calf, and more graphically in the envoys to the megalomaniacal aspirations of the 'card-yn-all's' 'wolvys hede' which 'gapythe over the crowne'. Yet what is crucial about such assertions is that, having established and clarified the basic premise, Skelton can do little else but reiterate it elsewhere. The poet, it must be remembered, knew little of the intimate dealings of King and Chancellor. Consequently, instead of being able to suggest specific instances of this unnatural dominance of servant over master, he is forced to disguise his

---

[35] See, for example, the account in Cavendish, *Life and Death*, pp. 25–8 of Wolsey's delight in entertaining Henry at his home.

[36] For a fuller treatment of Wolsey and Henry's respective roles in these trials, see my 'John Skelton and literary attitudes to the nobility', in G. W. Bernard (ed.), *The Early Tudor Nobility* (Leicester, forthcoming). For an alternative interpretation of the same evidence, which sees Wolsey as the instigator of the court action, see H. Miller, *Henry VIII and the English Nobility* (Oxford, 1986), pp. 108–9.

lack of exact knowledge by simply recycling that basic premise in subtly different ways. The effect of Wolsey's supremacy is described, in *Why Come Ye Nat?*, as we have seen, by the allegedly unnatural disparity which it creates in the queues of suitors at the respective doors of the King and Cardinal.

> The Kynges courte
> Shulde have the excellence;
> But Hampton Court
> Hath the preemynence! (406–9)

The relationship is also seen in pseudo-proverbial terms,

> Set up a wretche on hye,
> In a trone triumphantyle,
> Make him a great astate,
> And he wyll play checke mate
> With ryall majeste
> Counte himselfe as good as he. (585–90)

But for all these and other reiterations of the original assertion one learns little or nothing else of any value about either King or Cardinal from the text. What Skelton is attempting is not to expand his argument with any new factual material, because he has none, but to find support for his original allegation from as many sources and authorities as possible.

Yet, having made the point, Skelton was forced to attempt an explanation of how that situation had come about. How could 'Royal Henry the eyght', the 'so royall a kyng' of *Speke, Parott* (line 468), not have seen his own error in raising the 'bull-calf' to high office? To answer such a question was, of course, an extremely delicate exercise. In *Speke, Parott* the poet had simply refused to address it, offering only the implied explanation that it was Melchisedek's 'mercy', his generosity of spirit, which allowed Moloc's iniquity to flourish. Yet the question clearly troubled the poet, and in fairness to him it must be noted that he did not flinch in his later satires from grasping this particular nettle of his own devising. To criticise the Chancellor, even openly as Skelton increasingly did, was one thing. To criticise the King, particularly the King from whom he hoped to win patronage, was quite another. But, despite the accounts of some commentators who have suggested that Skelton's portrayal of Henry was entirely favourable,[37] it is clear that the poet came to be far from flattering in his treatment of Henry and the motives behind his continued support for Wolsey.

After the completion of *Speke, Parott* Skelton began to approach the im-

---

[37] Pollet, for example, observes that Henry is portrayed as 'beyond reproach' (*Poet of Tudor England*, p. 122), whilst Paula Neuss states that 'Skelton never wrote a word against Henry' (P. Neuss (ed.), *Magnificence* (Manchester, 1980), p. 36).

plications of his satirical assertions more seriously. Perhaps once his decision
to search for a patron in the City had been made he felt that it was no longer
realistic or necessary to appeal so directly to the King, and so felt free to
adopt a more critical attitude. Perhaps the need to convince the hard-headed
readers of the merchant community of the authenticity of his account forced
the poet to follow through this particular assertion more fully than he might
have wished. But whatever the motivation behind the move, Skelton's adoption of the guise of a jaundiced former courtier passing on his wisdom to the
masses beyond the Court saw him advance a number of different analyses of
the reasons for Wolsey's continued eminence. The most favourable suggestion offered was simply a fuller articulation of the assertion that Henry
had been merely too kind, too trusting,

> But, however he [Wolsey] was borne,
> Men wolde have the lesse scorne
> If he coulde consyder
> His byrth and rowme togeder,
> And call to his mynde
> How noble and how kynde
> To him he hathe founde
> Our sovereyne lorde, chyfe grounde
> Of all this prelacy,
> And set hym nobly
> In great auctoryte
> Out from a low degre. (*Why Come Ye Nat?*, 495–506)

In this analysis Wolsey's elevation reflected only honour on the King and
acted as a demonstration of his power.

> This man was full unable
> To reche to suche degre,
> Had nat our prynce be
> Royall Henry the eyght,
> Take him in suche conceyght
> That he set him on heyght,
> In exemplyfyenge
> Great Alexander the Kynge. (537–44)

> Suche is a kynges power
> To make within an hower,
> And worke suche a myracle,
> That shall be a spectacle
> Of renowme and worldly fame. (565–9)

No doubt this interpretation; that it 'pertayneth to a kynge / To make up
one of noght', and to place his trust in whom he chose, was the one which
Henry himself would have considered the most fitting, had he been confron-

ted with the question.[38] But for all the magnificence which Wolsey's elevation should have reflected on Henry in theory, Skelton had already said far
too much in his first two satires about the contrary effects of the Cardinal's
regime in practice for this explanation to carry any more than a token
weight. The simple counter to it would have been that Henry, if he were so
admirable a King, should have removed Wolsey from high office immediately that it became obvious that he was misusing his position. Since this
clearly had not happened the poet was forced to seek other explanations for
the Cardinal's continued favour, and in the process his supposedly flawless
treatment of his sovereign becomes decidedly tarnished. Henry did not withdraw his favour from Wolsey, Skelton asserts, because he was deceived by
the subtle guiles of the Cardinal who,

> . . . dyggeth so in the trenche
> Of the court royall
> That he ruleth them all.
> So he dothe undermynde,
> And suche sleyghtes dothe fynde,
> That the Kynges mynde
> By him is subverted;
> And so streatly coarted
> In credensynge his tales,
> That all is but nutshales
> That any other sayth,
> He hath in him suche fayth. (434–45)

Another possible means of such domination of the King's ear is offered. Perhaps, Skelton suggests, the Cardinal has employed witchcraft:

> It is a wonders case:
> That the Kynges grace
> Is toward hym so mynded,
> And so farre blynded,
> That he can nat parceyve
> How he doth hym disceyve.
> I dought, lest by sorsery
> Or suche other loselry
> As wychecraft or charmyng;
> For he is the Kynges derlyng
> And his swete hart rote,
> And is governed by this mad Kote! (657–68)

Thus Henry is described both as 'blynded', and thus as a fool, and beguiled, and thus as a dupe, and furthermore is alleged to be the victim of witchcraft. The assertion that Wolsey was 'his swete hart rote' also carries hints of

---

[38] *Why Come Ye Nat?*, lines 550–1. Note his angry defence of his honour during 1521 when
Wolsey had seemed to question his capacity to place trust in others. (B.L. Cotton MS Caligula D VII 153 (*St. P.*, I 38)).

a homosexual element to their relationship equally unflattering to a monarch vaunted at jousts and spectacles as *Coeur Loyal*. Any one of these suggestions would have been sufficient to expose a man to the full force of the royal wrath if spoken to the King's face. Clearly Skelton has moved a long way from his overt courtship of Henry's favour in *Speke, Parott*. Why should this have been? It is possible that simple frustration with the King's failure to offer him support might have prompted the poet's more cavalier attitude. But it is also interesting to speculate on just how popular criticism of the King would have been with Skelton's new City audience. Joan Kennedy offers the intriguing assertion that Henry had increasingly antagonised the City's governing elite during the early 1520s through his attempts to insert his own nominees into such influential civic offices as the Common Weigher at the Great Beam (unofficially annexed into the royal prerogative during June 1521), with the result that he became 'the subject of much popular hostility in the period 1517–21'.[39] Perhaps, then, Skelton's new-found boldness in his criticism of the causes of Wolsey's ascendancy can be seen as further evidence of the element of calculation behind his satires. In order to appeal to the substantial men of the City he may have decided to adopt not only their resentment over the loans of 1522 and Wolsey's role in their imposition, but their more general dissatisfaction with the Crown's demands on the City as a whole. To implicate the King as an unwitting accomplice in Wolsey's crimes rather than attacking him as the source of the objectionable policies was certainly the safest way of so doing.

Yet what of Skelton's allegations? We have already seen how much of Wolsey's activity can be attributed to his efforts on his King's behalf rather than his own prejudices. And it is clear that Henry could be extremely forceful when he suspected that his royal prerogatives were being encroached upon, or his person slighted. Does this suggest a strong King in command both of himself and his ministers, or rather, as a reading of Skelton's satires might suggest, an essentially malleable figure, a proud but irresolute man allowed an occasional public outing in which to indulge his taste for self-aggrandizement but kept for the most part away from the political arena in order that his Chancellor might manipulate events there as he chose?

The overall impression gained by the continental ambassadors, whose vocation called for their continual observation and analysis of affairs at Court, was that Wolsey ran the administration largely to his own design, and was able to manipulate his royal master without evident difficulty. On 28 December 1519, for example, Antonio Surian described Wolsey to the Venetian Signory as 'this individual who might be styled the governor of the King of

---

[39] J. Kennedy, 'The City of London and the Crown *c*. 1509–*c*. 1529', unpublished Manchester University M.A. thesis (1978), pp. 7–10.

England', whilst Giustiniani remarked that 'the Cardinal, for authority, may in point of fact be styled *ipse rex*.'[40] On 26 July 1519 the latter informed the Doge that 'the French ambassador, who acquainted us with everything, is also convinced that he shall receive the like reply [to that given to him by Wolsey] from his Majesty, as this Cardinal is King, nor does his Majesty depart in the least from the opinion and counsel of his lordship'.[41] This opinion was apparently shared in Rome, and by Juan Manuel, the Imperial ambassador there, who had thirteen days earlier informed Charles V that 'the pope said further to him that the Cardinal, who is "the governor of the King of England", is a very strange person, and makes the King go hither and thither, just as he likes'.[42]

So in part, at least, it seems that Skelton's suggestions struck a chord. Although Wolsey's dealings with the ambassadors may have been eminently successful in his own terms, in that they established a relationship favourable to him, in which he could manipulate them, summon them at will, dismiss, ill-treat or simply ignore them as the political circumstances dictated without provoking a diplomatic crisis, a by-product of his high-handed approach was their inference that his apparent arrogance was endemic in his character, and carried over into his dealings with the King. That his manner might have been entirely different, and entirely deferential, with Henry was a possibility which seemingly did not occur to them. The picture which they transmitted abroad was one of a Court dominated by its Chancellor, not by its King. And such accounts as they sent were readily accepted by their continental masters. As Francis I told Giustiniani as the two compared notes on the nature of Wolsey's character, 'by my fault, the Cardinal must bear this King light good will for it is not the office of a good servant to filch his master's honour'.[43]

So prevalent was this picture of Wolsey that it was utilised by the administration to justify his eventual fall, when in actuality the ease with which Henry dismissed the Cardinal from power might more properly stand as an example of the latter's weakness rather than his strength. Not only did the 'Lords' Articles' of 1529 include the charge that Wolsey had 'used himself more like a fellow to your Highnesse than like a subject',[44] but the new Lord Chancellor, Sir Thomas More, used the same argument in his opening address to the Reformation Parliament. Speaking in a characteristically biblical vein, More (rather less characteristically) incited a mood of anti-

---

[40] Rawdon Brown, *Four Years*, I pp. 115, 155; II 216; *L.P.*, II (ii) 3558, 4438.
[41] Rawdon Brown, *Four Years*, II p. 295 (*L.P.*, III (i) 397).
[42] *Sp. Cal. 1509–25*, 281. As late as 2 April 1529 the Venetian envoy, Vernier, was still reporting that 'The Cardinal of York is more than King' (*Ven. Cal. 1527–33*, 440).
[43] *L.P.*, III (i) 402.
[44] Lord Herbert of Cherbury, *Life and Reigne of Henry The Eighth* (London, 1649), p. 267.

Romanism amongst the members by expatiating on the duplicity of the fallen Cardinal.[45]

As you se that emongest a great flocke of shepe some be rotten and fauty, which the good sheperd sendeth from the good shepe, so the great wether which is so late fallen, as you knowe, so craftely, so scabedly, ye & so untruly juggled with the Kynge, that all men must nedes gesse and thinke that he thought in him self that the [King] had no wit to perceive his craftie doyng, or els that he presumed that the kyng wolde not se nor knowe his fraudulent juggeling and attemptes. But he was deceived for his Grace's sight was so quicke and penetrable that he saw him, ye and saw through hym, both with in and without, so that all thing to him was open; and accordyng to his desert he hath had a gentle correction.

Evidently by the time of his fall the feeling that Wolsey had usurped too much of the King's prerogative to rule was widespread. It must be noted, however, that it was most obviously prevalent amongst those with a vested interest in capitalising on that fall, and the bulk of the public attacks on the Cardinal were specifically directed at his legatine authority and at his administration of the Church, more in order to exert pressure on the Papacy and the English clergy than in genuine outrage at Wolsey's activities.

Many factors may have led to Wolsey's acquisition of such a reputation. Its popularisation may have owed much to the circumstances surrounding the abandonment of the inaptly named Amicable Grant of 1525. Here the Cardinal was forced, again in the role of the political lightning conductor, to protect the Crown from the dishonour (and the dangerous precedent) of being seen to withdraw its financial demands in the face of popular opposition, by publicly accepting the blame for having secretly fostered and advanced the scheme without the King's knowledge – an improbable notion. This public assertion by both King and Cardinal that the latter had both the freedom and the power to produce and execute so ambitious a scheme without royal authority and without Henry's knowledge would clearly have reinforced the idea that he was given too great a licence in matters of state, and was inclined to take advantage of that freedom to run the government for his own ends. Even if the public charade of Wolsey's admission of responsibility for the scheme was not universally believed, it at least implied that such a view of the Cardinal as an over-secretive and over-powerful minister would not be frowned on by the King. In addition Skelton himself, through his satires, may have had no small effect in popularising the picture of a subservient King and a dominant minister. But our interest here is with the validity or otherwise of this model at the time at which Skelton made use of it, not with its subsequent popularisation. The ambassadors' accounts cited above suggest that at least some elements of Court society felt that such a model was realistic. But is this impression of Wolsey as the Great Juggler a

---

[45] Hall, *Union*, p. 764.

fair reading of his relationship with the King, or merely an exaggerated reflection in ill-informed minds of his ability to read and manipulate lesser men to good effect in the service of the Crown?

George Cavendish, the Cardinal's least hostile contemporary critic, gives an account of Wolsey's dealings with Henry which has been widely accepted by subsequent writers. Once he gained the King's confidence, his biographer asserts, Wolsey played on the youthful King's delight in the hunt and other pursuits to acquire power and responsibility for himself.[46]

The Kyng was young and lusty, disposed all to myrthe and pleasure & to followe his desire & appetyte no thyng myndyng to travell in the busy affayers of this Realme / the wiche the Almosyner [Wolsey] perseyved very well / toke uppon hyme therefore to disborden the Kyng of so waytie a charge & troblesome busynes puttyng the Kyng in Comfort that he shall not nede to spare any tyme of his pleasure for any busynes that shold necessary happen in the Councell as long as he beyng there havyng the Kynges auctorytie & commaundment doughted not to se all thynges sufficiently furnysshed and perfected . . . and so fast as thother Councellors advised the Kyng to leave hys pleasure / and to attend to the affayers of his realme / so busylie did the Almosyner perswade hyme to the contrary.

Thus, as the traditional account would have it, as Henry played, Wolsey began to monopolise power and authority in his absence.

Certainly Cavendish as a man familiar with Wolsey's methods deserves our attention. Yet to leave such a suggestion unqualified would be naive in the extreme. Cavendish did not enter the Cardinal's household until after 1520, long after Wolsey had been drawn into royal service and the terms of his relationship with Henry established. Thus he was reliant for the early part of his biography on reminiscence and gossip. Moreover, when Cavendish does describe instances of Henry and Wolsey's meetings from his own experience, the relationship portrayed does not entirely tally with the simple account given above. The biographer's perspective on their relationship was both extremely limited, and moreover, further distorted by his own almost total ignorance of their political dealings. Perhaps Pollard was unkind to condemn Cavendish's biography as 'the classic example of history as it appeared to a Gentleman Usher'.[47] Yet one must be aware that, although it is not quite the endless recitation of domestic etiquette which such a description implies, neither is it the analysis of a commentator familiar with the political business with which Wolsey was primarily concerned.

In support of Cavendish's account it must be observed that Henry did not possess the temperament to dedicate himself exclusively to business. He was no Henry VII who could sit up into the night reading reports, minutes of committee meetings and despatches and personally oversee the keeping of the royal accounts. But this need not necessarily imply that he was the sort of

---

[46] Cavendish, *Life and Death*, p. 13.
[47] Pollard, p. 2.

incompetent monarch which Skelton's satires might suggest. Such kings as Henry VII were the exception, not the rule, and they may well have done their estate as much harm as good through their diligence in conducting administrative business, by neglecting the equally important social and ceremonial functions of the Crown. The King shared the social and recreational tastes of his noblemen and a taste for hunting need not preclude an aptitude for and an attention to more serious pursuits at other times. Thus when even in his maturity Henry rode to hounds and led, to Spanish eyes, 'his normal life, leaving all the cares of State to Wolsey',[48] this need not indicate a complete neglect of his royal responsibilities. His riding with and entertainment of his leading magnates and eminent foreign visitors was as much a part of his royal duties as attendance at meetings of the Council or listening to a royal secretary reading the latest despatches from Denmark or Venice or the customs returns from the Cinque Ports. These last were the proper concern of the Crown's bureaucratic servants and Henry can hardly be censured for neglecting to involve himself with them. It is not to the conduct of routine business which one must look to find evidence of royal shortcomings but to the formulation and execution of policy, and in these areas Henry can be seen to play an extremely active, and indeed crucial, role.

The royal secretaries, who were intimately familiar with the King's role in government, were under no such illusions as those harboured by the foreign ambassadors. Richard Pace, for example, was fully aware that his royal master took a lively interest in the latest diplomatic news. In April *c.* 1518 he informed Wolsey that 'your Grace shall understande that no lettres be sende unto hys Highnesse undre your Grace's pacquett, but hys Highnesse doth rede them every wurde'.[49] Furthermore that he understood what he read and was more than capable of producing his own interpretation of events, often at variance with Wolsey's is revealed in many of the letters which passed between the two through the offices of their secretaries. A case in point is More's account of Henry's desire to point out his own shrewdness to Wolsey *c.* 1523. 'As touching the demeanure of the Cardinall Sedunense', wrote More,[50]

concernyng the truste that the King's Grace did put in hym, his Grace commaunded me to shew your Grace that he mystrusted the same hymselfe byfore; and he shewed your Grace at Richemount, and though he be not glad at the Cardinal's delyng, yit is he glad he saith that your Grace may see that he fore saw it, wherby he thinketh your Grace will the bettre truste his conjecture hereafter.

For all Skelton's claims that Wolsey 'ruleth all at wyll' (*Why Come Ye Nat?*, line 489) and that 'The Kynges mynde / By him is subverted; / And so streatly

[48] *Sp. Cal. F.S.*, p. 164.
[49] Ellis, *Letters*, third series, I p. 187.
[50] B.L. Cotton MS Galba B V fo. 269 (Ellis, *Letters*, first series, I 70).

coarted / In credensynge his tales, / That all is but nutshales / That any other sayth' (lines 440–5) it is clear that, as the previous chapter demonstrated, Henry and Wolsey did have disagreements over the detailed implementation of policy and that Wolsey, as the humility of his despatches reveals, was always careful to respect his master's wishes. Such disagreements arose not because Wolsey 'wylfully' wished to 'rule' the King, but on specific occasions when the former felt obliged to point out the practical difficulties created by the measures which Henry suggested.

It is equally evident that Henry, although he relied on Wolsey as his chief minister and as his major channel of information, was not prepared to allow the latter a monopoly of his ear or of his time. That he sought other advice and kept open other channels of information, separate not only from his chief minister but even from his personal secretary, is made clear in the following despatch from More to Wolsey of 29 November 1524. 'Hit may lyke your Grace to be advertised', he informed the Cardinal,[51]

That yisternyght at my cummyng in to the King's Grace's presence, after that I had made your Grace's recommendations and his Highnes showed hymselfe very greatly glad and joyful of your Grace's helthe, as I was abowte to declare ferther to his Grace what lettres I had brought, his Highnes, perceiving lettres in my hand, prevented me ere I could begyn, and saied 'Ah ye have lettres nowe by John Joachym [the French envoy] and I trow sum resolution what they will do'. 'Nay veryly Sir' quoth I 'My lord [Wolsey] hath yit no word by John Joachim nor John Joachim as far as my lord knew had yet no worde hym selfe this day in the mornyng when I departed from his Grace'. 'No had' quoth he, 'I myche mervaile thereof, for John Joachim had a servaunt come to hym two dayes ago' . . . 'Sir' Quoath I 'If it lyke your Grace this mornyng my lord's Grace had no thing herd thereof'.

The King then read More's letters and 'forthwith he declared the newes and every materiall point which uppon the reding his Grace well noted unto the Quenys Grace, and all other abowt him, who were mervelous glad to here it'.

The likelihood that this instance of a well-informed Henry confounding his usual sources of news was an exception rather than the rule is suggested both by the surprise evident in More's lengthy recapitulation of the interview, and by Henry's good humoured triumphing at his own achievement. But it serves to illustrate that the King was not without a mind or channels of information of his own when it came to political events. It also clearly demonstrates both his own interest in such events and his desire to display his informed opinions, both of which help to refute the suggestion that Henry was prepared to let his minister conduct all the business of the realm and formulate its policies whilst he himself concentrated on sport and revel.

Despite their apparent conviction that Wolsey was in effect 'the governor of the King of England', the continental ambassadors resident in England provide, through their despatches, ample evidence of a king who involved

[51] B.L. Cotton MD Galba B VIII fo. 132 (Ellis, *Letters*, first series, I p. 253).

himself in policy-making and who took seriously his consultations with his chief minister and with the other members of his Council. Moreover their reports suggest that these consultations did not involve simply the perfunctory agreement to and 'rubber-stamping' on Henry's part of decisions already determined by Wolsey. Often such discussions were protracted.[52] The assertion that Wolsey considered himself the King's governor, or that he ruled Henry at will seems even less plausible in the light of his letters to the King and his handling of Crown business.[53] In reality, regardless of the impression gained by others, Henry was very much the master, and Wolsey very much his servant. That the Cardinal was keen to advance his own interests cannot be denied. But even these would take second place if and when the interests of the Crown dictated. As he 'expressly' informed the Imperial ambassadors on 5 February 1523, when negotiations over the payment of Spanish pensions had reached a delicate phase, 'neither he nor any other Englishman will accept a penny until Henry is paid'.[54] If he occasionally forgot himself in public and appeared to presume too much power, in boasting of what he could do in foreign affairs, or in giving the impression that he and not Henry determined policy,[55] for far the greater part of his career he was scrupulously careful in his presentation of Henry as the instigator of policy and the commanding voice in the determination of affairs. Thus even in so small a matter as promising the Imperial envoy Lachaulx that his own sympathies lay with the Emperor, he did so only after giving due precedence to the King as the source and the epitome of that inclination. As Lachaulx subsequently informed the Emperor on 13 March 1522, Wolsey 'begged me to write [to] you assuring you that, except for Henry himself, there is no one more earnest in your service than he'.[56] Such lapses into apparent arrogance as there were were only flaws in presentation, for Wolsey was essentially a deeply loyal Crown servant. No doubt much of his loyalty stemmed from his realisation of the fact that the Crown was the chief, and indeed in practice the only, source of his wealth and influence. But such loyalty was no less valuable to his King for that. Perhaps no better example of this usefulness can be found than the already cited case of the abandonment of the Amicable Grant. There Wolsey by taking the blame for the abortive demand himself allowed Henry, who shared the responsibility for the scheme, to escape the affair apparently untouched by public criticism.

[52] See, for example, *Sp. Cal. F.S.*, pp. 14–16, 123.

[53] For Skelton's assertion, see *Why Come Ye Nat?* lines 670–9. For the reality, see, B.L. Cotton MS Galba B VII fo. 264 (*St. P.*, I 53).

[54] *Sp. Cal. F.S.*, p. 189.

[55] See the oft-quoted remarks of Giustiniani to the effect that, in 1515 Wolsey had used to tell him that 'his Majesty would do so and so', a phrase which as he gained power and assurance became transmuted into '*we* shall do so and so' and finally '*I* shall do so and so' (Rawdon Brown, *Four Years*, II p. 314 (*Ven. Cal. 1509–19*, p. 560).

[56] *Sp. Cal. F.S.*, p. 86.

Wolsey was clearly not a traitor then, for all Skelton's allusions to Judas Iscariot (*Speke, Parott*, line 133). Nor was he a dictator. He did not sufficiently 'subvert' the King's mind that he could determine policy himself. He could only offer advice and counsel. Nor was his the only voice to be heard in the Council.[57] His dominance of the Court was of a different order. He was the realm's chief minister and the greatest single attractor and conductor of business purely because he was the ablest and most willing Crown servant. His 'domination' of Henry existed only in so far as he had convinced the King that he, and only he, could be trusted to carry out the most important and demanding governmental and private missions, and in so doing he had probably only succeeded in convincing Henry of the truth. Thus his position depended on his continued ability to get things done swiftly and efficiently. And as his ambitions increased, so the scope of his prerogative and the number of tasks laid before him increased correspondingly. Hence his continual 'besynes' and increasingly regular bouts of ill-health, as he strove to limit the King's reliance on others (and so ensure his own indispensability) through continued activity. The sheer range of these activities is a good indication of how much Henry relied on, or exploited, Wolsey, and how much the latter needed to absorb into his portfolio in order to maintain his position.

His conduct of foreign policy is only the most public and obvious of his fields of operation. Even, as in 1523, when he was involved in complex negotations with the agents of both France and the Empire, he was called on to perform a vast range of other tasks to satisfy the King's demands. More informed him, for example, on an undated occasion *c.* 1523, that Henry wished him to settle a dispute between the towns of Waterford and New Ross in Ireland over wine franchises. It was not that the problem was too complex or too intractable for the King to deal with. Henry knew what actions the situation required and what avenues of solution were available. It simply was not his responsibility to settle the issue himself. So he passed on the problem to his chief minister with the recommendation that he 'either in the Starre Chambre . . . examine the matter of the said Citee, or ellis committe the same to the examination of sum justices or other, such as your Grace shall thynke convenient'.[58] Henry understood what his royal estate required him to do, and what he could legimately remit, and he was fully aware of what his servants were for. The fact that he passed so much business to Wolsey does not suggest that he himself was incapable of performing any serious governmental function. Quite the reverse, it demonstrates that

---

[57] Ruthal, Norfolk, Surrey, Suffolk, Sir Thomas Lovell, Sir William Compton and the 'minions' are just some of those who were described by Giustiniani as exercising considerable power during Wolsey's ascendency (Rawdon Brown, *Four Years*, II 114, 138, 252, 270).

[58] B.L. Cotton MS Titus B XI fo. 391 (Ellis, *Letters*, first series, I p. 195).

he was the master of his own vocation: a man who, unlike his Chancellor, could delegate effectively to relieve himself of unnecessary burdens. That he chose Wolsey as the chief recipient of so much business simply indicates that he could recognise an able servant when he saw one. And that Wolsey was an able servant is revealed by the scope of the talents which he was expected to exercise, and which he exercised successfully.

Having already referred the Waterford dispute to a minister already engrossed in the internecine coils of Franco-Imperial intrigue, Henry was not averse to delegating more intimate problems too. As More wrote on a subsequent occasion *c.* 1523–4;[59]

Hit may lyke your good Grace to be advertised that the King's Highnesse this nyght, going to his souper, called me to hym secretly, and commaunded me to wryte unto your Grace that where as hit hath pleased our lord to call to his mercy mr Myrfyn, late Alderman of London, his Grace very greatly desireth for the speciall favour which he bereth toward Sir William Tyler, that the same sir William should have the widow of the said late Aldreman in marriage. For the furtheraunce whereof his Highness considering your Grace's well approved wisedome and dexteritie in th'achieving and brynging to good passe his vertuouse and honourable appetites, commaunded me with diligence to advertise you Grace that hit may lyke you, at the contemplation of this his affectuouse request, by your high wisedome to devise, put in ure, and persue, the moost effectual meanys by which his Grace's desire may in this mater best be brought about and goodly take effect.

This is not the tone of a king cowed or beguiled into submissive indulgence of Wolsey's personal desires. It is that of a monarch used to having his will performed who is letting that will be known to his chief executive officer: Wolsey. That he instructed the Lord Chancellor and effective head of the Church in England to 'devise, put in ure, and persue' so trivial a matter as the proxy-wooing of an alderman's widow is similarly good evidence that Henry had little time for any pride or presumption on his minister's part. The Cardinal may well have been *alter* (or *ipse*) *rex* in the eyes of Europe's ambassadors, but in the eyes of his King it is clear that he was simply the most effective and trustworthy servant at his disposal. His offices and titles were merely his rewards for that service and the means by which he could conduct it the more effectively.[60]

---

[59] B.L. Cotton MS Titus B I fo. 270 (Ellis, *Letters*, first series, I p. 207 (undated).

[60] That even his Legacy, the one title seemingly exempt from royal pressure, was seen by both King and Cardinal as merely a temporary product of Henry's favour is suggested by Cavendish's account of Wolsey's fall. In the *Life and Death* he details a conversation between Wolsey and Norfolk held after the prorogation of the Blackfriars Court, in which both speak of the legatine honour in the past tense. Wolsey remarked (p. 116) that the Legacy, 'wherein consisted all my honour', was lost, to which the Duke replied 'a strawe for yor legacye / I never esteemed yor honour / the more or higher for that'. Clearly no indication had been received from Rome that the title had been revoked, nor could such indication have had any validity, the title having been confirmed for life in 1524. All that had been removed from

If, as Hall remarks, Wolsey 'bare all the rule aboute ye Kyng, and what he said was obeyed in all places',[61] it was more because he was known to be the major repository of the King's favour than because he overbore or cajoled the Court into obedience. Indeed the latter would not have been possible without the former, as Skelton himself attested, albeit obliquely, in the satires. In *Speke, Parott*, for example, Wolsey's ability to subdue the nobility, to make them 'bere babylles' and to 'stowpe and to play cowchequale', is attributed to his possession of the trump card of royal favour,

> He caryeth a kyng in hys sleve, yf all the world fayle;
> He facithe owte at a flushe with 'shewe, take all'. (429–30)

In *Why Come Ye Nat?* the point is reiterated, only with more vehemence, in the claim that

> He is in such elacyon
> Of his exaltacyon,
> And the supportacyon
> Of our soverayne lorde,
> That, God to recorde,
> He ruleth all at wyll
> Without reason or skyll. (482–8)

Skelton's point seems to be that Wolsey's very eminence, and the fact that he could so flaunt royal favour in the faces of his rivals and dare them to oppose him (symbolised by his defiant taunt 'shew, take all'), inevitably made the Cardinal unpopular. And historians have tended to accept such logic. But the evidence used to support this argument is hardly convincing. Certainly Wolsey was unpopular in certain quarters at certain times. As the previous chapter suggested, his stock amongst the tax-paying community, particularly in London, was extremely low following the imposition of the loans and assessments of 1522. But it is vital that one does not mistake evidence of the (understandable) resentment of certain groups concerning certain specific policies for proof of a more general and more enduring personal unpopularity. Only during those unwelcome financial demands and in their immediate aftermath does one find concrete evidence of Wolsey's unpopularity, such as the account of the London butcher 'who had four pounds a year from the King' who had heard 'from a substantial man, who would abide by it' that Wolsey had informed the King that 'all london wer tratores unto his grasse'.[62] Such personal attacks on the Cardinal as surfaced in the

Wolsey was Henry's favour. Seemingly that was accepted by both Norfolk and Wolsey to be sufficient to strip the latter of all of the titles which it suited the King to remove, whatever their point of origin.

[61] Hall, *Union*, p. 581.
[62] P.R.O. SP1/27/319/21 (*L.P.*, III (ii) 3076) (4 June 1523).

City during 1522–3 were attacks on the loans, not morally motivated criticisms of Wolsey's personal vices or his alleged failings as a churchman. The opposition to Wolsey's demands in the Parliament of 1523 and the Commons' refusal to debate the Subsidy Bill in the Cardinal's presence, stemmed from the same grievances,[63] not from any constitutionalist opposition to Wolsey's regime, or from an attempt by displaced Court nobles to outflank Wolsey's domination of the Council through their clients in the Commons. It was not Wolsey's alleged tyranny which was objected to, as that was largely a myth. Opposition to Wolsey in 1522–3 was primarily opposition to the financial demands for which he was the vehicle, and Skelton's more general, and more moralised, critique of the Cardinal was simply his attempt to bring his considerable literary and poetic resources to bear on the task of producing a satire to capitalise on that opposition and protest. This resentment among the substantial men of the City and elsewhere created a fierce but temporary furore, not, as some critics have suggested, a rising opposition to the Cardinal which would eventually bring about his fall.

If Wolsey appeared genuinely tyrannous it was only to the ambassadors with whom he could afford to indulge his theatrical bent with royal approval. When, for example, Manuel reported on 22 May 1521 that 'it is generally believed that the violent manner in which the Cardinal governs England will produce inconvenience in that country',[64] the impression created in the ambassador's mind was more a product of Wolsey's treatment of his fellow ambassadors than of his supposed persecution of the Duke of Buckingham. It would not, for instance, have alarmed the nobility that Wolsey had 'laid hands upon' the papal Nuncio, Chieregato, in 1516, or that in 1525, infuriated by the collapse of his intrigues with France and the discovery of his letters in Francis I's tents at Pavia, he had placed the Imperial ambassador under house-arrest and prevented him from communicating with his government. Such evidence of the Cardinal's violent temper when frustrated would only appear terrible to the diplomatic community at which it was aimed. His relationship with the noblemen of England seems to have been of another kind, despite Skelton's claims of tyranny.

And yet if one cannot conclude with Skelton that 'thwartyng over them, / He rulyth all the roste / With braggynge and with bost' (*Why Come Ye Nat?*, lines 200–2) neither is it possible entirely to agree with Peter Gwyn that 'what evidence there is suggests that Henry VIII got on well with most of his noblemen, as did his chief servant, Thomas Wolsey',[65] at least not with the second part of his assertion. What Wolsey had with the nobility seems to

---

[63] *L.P.*, III (ii) 3024.
[64] *Sp. Cal. 1509–25*, 336.
[65] P. J. Gwyn, 'Why Come Ye Not To Court: Wolsey and the nobility', p. 20. I am grateful to Peter Gwyn for the opportunity to read and cite this unpublished paper.

have been a practical working relationship, no more. His ability to appear as a good friend to many individuals has already been noted, but it is significant that all of these relationships existed for practical political purposes. Wolsey had no faction *per se*, and no permanent allies among the nobility. He did not need aristocratic friends and so made little effort to cultivate them in anything other than an *ad hoc* fashion.

In essence then, the basic assumption underlying many of Skelton's allegations concerning Wolsey's dominance is quite valid, despite the inaccuracy of many of the arguments which he develops from it. Whilst the Cardinal could command the King's favour and support he could, as the poet asserts, outface anyone. But once that support was removed he could not call on any significant allies. Unlike the King he could not rely on any innate sense of loyalty or fellowship amongst those nobles with whom he shared none of the conventional affinities of blood, class or marriage, and whose alliance he took no pains to cultivate. With Wolsey it was the office and, more significantly, the office as a symbol of royal favour, and not the man, which commanded respect.

Once Henry, perhaps only temporarily, lost faith in Wolsey's integrity and usefulness as an agent, perhaps when the failure of the legatine Court at Blackfriars seemed to reveal the betrayal of a promise to settle the 'Great Matter' entrusted to him, then suddenly he became of no further use to the nobility. Then those few who may have harboured grudges against him or, like lord Darcy, against the clerical domination which they perceived in the administration of the north and for which Wolsey was a convenient symbol, and those others who saw in the King's dissatisfaction with his chief minister the chance to advance their own fortunes, took up the cudgels, whilst the indifference of the majority gave them free rein so to do. Once the man who had got things done, for nobleman as well as monarch, could no longer do so, he was no longer of use, and few felt sufficient affection to defend him. Thus Wolsey became the scapegoat for the royal spleen, and was trampled by the rush to fill the vacuum of vacant royal favour created by his fall. In this analysis there was no prolonged factional intrigue pursued to unseat Wolsey. Simply put: when the chance appeared to replace him those lords who saw the opportunity for self-advancement leapt at it. How else can one explain the sudden reversal in the attitudes of men like Suffolk and More who, prior to 1529, were, to all intents and purposes, content with if not bound to Wolsey, yet suddenly, after the prorogation of the Blackfriars Court, having taken their lead from royal displeasure, made such public display of opposition to him, declaring to the assembled Court that 'there was never Legate nor Cardynall, that dyd good in Englande',[66] and gathering to

---

[66] Hall, *Union*, p. 758. For a detailed exposition of an alternative, factionally driven, view of Wolsey's fall, see E. W. Ives, *Anne Boleyn* (Oxford, 1986), pp. 122–60.

collect and endorse a series of the most savage articles against him? Wolsey's 'enemies' seem to have sprung up from nowhere. As Chapuys reported on 4 September 1529, 'formerly noone dared say a word against him, but now the tables are turned, and his name is on everybody's lips'.[67]

In a personal monarchy the ability to catch the mood of the Monarch was often the surest path to advancement.[68] In 1529–30 those lords ambitious for power and favour would vie with each other to display their loyalty to the fountainhead of those commodities through attacks on Wolsey's mishandling of Blackfriars and other failings, joined by those who acted from simple loyalty, because they thought that that was what Henry wished them to do, as perhaps, just at that moment, he did. Once Wolsey was hounded from the Court, and rewards were to be gained by those who denounced him the loudest, his own voice had little chance of gaining a second hearing, and so the slip at Blackfriars turned into a fatal fall.

In part then, Skelton was correct in his assessment of the nature of and the weaknesses inherent in Wolsey's political power. Indeed the Cardinal's eventual fall could even be described as the vindication of the poet's political judgement. Skelton had anticipated that fall in 1521 and constructed *Speke, Parott* as a means of capitalising on it, and he had spent much of *Collyn Clout* and *Why Come Ye Nat?* predicting it. His only miscalculation was that of timing. He had expected the Cardinal's fatal slip to come at Calais, because he had misread the level of Henry's personal commitment to the Universal Peace which was the ostensible objective of that conference. In the event it was not until Wolsey's failure at Blackfriars, over which Henry's concern was both more personal and markedly more intense that the fall was

---

[67] *Sp. Cal. 1529–30*, 135. For Thomas Howard II's enmity toward Wolsey there is some evidence, mostly from the dubious source of Vergil's *Anglica Historia*, but there is also his own observation from the Tower in 1546 that 'The Cardynall did confes to me at asher that he had gone aboutes XIIII years to have destroyed me' (B.L. Cotton MS Titus B I fos. 99–101. Yet even if this statement, unconfirmed by Cavendish's account of the interview, and made with hindsight in circumstances particularly conducive to paranoia, can be accepted, it is no proof of Howard's active intriguing against Wolsey in the early 1520s, quite the reverse for the Duke's tone implies outraged innocence on his part. Significant perhaps of the state of the Duke's mind at this time is the fact that he suggested that it was at Suffolk's instigation that Wolsey acted against him. He also claimed to have identified Cromwell, Buckingham, Exeter, Lord Sandys and his own nieces Anne Boleyn and Katherine Howard as conspirators against him. The only other statement concerning long-term enemies of Wolsey is provided by Chapuys who referred on 15 November 1530 to Shrewsbury as Wolsey's '*ancien malveuilliant*' (*Sp. Cal. 1529–30*, 492). This, however, need mean no more than 'his enemy who is old', which the sixty-one-year old Earl certainly was. There is no indication that Shrewsbury opposed Wolsey during the 1520s. Indeed Cavendish's account of the Earl's reception of the Cardinal at Sheffield Park during the last stages of his fall indicates rather that the former remained formally well-disposed toward him (Cavendish, Life and Death, pp. 163–4).

[68] Wolsey had followed this path to power himself, by supporting and furthering war with France in 1513. See *L.P.* i 1201, 1247, 1327, 1422; Cavendish, *Life and Death*, p. 12.

to come. Regardless of the numerous miscalculations and wilful obfuscations which litter the satires, Skelton's recognition of the basic truth that Wolsey's dominance of the Court relied purely on his continued ability to satisfy a demanding king was impeccable.

But more important for this study than his recognition of this general principle is the fact that Skelton's specific examination of Wolsey's personality and policies is far from perfect. Yet this is the inevitable consequence of the circumstances of the satires' creation. They were neither a labour of love nor the culmination of a long-prepared political campaign. The decision to write 'against' the Cardinal was reached very quickly during the late summer of 1521, and the poet was forced to utilise what resources he had to hand. This is most readily apparent in *Speke, Parott*, in which his wit and scholarship compensated for his lack of any detailed charges with which to berate his target beyond those provided by the apparent signs of royal disfavour emanating from the Court. By the time he came to write *Collyn Clout* and *Why Come Ye Nat?* he had had more time to prepare, to research the grievances of his intended audience and this is evident at times in the inclusion of better-supported allegations in those texts. Yet there were still large blind spots in the poet's knowledge and clear signs that when he had not the information at hand, or could not risk the implications of scoring a political point against the Cardinal, he was satisfied with registering a purely literary one in the guise of a political comment.

Skelton's satires are not, then, a fair picture of Wolsey. Neither are they evidence of a personal hatred for the Cardinal on the part of the poet. They are a collection of writings aimed at the vilification of Wolsey, written to further the poet's own fortunes. The latter's lack of first-hand knowledge of the higher affairs of the Court, evident in the false assumptions apparent in *Speke, Parott*, in his constant reiteration of basic premises without exemplification in the later texts and, in part at least, in his recourse to literary convention, must also compromise the value of the satires as historical source material for the period. It has been suggested that Skelton was not, strictly speaking, a 'Court Poet', and was not enjoying royal favour in the period 1515–21. Thus it is no longer possible to talk of the satires as intimate and penetrating indictments of Wolsey's public and private lives. Supposedly intimate details there are, but these are often prompted more by extrapolation from the conventional literary types which Skelton drew on than by any actual insight into Wolsey's character or administration. Skelton was conscientious in his gathering of material, particularly for *Why Come Ye Nat?*. But he was too limited by his position to gather much more than what was public knowledge. Hence the fact that a remarkable amount of his evidence is confirmed by ambassadorial reports and in the chronicles of the period which also drew on gossip and rumour. When he did have the material the lessons which he drew from it were often too compromised by the overall antipathetic and satirical intentions of the texts to be of any serious historical value.

It is evident, then, that the use to which Skelton's poety has been put by historians and other commentators in the past has been fundamentally misleading. The lack of support for the satires in 1521–2 is really evidence of how little opposition to Wolsey there was in the period, not of how wide that opposition was. It is easy, after a superficial examination, to see Skelton's verses as adding another link to a consistent chain of anti-Wolsey opinion. They neatly fill the gap between the domestic opposition to Crown foreign policy in the period after 1515 (which can be stretched out and distorted to include the affair of the 'minions', who were said to be 'too partial to the King of France', and the fall of Buckingham who had criticised the cost of the meeting at the Field of the Cloth of Gold), and the furore against the loans and financial initiatives taken between 1522 and 1525. But such apparent continuity is misleading. In 1516 it was Wolsey's fellow Councillors who were most opposed to his costly intrigues against the French and his support for the Emperor Maximillian. Fox, Warham and others (possibly including Suffolk) had, it was said, withdrawn from Court, whilst Shrewsbury was still feigning illness in his locality and Wolsey thus 'perceived that all the grandees of England were opposed to his policy'.[69] But in 1522, and particularly during 1525 during the attempt to raise the Amicable Grant, the nobility, and the Councillors generally, seem to have been loyal to the regime, and to have worked hard in their localities to raise the sums demanded, only protesting once it became obvious that the shire communities were finding it impossible to pay. It was the Commons, the East Anglian cloth workers and their employers the clothiers, the London tax-payers and those of Kent, who reacted, in some cases violently, to the imposition.[70] The two periods of opposition were clearly separate and unconnected. They involved different social groups and concerned entirely unconnected issues. Even if one attempted to suggest the covert involvement of the dukes of Suffolk and Norfolk in the opposition of 1525 (a supposition which runs entirely contrary to the available evidence), Skelton still could not be seen to provide a link for, as has been demonstrated, he was not the mouthpiece of the Howards or of the 'traditional' nobility.

Indeed, paradoxically, as chapter 6 will suggest, by 1525 Skelton, despite his temporary espousal of the grievances of the tax-paying community during 1522, would probably have conveniently forgotten any notion of cri-

[69] Rawdon Brown, *Four Years*, I pp. 252, 264, 307–8.
[70] G. W. Bernard, *War, Taxation and Rebellion in Early Tudor England*, (Brighton, 1986), pp. 76–95, 110–49.

ticising Wolsey, however outrageous his demands, for the poet had finally found his berth on the vessel *The Bowge of Court* as Wolsey's guest and his only thought was to praise the 'most honourable, most mighty, and by far the most reverend father in Christ . . . Lord Thomas', my 'most worthy patron'.[71]

[71] *A Replycacion*, Introduction, trans. Scattergood, p. 372 xxiv.

6

'Obsequious et Loyall': Skelton's political work under Wolsey's patronage

After the completion of *Why Come Ye Nat?*, Skelton's public attitude towards Wolsey changed dramatically. In the space of months the poet ceased his reviling of the Cardinal and began instead to offer him praise and to court his favour. In a Latin epilogue *The Garlande of Laurell*, printed by Richard Faukes on 3 October 1523, one finds not criticism of Wolsey but a contrite dedication of the text,[1]

To his most serene majesty the King, also with the Lord Cardinal, the most honoured legate *a latere*, etc, Go, book, and bow down before the famous King, Henry VIII, and worship him, repeating the rewards of his praise. And in the same way you should greet with reverence the Lord Cardinal legate *a latere* . . .

Such sentiments were repeated in *Howe The Douty Duke of Albany*, written (as what follows will demonstrate) in the second week of November 1523, commended by 'Skelton Laureat: *Obsequious et loyall*. / To my Lorde Cardynals right noble grace' (between lines 523–4), and in the *Replycacion* against the heretical scholars Thomas Bilney and Thomas Arthur, written *c.* 1528. In this last work the reversal of attitude is most clearly demonstrated in the fulsome dedication to[2]

the most honourable, most mighty, and by far the most reverend father in Christ and Lord, Lord Thomas, in the title of St Cecilia priest of the holy Roman Church, the most illustrious legate *a latere*, etc. The laureate Skelton, royal orator, makes known his most humble obeisance with all the reverence due to such a magnificent and worthy prince amongst priests, and the most equitable dispenser of every justice, and, moreover, the most excellent patron of the present little work, etc, to whose most auspicious regard, under the memorable seal of glorious immortality, this little book is commended.

This *volte face* in the poet's attitude makes a nonsense of the Howard-factional interpretations of the satires. And the members of the Howard school have found it impossible to explain convincingly why Skelton should

---

[1] Trans. in Scattergood, p. 512.   [2] *Ibid.*, p. 517.

have suddenly 'defected' at this point. Was he frightened off, brought to accept Wolsey as the lesser of two evils in the face of the rise of Protestant heresy; or did the withdrawal of the Duke of Norfolk to his estates in 1523 leave the poet with no alternative but to sue for peace with his erstwhile enemy? These and other explanations have been offered, with varying degrees of plausibility.[3] But if, as this study has argued, the satires ought to be seen as prompted rather by Skelton's lack of patronage than otherwise, there is no dilemma. Skelton wrote against Wolsey for opportunist reasons; not from any strong conviction in a cause, but in order to attract patronage. And when Wolsey offered him that patronage, he promptly accepted it. There was no barrier, other than initial surprise at the offer perhaps, which prevented him from so doing.

It is not possible to state with certainty why Wolsey should have made such an offer. But the analysis of the political background to *Why Come Ye Nat?* offered in the previous chapter raises a number of suggestions. With that text, the last of the satires against the Cardinal, the poet seems at last to have reached a wider audience and to have taken up the genuine grievances of the citizens of London against the forced loans of 1522 and given them a voice in a powerful invective which 'thousands quote[d]'. It is impossible either to confirm or to refute Skelton's assessment of his own readership from external evidence. As both of the later satires circulated entirely in manuscript form at this time one can know nothing of their numbers or degree of circulation. The internal evidence, however, argues strongly for a wider popular success for these two poems than that enjoyed by *Speke, Parott*. Whether Wolsey himself was aware of Skelton's attacks, and, if so, at what point in the series, is another point which requires greater investigation than the available evidence allows. It is conceivable that the Cardinal was entirely ignorant of the poet's activities and chose to employ him in 1523 purely as a result of his work in 1513. Yet what evidence there is militates against such a possibility. It seems entirely possible that Wolsey was unaware of the existence of *Speke, Parott*, which circulated in limited numbers, and was largely ignored whilst he was absent in Calais. But that he was aware of, and indeed concerned at, the contents of *Collyn Clout* is suggested by Francis Thynne's assertion that the chief cause of Wolsey's enmity toward his father was that he had 'furthered' Skelton to write *Collyn Clout* at his house in Erith. And that he was ignorant of the apparently even more popular and volatile *Why Come Ye Nat?* seems extremely unlikely. With this last text it seems that the poet became a potential nuisance to the Crown, notably at a time when the latter, preoccupied with providing for costly military cam-

[3] Edwards, pp. 222–5; M. Pollet, *John Skelton: Poet of Tudor England*, trans. from the French by J. Warrington (Lewisberg, 1971), pp. 145–8; M. J. Tucker, 'The ladies in Skelton's Garland of Laurel', *R.Q.*, 22 (1969), p. 344.

paigns, and with financial problems at home, had no time for nuisances which might aggravate its problems.

It should be no surprise, therefore, that Wolsey chose to act *when* he did. That he acted in the *manner* in which he did is of more interest. For one might have expected him to have arranged some corrective punishment for the poet of the sort which Polydore Vergil or Baron North suffered for their critical writings. Yet Wolsey chose to buy rather than to enforce Skelton's silence. Rather than play the tyrant, he chose the path of least resistance to his desired end, which both suggests an element of shrewdness in his appraisal of the poet's motivation and further supports the argument that the Cardinal was a skilled manager of men rather than an intemperate dictator.

That Skelton accepted such an offer also underlines the assertion that it was calculation and a desire for self-advancement which lay at the heart of the poet's campaign of invective, not any more genuine concern for his theme. He seems to have swiftly considered the advantages to be gained from aligning himself with his erstwhile target, compared them with the less certain gains to be won by continuing his wooing of patronage from the City, and promptly thrown in his lot with Wolsey. Thus a bargain seems to have been struck between the poet and the Cardinal soon after the completion of *Why Come Ye Nat?*, by which the former agreed to terminate his vitriolic satiric campaign against the latter, and in return receive some measure of the patronage and recognition which he craved.

Wolsey's offer seems to have involved three distinct elements. First and most obviously there was clearly the promise of a second clerical living for the poet. So much is made evident by the latter's references to such a promise in his subsequent poems. For the dedicatory portion of *The Garlande*, cited above, continues to 'beg him [Wolsey] to remember the prebend he promised to commit to me, and give me cause to hope for the pledge of his favour',[4] whilst *The Douty Duke* concludes with the lines,

> Go, lytell quayre, apace,
> In moost humble wyse,
> Before his noble grace
> That caused you to devise
> This lytel enterprise;
> And hym moost lowly pray,
> In his mynde to comprise,
> Those wordes his grace dyd saye
> Of an ammas gray. (523–31)

This promise of an 'ammas gray' may never have been fulfilled, for no evidence of such a preferment is extant. It is possible that no suitable post became available. But it seems more probable that Wolsey simply deferred

----

[4] Trans. in Scattergood, p. 512.

the satisfaction of Skelton's desire in order to ensure his continued loyalty. While the poet continued to hope for the financial security and official recognition which Wolsey held tantalisingly before him, his loyalty to the Cardinal and to the Crown could be guaranteed. Should Wolsey have actually provided such a living he could not have been certain that future events would not prompt a renewed outbreak of poetic invective.

But if Wolsey had good reason not to satisfy Skelton in the first part of their bargain, he seems swiftly to have complied with the other two clauses. These seem to have involved the opportunity to publish his self-justifying masterpiece *The Garlande of Laurell* through the presses of Faukes, a printer often employed by the Crown, and the promise to provide official commissions for the poet's work in the future. The fact that *The Garlande* should have been published during 1523, at most eleven months after the completion of *Why Come Ye Nat?*, strongly suggests that the agreement with the Cardinal was the crucial factor in the termination of Skelton's barren decade at the printers. This suggestion is further strengthened by an examination of the text of *The Garlande* which is, as the previous chapters have indicated, largely an allegorical celebration of the poet's career and genius, in which he (over)compensates for years of neglect with a remarkable display of self-eulogy. Throughout the poem there are references to the poet's lack of publication and preferment, which clearly imply that Skelton intended to make good the lost time henceforward.[5]

Having provided the poet with the opportunity to publish his *apologia*, Wolsey did not need to wait long before he could begin to fulfil the final part of their bargain. It may have been that the Cardinal had not seriously intended to patronise the poet himself, on behalf of the Crown, but meant simply to use the possibility of such patronage, like the offer of a prebend, to ensure Skelton's future good behaviour. But, whether fortuitously for the poet or not, the opportunity for Wolsey to call on his singular talent for popular invective arose almost immediately.

In 1513 Skelton had shown his aptitude for writing ribald vernacular propaganda with his verses on the victory at Flodden. And the evidence of *Why Come Ye Nat?* suggests that he had demonstrated again in 1522 that he could capture the attention of a popular audience with his political invective. Both of these talents were to be called upon in November 1523 when Wolsey commissioned the poet to write an invective against the Scots Regent, John Stuart, duke of Albany, on the occasion of his abortive invasion of England.

---

[5] Fame rebukes Skelton for being 'wonder slake' in the custom of poets, which is 'them selfe to embesy with all there corage / So that there workis myght famously be sene' (lines 64–72). See also lines 82–4 for reference to Skelton's 'dum mouthe' and failure to 'gloryously publisshe his matter', and lines 118–9. The entire logic of the allegory involves Skelton making good Fame's ignorance of his writings through the revelation of the number of works which he has written unbeknown to her (hence the bibliography contained in the text).

As what follows will demonstrate, Wolsey seems to have played a significant part in the creation of *The Douty Duke*, one of the most neglected of Skelton's so-called minor works. He did not simply commission the poet to produce a ribald rhyme suitable for the occasion. At the very least he provided detailed instructions concerning the subject matter to be treated and the points which he required to be made within the text, and he may well have gone as far as to make available to Skelton extracts from official documents relating to the Scottish campaign. Why the Cardinal should have taken such an interest in the project will be considered below.

Before examining the details of the text, however, it is important to note its outward form. It is remarkably similar in terms of style to the last two satires against Wolsey, *Collyn Clout* and *Why Come Ye Nat?*. Skelton is still posing as the pseudo-prophet-cum-gossip, the hybrid purveyor of news and revelation, speaking out in the short 'Skeltonic' lines ideal for public performance and popular consumption. That Wolsey should have commissioned such a work when he wished to have a point publicly made is a further testimony to the popularity of Skelton's later satiric style. If the Cardinal felt that the best method of broadcasting propaganda was through Skelton's verse, that is a sure sign that such verse had proven popular and that the later Wolsey satires had found their mass audience. With *The Douty Duke*, however, the message which that verse carries has been altered. Instead of the forebodings of doom and the declaration of grievances crying out for redress which had been his burden in the earlier invectives, the tidings which Skelton now offers are, he asserts, glad and worthy of celebration. Gone is the lone voice in the wilderness with its prophetic cry of

> All noble men of this take hede,
> And believe it as your crede. (*Why Come Ye
> Nat?*, 1–2)

Instead one hears the ringing tones of the town-crier;

> Rejoyse, Englande,
> And understande
> These tidinges newe,
> Whiche be as trewe
> As the gospell. (*The Douty Duke*, 1–5)

As will become apparent, all is not exactly as it appears in the text, but the town-crier analogy is a valid one. For here Skelton is, for the first time since 1513, truly performing the role of *Orator Regius*, speaking to the populace as the mouthpiece of the Crown, and passing on the latest news almost immediately that it reached London.

As Skelton states, it was Wolsey 'That caused you to devise / This lytell enterprise' (lines 526–7). But why should the Cardinal have wished to become involved with such a 'lytell enterprise'? What was it which prompted him to commission such a work? In the past commentators have been reluctant to grasp this particular nettle; being in the main content to suggest that the occasion of an English victory such as the repulse of Albany's assault upon Wark Castle was in itself sufficient to warrant celebratory verses, as was the case in 1513. Yet, even if it was true, such an observation would beg too many questions. If this victory over the Scots, achieved after an extremely limited engagement and comparable in terms of casualties with many of the continuing series of border raids by both sides which marked this period, was worth celebrating in verse, why were not the other significant military campaigns of the period? What of those of Surrey and Suffolk in France during 1522 and 1523, or the diplomatic triumphs such as the Treaty of London of 1518, the Field of Cloth of Gold of 1520, or the Calais conference of 1521? What becomes readily apparent from a study of such 'triumphs' as these is that Wolsey was concerned with the realities of the situation, not with any trumpeting of the achievements after the event. Why then should the Cardinal have been interested in vaunting the victory at Wark, if Skelton's text was simply the victory poem which previous commentators have alleged? A closer reading of the text, and a comparison between its details and its historical context serves to answer such questions. For on such a reading it becomes apparent that *The Douty Duke* is, despite appearances, not a victory poem at all but was designed for quite another purpose. To understand the nature of the poem, and the reasons for its commission it is necessary to look primarily, not at the siege of Wark itself, but at the events which preceded and immediately followed it, and at how they were perceived both on the borders and in London.

The figure of John Stuart, duke of Albany, is the key to any understanding of Wolsey's role in Skelton's poem. An earlier attempt to invade England during September 1522 had illustrated his ability to distract English attention from her continental concerns. But this was not the limit of the threat which he posed to English foreign policy. For not only did Albany have temporary control of Scottish policy-making whilst he held the Regency, but, as the nephew of James III, he was also himself heir presumptive to the Scottish Crown. Thus only the life of the boy King James V stood between Albany and the throne, and as Regent he controlled that frail life in his own hands. Hence the recurrent English concern for the young King's personal safety whenever Albany entered the country, and hence the continued efforts of Wolsey and the English commanders in the north, such as lord Dacre, to have the keeping of his person placed in the hands of the Regent's rivals. For Albany's succession would have ended the Anglo-French rivalry for the disputed title of protector of Scotland, and turned Scotland into a French satellite, which would bring with it the prospect of a permanent French presence

on the British mainland. With Albany on the Scottish throne any attempt by
England to intervene in Europe against French interests would be rendered
impotent.[6] Hence the anxiety with which the English government viewed
Albany's return to Scotland on 24 September 1523. Clearly Albany's presence in Scotland posed a serious long-term threat to English security and to
Henry's ambitions to play a role in European diplomacy. And yet, while he
remained merely Regent, he could not entirely fulfil such potential as he possessed. He needed to secure the loyalty of the Scots magnates before he could
enjoy in practice the powers to which his position theoretically entitled him,
and the English were determined to prevent him from so doing. This explains
the intense activity on both sides of the border during the autumn of 1523.

From the moment of his arrival in Scotland Albany had been conducting a
potent anti-English propaganda campaign, the main thrust of which was
aimed at convincing the Scots that a war on English soil, or at least a single,
decisive battle ('some signal blow'[7]) could be fought and won. This was not
simply aimless bravado on the part of the Regent, the 'bragge and boost' and
'waste wynde' (lines 207–8) of Skelton's poem, but an essential part of
Albany's campaign. D. M. Head may well be correct in his assertion that,
when Albany arrived in Scotland with French troops and funds, Queen Margaret's 'flimsy [pro-English] party collapsed at once, and the possibility of an
effective invasion under Albany's leadership began to dawn upon the
English',[8] but possibility and reality are far from identical, and Albany was
fully aware of the difficulties which faced him if he wished to raise a force
which would cross the border in convincing strength.[9] During the Duke's
absence in France the French ambassador, Langeac, had repeatedly spoken
of the difficulties of 'keeping the Scots faithful to France' in the face of
English efforts to sever the 'auld alliance', and Francis I had thought it
necessary to write in person to the Scottish Estates on 30 May 1523, urging
them to continue in their resolve to remain on 'the accustomed path' and to
beware 'the ambiguous promises of England, calculated to deceive [them]'.[10]
Prior to Albany's arrival, as the contemporary historian Buchanan noted,
Scotland was in a 'wretched state', with 'the nobles at variance with each

---

[6] For the benefits which the French government saw in such a succession, note the reaction of
     their representatives in Rome to the false rumour that James V had died and Albany
     succeeded to the throne in December 1521. 'The French rejoice very much at this news',
     reported Imperial ambassador Manuel to Charles V, 'and threaten all the world', *Sp. Cal.
     1509–25*, 368.

[7] J. Aikman (trans.), *The History of Scotland of George Buchanan*, 4 vols. (Edinburgh, 1827)
     (hereafter, Buchanan) p. 287.

[8] D. M. Head, 'Henry VIII's Scottish policy: a reassessment', *The Scottish Historical Review*,
     LXI (1982), pp. 1–24, 17.

[9] See G. Donaldson, *Scotland: James V to James VIII*, The Edinburgh History of Scotland
     series, (Edinburgh, 1965), III, pp. 35–6.

[10] R. K. Hannay and D. Hay (eds.), *The Letters of James V, 1513–42* (Edinburgh, 1954), pp.
     93–4.

other' over Scottish support for France. Thus, even if the pro-English faction did dissolve as swiftly and completely as Head suggests, the difficulties facing Albany were still significant if he was to turn apathy, reluctance to fight and even Francophobia, into active support for a war. Hence his immediate instigation of a campaign of propaganda in speeches and proclamations, in order to reinforce and capitalise on the boost to national morale provided by his appearance in Scotland. As Buchanan records,[11]

The news of the regent's arrival diffused great joy among his friends, confirmed the wavering and deterred many from joining the English alliance who were inclined to espouse it. Having sent his warlike stores by the Clyde to Glasgow, he reviewed his army there, and issued a proclamation for the nobility to meet him at Edinburgh, where, in a flaming oration, he praised their constancy in adhering to their ancient league, and their prudence in refusing the perfidious promises of the English, and expatiated on the affection, and liberality, of the French King towards the Scottish nation, and exhorted them to lay aside their private animosities, and, now that foreign assistance had arrived, avenge their injuries and check, by some signal blow, the insolence of the enemy.

As Edward Hall reports the oration, Albany encouraged the Scots to[12]

together revenge the hurtes done to us and our countrey: And I on myne honor shal go with you, and therefore I have brought with me bothe treasure, men and artillerie into this realme. I thinke not but we shall do that all Christendome shall speake of our noble conquest.

Such rhetoric was evidently necessary if the reluctant Scots lords were to be persuaded to follow Albany into battle. And battle quickly became the only option short of complete withdrawal from the realm once it became clear that Henry and Wolsey would not countenance a peaceful settlement whilst Albany remained in Scotland. The negotiations conducted between the Lord Regent and the English Crown between September and October 1523 identified the English position unequivocally.[13] Thus Albany was forced to choose between battle at a time of his own choosing, or at a moment more convenient to the English, who were, as a prelude to that moment, pursuing a diplomatic policy designed to detach the Scots lords from his side. The events of November 1523 indicate that he chose the former option and determined to win the support of the Scottish nobility by offering them a successful military campaign in England.

Evidently if Albany was to raise any force of considerable size, he needed to convince the Scots, first that an invasion was in their own interests,[14] and

---

11 Buchanan, p. 287.
12 Edward Hall, *The Union of the Two Noble Families of Lancaster and York*, ed. Henry Ellis (London, 1809), p. 665.
13 *L.P.*, III (ii) 3423, 3438, 3443, 3447, 3449, 3461.
14 Hence his stress on the need to avenge the 'great murders, slaughters and burnynges done by the Englisemen', Hall, *Union*, p. 665.

second that a victory could be achieved at little cost as the English were either too weak or too distracted to resist them effectively. He also needed to convince them quickly in order that a force might swiftly be raised to invade at once, both as the campaign season was rapidly disappearing and as his limited resources would soon be exhausted.[15] Hence Albany's need to inspire the Scots through potent propaganda; the 'boasts' of which Skelton was to make so much, which, as Surrey observed, convinced and cajoled the Scots lords into line.[16]

News of Albany's rhetoric, and of its effectiveness, began to reach Wolsey early in October, and clearly gave him cause for concern. On 23 October he informed Surrey that it was only the Regent's 'bragges' which had prevented the Scots lords from suing for peace rather than launching an invasion. And, after the unsuccessful siege of Wark, the undoing of all Albany's 'greate preparacions, bragges and bostes' was a major theme of the Cardinal's correspondence.[17] Clearly a major reason for Wolsey's commissioning of Skelton to write *The Douty Duke* was the need to counter the effects of Albany's propaganda as it filtered into England. Yet it was not simply that the Duke was weakening the morale of the English forces with his exaggerated claims for Scottish martial prowess and desire for revenge. Wolsey was well assured on that point, for the morale of the troops along the borders was exemplary.[18] The Cardinal's concern was more specific and involved more than a simple fear for the outcome of the fighting along the border. His major fears seem to have been two-fold: for, in roughly equal parts, the internal security of the realm and the honour of its King. For a prime element in Albany's propaganda was the claim that Richard de la Pole, self-styled duke of Suffolk and pretender to the English throne was involved in his plans and would secretly enter England to stir up insurrection and seize the Crown.

On his arrival in Scotland Albany had claimed, as Surrey informed Wolsey on 27 September,[19]

that Richard Delapole, calling hym his cousyn the noble Duke of Suffolk, departed from hym upon the see with XXX sayle of great ships full of men, and should have landed in Inglond upon Mondaye last, where he shuld have somoche helpe of Englishmen that he shuld not be resisted.

At this point Surrey was inclined to discount such claims: 'If any part [of] hy saying bee true', he wrote, 'your Grace is advertised thereof or nowe: but I neyther believe that he is landed, nor that he shalhave any assistance'. By 19 October, however, his despatches contain no such confident denials. He

---

[15] Note Surrey's report of 2 October, B.L. Cotton MS Caligula B VI fo. 284 (*St. P.*, IV 23).
[16] *St. P.*, IV 26.
[17] *L.P.*, III (ii) 3461; *St. P.*, VI 70.
[18] See Surrey's report of 19 October, *St. P.*, IV 26.
[19] B.L. Cotton MS Caligula B VI fo. 313 (*St. P.*, IV 21).

simply noted of Albany on that date that 'contynuall boste he doth make, that Richard de la Pole woll either come to joyne with hym, orels not faile to lande in England, by that tyme he shalbe come to the Border of England', whilst in a hasty postscript to the same report he remarked that 'suerly either the seid Duke doth mervelously dissymell with Scotland, orels Richard de la pole hath vi or vii M men redy to invade this realme'.[20] Four days later even Surrey was clearly convinced that there was some substance in such claims. For he warned Wolsey that 'He [Albany] doth make grete booste off the landyng of Richard de la Pole in Scotland assewryng the lords off Scotland that he shall have great help in this realme'. More specifically de la Pole was said to be making for the Welsh coast. Surrey therefore advised the Cardinal to instruct Sir Rice Ap Thomas to look to the defences of the principality, and to take precautions himself against potential insurrectionaries.[21]

yff your Grace know any man suspect I doubt not ye woll provyde that he shall not shyp away. I know no man lyvyng that I shuld mystrust, but he [Albany] hath spoken so largely and dayle doth, that I know not what to thynk.

Clearly Wolsey had cause to fear the potency of Albany's rhetoric if it could cause the English commander in the field to alter his opinion and to give credence to the Duke's claims, particularly as that rhetoric raised the spectre of the Yorkist pretender Richard de la Pole.

From the comfortable perspective of historical analysis it is possible to dismiss de la Pole as an insignificant threat to the Tudor dynasty, but to Wolsey he would hardly have appeared the paper tiger which hindsight paints him. His credentials as a pretender were certainly impressive. As the seventh son of John de la Pole, second duke of Suffolk (d.1492) and Elizabeth of York, sister of Edward IV, his claim to the English throne was clearly more valid than that of the Yorkist impostors of the previous reign, Simnel and Warbeck, who had posed no little threat to the early Tudor monarchy. And with foreign support, such as the backing from the French which he had been receiving since 1513, his potential as a focus for internal disaffection and residual Yorkist sympathies could not be ignored. Certainly the French were prepared to utilise the self-styled 'White Rose' for all that he was worth to discomfort Henry and England when it suited them. Consequently the prospect of a French-backed invasion proved a serious worry to the English Crown. Throughout 1522 rumours abounded in England and on the continent that an invasion led by de la Pole and financed from Paris was imminent, or had already occurred.[22] More serious still were the rumours that de la Pole would find substantial support within England once he had launched

---

[20] *St. P.*, IV 26.
[21] B.L. Cotton MS Caligula B VI fo. 289 (H. Ellis (ed.), *Letters Illustrative of English History*, 3 vols. (London, 1824, 1827, 1846), I p. lxxxi).
[22] *L.P.*, III (ii) 2708, 2340, 2707, 2870, 2755, 2768, 2798, 2799, 2800, 2856, 2869.

his invasion; rumours which were founded not only in Albany's rhetoric but also in more objective evidence. Early in 1523 the arrest and interrogation of one Simon Jones, an agent in de la Pole's employ, raised the disturbing possibility that the households of the English lords Stafford and Derby might be sympathetic to the pretender's cause and an embryonic conspiracy might be forming in the Low Countries, whilst in September of that year it was widely accepted in Scotland, as Queen Margaret informed Surrey, that de la Pole would find adherents in England.[23] In the atmosphere of doubt created by such rumours it was not sensible to ignore the possibility of an insurrection. More particularly it was not possible to counter Albany's claims that England was a nation ripe for defeat simply by contemptuous diplomatic indifference. This was the context in which Wolsey provided Skelton with his first Crown commission since 1513.

Wolsey was, moreover, in the midst of something approaching a financial crisis during the summer and autumn of 1523. He had already seen the demands of the Crown for a subsidy of 4s in the pound to support the war dramatically resisted in the Parliament of April to August of that year by 'the grettiste and soreste hold in the lower house . . . that ever was sene . . . in any parliamente',[24] and may also have heard the policy of war with France itself comprehensively criticised in a stinging speech from the Commons benches.[25] By autumn he was attempting to raise by 'Anticipation' (a term, as Hall observes, 'new to ye cominaltie') 'the whole subside before graunted out of hand and bifore the dayes of payment', in an attempt to circumvent Parliament's decision to grant the sum over four years[26] and thus support the two costly armies in France and on the Scottish borders. If Albany's claims of potential insurrection and threats of the arrival of de la Pole had found credence among a potentially disaffected populace, the least that the Cardinal could have feared was resistance to the Crown's latest demands and thus the collapse of those campaigns for want of supply. Hence there was a premium on the swift countering of such claims and the defence of Henry's slighted honour, not in a costly and slow-to-prepare pageant series or disguising, which were the normal vehicles for Crown propaganda, but in quickly prepared form which could, if necessary, be made available to far wider audiences. This was the service which Skelton was to provide.

With such a context in mind, a close reading of the text makes clear the

[23] *Ibid.*, 2769, 3368.
[24] B.L. Cotton MS Titus B I fo. 112 (Ellis, *Letters*, first series I, p. lxxix).
[25] R. B. Merriman, *The Life and Letters of Thomas Cromwell*, 2 vols. (Oxford, 1902), I, pp. 30–44 (*L.P.*, III (ii) 2958). Even if this speech was never read in the Commons, the fact of its drafting suggests a mood of criticism towards the cost of the French war among at least a substantial minority of the members. It is unlikely that such a speech could have been conceived in an atmosphere of wholehearted support for the war.
[26] Hall, *Union*, p. 672.

real nature of Skelton's commission from Wolsey. It was not simply to provide a partisan narrative of the unsuccessful siege of Wark by the Scots, but, more specifically, to refute Albany's grandiose claims, to deflate his reputation through ridicule, to defend Henry's honour, and to proclaim, and thus reinforce, national morale in the face of attempts to disrupt it. It would be easy to dismiss the poem as a simple narrative, embellished and enlivened with a plethora of racial insults, as other commentators have done, were it not for the fact that the bulk of the larger, second portion of the text is concerned, not with the Scottish invasion, but with the nature and qualities of Henry's kingship. This imbalance of material is far from accidental and reveals much about the true purpose of the text.

Before considering that second portion of the text, however, it is important to examine the earlier, overtly narrative section, and its treatment of the siege of Wark Castle, which was the occasion rather than the true subject of the poem. What follows will reveal just how specific was the knowledge which Skelton possessed of events at Wark, and how clearly his poem conformed to the information available to and the opinions expressed by the work's patron, Wolsey. Furthermore a close comparison of the state of knowledge revealed in the text with the extant correspondence of the campaign will not only reveal just how close and efficiently organised the co-operation between poet and patron must have been, it will also enable the poem to be dated more effectively than has hitherto been possible.

As this is a narrative designed to denigrate and degrade an enemy, a far greater emphasis is placed on Albany's retreat from Wark than on the siege which preceded it. Yet the details of that siege remain illuminating for the present study owing to their correspondence with the information provided in Surrey's first report of the event, written from a camp two miles from the castle on the night of 3 November 1523.[27] Skelton's account of the heroics of the commander of the castle, Sir William Lisle, and of his garrison, for example, seem to have been taken directly from the Earl's despatch. The poet asserts that Albany is to be reviled,

> For Sir William Lyle
> Within shorte whyle,
> That valiavnt kuyght,
> Putte you to flyght
> By his valyaunce.
> Two thousande of Fraunce
> There he putte backe
> To your great lacke
> And utter shame
> Of your Scottysshe name (38–47)

---

[27] B.L. Cotton MS Caligula B VI fo. 301 (Ellis, *Letters*, first series, I p.lxxxii), Surrey to Henry VIII).

Though he condenses the action from two stormings, first of the outer then of the inner ward, into one, the details of the engagement as described by the poet correspond remarkably with Surrey's report of how,[28]

at iij a cloke at aftir none, the water of Twede being soo high that it could not be riden, the Duke sent over ij M Frenche men in bootis to gif assault to the place, who with force entred the bas court, and by Sir William Lizle captain of the Castell with a hundred with him were right manfully defended by the space of one houre and an half, without suffring theym tentre the Inner ward: but fynally the seid Frenchemen entred the inner warde, which perceived by the seid Sir William and his company, frely set upon theym and not onely drove theym oute of the inner warde, but also oute of the uttir warde, and slewe of the seid Frenche men X personys.

That Skelton could name the Captain of Wark, and was able to describe a battle lasting only one and a half hours as being conducted 'Within shorte whyle' need not in itself be significant. One might dismiss the former as common knowledge and the latter as an obvious propaganda point made additionally attractive to the poet by the rhyme which it provides for 'Lyle'. But the observation that the force which attempted to storm the castle consisted of 'Two thousande of Fraunce' is more significant. Not only does this figure correspond exactly with the estimate in Surrey's despatch but, more importantly, only in this one document does the Earl specify an enemy strength of 'ij M Frenche men'. Before 3 November the estimates which he had sent to Wolsey had suggested a far larger contingent of Frenchmen in the Duke's army. On 27 September he had heard a rumour, confirmed by 'moo then XX dyvers espies' to the effect that Albany had brought 8,000 men with him from France. Surrey was, however, reluctant to accept such a figure and confided to Wolsey that 'I believe not the nombre to bee so great, for me think they shuld not bee carried in soo fewe ships, onles they were gretter than any maye be brought unto that haven'.[29] By 2 October the evidence of three further spies had forced him to revise his opinion, as 'all the seid espies saye he [Albany] hath brought with hym VIII M fotemen: II M men of armys, and CCC light horsis'.[30] Conversely within two days *after* the relief of Wark, having had time to collect more accurate information from the actual participants, Surrey's estimate of the number and nationality of the troops involved in the storming had been reduced to 'above 1000 Frenchemen and 500 Scottis'.[31]

It is conceivable, of course, that Skelton was aware of Surrey's second, lower, estimate but chose to ignore it in favour of the more dramatic, earlier,

---

[28] B.L. Cotton MS Caligula B VI fo. 304.
[29] B.L. Cotton MS Caligula B VI fo. 313 (*St. P.*, IV 21).
[30] B.L. Cotton MS Caligula B fo. 284 (*St. P.*, IV 23).
[31] *St. P.*, IV XXVIII, Surrey to Wolsey, 5 November 1523. By 4 December Wolsey was exaggeratedly referring to an army of '3,000 Frenchmen and 1,500 Scots' in despatches to the Imperial Court, *St P.*, VI 70.

figure. But it seems more plausible that the poet's 'tidinges newe / which be as trewe / As the gospel' were just that, the latest and truest account of the engagement which he could provide. Thus, at the very least, the poet's use of the phrase 'Two thousande of Fraunce' indicates that he had read, or was familiar with the contents of, Surrey's despatch of 3 November, for otherwise he could not have so accurately matched the Earl's estimate of the strength of the enemy. He cannot have conjured the figure from nowhere. For guesswork to have hit on the same figure as Surrey's report is possible, if unlikely. For Skelton to have, by sheer coincidence, similarly forecast that the enemy force consisted entirely of Frenchmen, when one might have expected a considerable contingent of Scotsmen, is virtually unthinkable. The army itself was, after all, predominantly Scottish. Neither could the poet have had an independent source of information from Wark. If he had, one would have expected his figures to have matched, not Surrey's first guess, but the more accurate assessment provided on 5 November, which would have made it clear that Scotsmen *were* involved (a fact which would have ideally suited the anti-Scots tone of Skelton's poem). Clearly only Surrey's despatch can have been the ultimate source of the poet's information, a fact which reveals the extent of Wolsey's involvement in the satiric project, as it could only have been the Cardinal's hand which passed on the relevant documents (or summaries) to the poet.

Further information within the text serves to confirm such conclusions concerning its creation. The account of Albany's retreat from Wark can also be traced back to Surrey's report of 3 November, and to a supplementary account written the following day. 'Your chefe cheftayne, / Voyde of all brane', Skelton taunts,

> Duke of Albany,
> Than shamefully
> He reculed backe,
> To his great lacke,
> When he herde tell
> That my Lorde Amrell
> Was comyng downe
> To make hym frowne
> And to make hym lowre (48–58)

It is a point which he repeats on two further occasions.

> Thou hast to lytell myght
> Agaynst Englande to fyght.
> Thou art a graceles wyght
> To put thy selfe to flyght.
> A vengeaunce and dispight
> On the must nedes lyght

> That durst nat byde the sight
> of my Lorde Amrell,
> Of chivalry the well,
> Of knighthode the floure
> In every marciall shoure,
> The noble Erle of Surrey,
> That put the in suche fray.
> Thou durst no felde derayne,
> Nor no batayle mayntayne,
> Against our stronge captaine;
> But thou ran home agayne
> For feare thou shoulde be slayne
> Lyke a Scottyshe keteryng. (230–48)

> Wherto shuld I more speke
> Of suche a farly freke,
> Of suche an horne keke,
> Of suche an bolde captayne
> That dare nat turne agayne,
> Nor durst nat crak a worde,
> Nor durst nat drawe his swerde
> Agaynst the lyon white,
> But ran away quyte? (302–10)

Again the details behind all this seem clearly to have been taken from Surrey's account of 3 November, in which he reported that, once the Captain of Wark had driven the 'ij M Frenche men' from the base court,[32]

incontinent the seid Sir William advertised me of the said assaulte, desiering too have reskue this daye, or else the place wold be no lenger kepte, whereof I being advertised by thre a clok this mornyng avaunced forward with the hole army, by the breke of daye. And the Duke hering that I cam towards hym toke away his ordynance and in likewise departed hymself with his hoole company.

Not only does the poet's account of the retreat from Wark further endorse the assertion that he must have been working from the account provided by Surrey on 3 November and that the vast majority of the substantial subject matter and interpretative passages in the text were selected, not by Skelton himself, but by his patron, Wolsey, it also includes a new piece of information which allows one to date the poem with some degree of accuracy. For in two of the three accounts of Albany's retreat the poet adds the additional assertion that that retreat was conducted under cover of darkness. As he observes of the Duke,

> For all his crake and bost,
> Lyke a cowarde knyght
> He fledde and durst nat fyght;
> *He ran away by night.* (68–71, my italics)

[32] B.L. Cotton MS Caligula B VI fo. 304 (Ellis, *Letters*, first series, I, p. lxxxii).

The point is reiterated in the observation that,

> He ran away by nyght
> In the owle flyght
> Lyke a cowarde knyght. (311–13)

Now for all the conciseness of Surrey's report of 3 November, there is nothing there to indicate that Albany's retreat was conducted by night. Indeed the impression to be gained from the Earl's account is rather that the Scots withdrew from Wark by day, or more specifically in the early morning. For, as Surrey stated, he was reached by Lisle's messenger 'by thre a clok this mornyng' (Tuesday) and 'avaunced foreward with the hole army *by the breke of daye*. And the Duke hering that I cam towards hym . . . departed hymself with his hoole company.'[33] This reading is supported by the testimony of Buchanan, a participant at the siege, who in his *History* observes that 'the regent when he perceived the Scots averse to war, and at the same time receiving certain information that the English were advancing with an army much more numerous than his own . . . he decamped on the 11 November to Eccles, a monastery about 6 miles distant'.[34] Clearly Buchanan's assigning the retreat to 11 November is a mistaken recollection (or a mistranscription of 11 for an original ii). But whereas it is possible that the historian could have muddled the exact date of the withdrawal, it is unlikely that he would have forgotten whether it was conducted in light or darkness. Thus it is surely significant that he makes no mention of a night march from Wark. Where such a march does enter his narrative is on the following day, when Albany withdrew, not from Wark to Eccles monastery, but from Eccles towards Edinburgh, as news reached him of Surrey's continued advance. As the historian relates, having reached Eccles Albany continued to withdraw as, from 'thence, at the third watch, by nocturnal march, he retreated to Louder'. This account is confirmed by Surrey's letter to Henry VIII of 4 November from Lowick village, in which he stated that the Prioress of Coldstream, an English agent, had told him that Albany had left Eccles *at midnight*, taking his ordinance with him and was now 'clearly gone'.[35] This is the first means by which news of a night withdrawal could have reached London, and so is the earliest document from which Skelton could have gleaned the information included in his text. Hence the very earliest moment that the poem could have been completed was on the receipt of Surrey's second, supplementary, battle report of 4 November, which would not have reached London until at very least 10 November, allowing six days for the

---

[33] B.L. Cotton MS Caligula B I fo. 307. My italics.
[34] Buchanan, p. 288.
[35] B.L. Cotton MS Caligula B II fo. 169 (*L.P.*, III (ii) 3508).

journey,[36] but which (as will become apparent) seems not to have arrived until a slightly later date.

Is it possible, however, given that Skelton describes not the retreat from Eccles but that from Wark as being 'by night', that this was a simple piece of guesswork on the poet's part designed to reflect further shame on Albany's action and so need not have been influenced by the official documents available to Wolsey in Westminster? This might have been a possibility were it not that Wolsey himself seems to have been the source of Skelton's confusion. For on 4 December the former stated in his account of the siege prepared for transmission to Charles V that Albany's withdrawal from Wark was conducted 'in the night, with all celeritie'.[37] Thus Skelton's conflation of the two stages of the Duke's retreat, the one by day from Wark to Eccles, the other by night from Eccles to Lauder, seems to have been neither the result of his own artistic tinkering with the facts for effect, nor of a genuine mistake on his part, but of direct misinformation from Wolsey. The latter had himself either misread Surrey's accounts or determined that a night retreat better suited his propaganda aims and so passed on that misreading to Skelton: a fact which provides further evidence of the Cardinal's active role in the production of the text.

Similarly other apparently incidental details in the poem tend to confirm the suggestion that Skelton was being provided with official information to aid him in the construction of his invective. His treatment of the composition of the Scots army has already been touched on, but the poet's references to the English host also deserve some attention. When he mentions that Surrey was 'comyng downe / To make [Albany] . . . frowne' (lines 56–7) he goes on to state that he was coming, not alone, but

> With the noble powre
> Of my Lorde Cardynall,
> As an hoost royall
> After the auncient manner
> With Sainct Cutberdes banner. (59–63)

This is not simply a passing reference to a token body of Yorkshiremen in the English army included in the text to compliment its patron, but an an allusion to a key unit in Surrey's force, as anyone who was familiar with the contents of his despatches would know. As the Earl informed Wolsey on 3 October, he needed to raise a large body of men quickly if he was to resist Albany's incursions, 'whiche cannot bee withoute spedy setting forewardes of a sufficient poure tencountre hym'. Thus he needed, in particular, the

---

[36] This was the journey time allowed for by Dacre when, on 4 January 1522, he established a chain of post riders between Morpeth and London, although eight days was considered more realistic for moonless nights in winter. *L.P.*, III (ii) 1986.

[37] *St. P.*, VI 70.

Yorkshiremen whom Wolsey could provide from his archbishopric, both for the beneficial effect on further recruitment which their arrival would provide, and for their importance in actual numbers. As he begged of Wolsey,[38]

I beseeche your Grace too send commaundement to your retinue in Yourkshire to bee in arredynes too bee of the furste that shall come forewardes, whiche shall not onely bee a good ensample to thoders, but alsoo they shalbe very welcome to me; for in theym consisteth a greate part of the poure that I shall have.

By 30 October he was able to inform the Cardinal that, with the troops provided by lords Northumberland, Clifford and Latimer, the Yorkshiremen would provide 8,000 men 'besides the bishopric', and would have pride of place in the proposed battle formation at Surrey's right hand.[39] Again Skelton's inclusion of a piece of information suggests that he possessed a detailed knowledge of the situation on the borders, and Surrey's despatches or summaries of them, provided by Wolsey soon after their receipt in Westminster, again seem to be the most likely sources of that knowledge.

The poet's reference to 'Sainct Cutberdes banner' in the same passage, hitherto seen by commentators as simply a quaint reference to English military folklore included, again, simply to flatter Wolsey, as 'technically, he would have had possession of St Cuthbert's banner in his capacity as Bishop of Durham',[40] similarly betrays a closer knowledge of Surrey's military preparations than it at first suggests. For it seems that the beneficial effects on the morale of the English troops of the presence of the banner among them was considered an important factor in the plans of both Surrey and Henry. On 30 October the Earl had thought fit to inform Wolsey that the banner was to be included in his battle-line, whilst on the same day in a letter to Henry he acknowledged the latter's insistence that the army should advance no faster or further than the banner could accompany it.[41] Thus here again it is hard to avoid the inference that the details of the poem are there, not because Skelton decided so, but because his patron decided that they should be. Indeed it might be noted in this context that Skelton did not refer to St Cuthbert's banner in his anti-Scots poems of 1513, despite the fact that it was present in the field at Flodden, and despite his reference in *The Douty Duke* to its 'auncient' heritage. The clear inference to be drawn is that in 1513 the poet was not aware of the banner, the legend surrounding it, or its importance to English morale, whereas in 1523 he was. This suggests once again that he was kept well-informed of the latest events and of official attitudes to the

[38] *St. P.*, IV 24.
[39] *L.P.*, III (ii) 3482.
[40] Scattergood, p. 514, nn. 63–4. The banner was alleged to have been created, under saintly direction, before the Battle of Neville's Cross (1347), and to have brought English armies victory over the Scots ever since.
[41] *L.P.*, III (ii) 3482, 3481. See also, B.L. Cotton MS Caligula B VI fo. 304.

campaign during the writing of the later work in a way in which he was not in the earlier period. Such information could only have been gained with Wolsey's co-operation. Thus it seems that when the Cardinal turned to the newly compliant satirist with his commission he was careful to make clear exactly the points which he wished the text to make, and to provide the poet with as much relevant material as he felt was necessary. Skelton then set about the task of completing the required work while its subject matter was still the latest news, bringing to the project both his own enthusiastic anti-Scots feeling and a canon of previous invectives from which to plunder his material.

It is readily apparent from the looseness of many of the poet's arguments, from the continual repetition of phrases and the frequently lacklustre quality of the invective, that this is far from Skelton's greatest artistic achievement. It has to be accepted that the exigencies of the time available (perhaps as little as two days), caused the poet to sacrifice quality for the material satisfaction of presenting his patron with a finished product. Hence the number of rhymes, phrases and allusions lifted directly from his earlier invectives and satires[42] which suggest that he cobbled together the text from the materials to hand rather than spending long hours in search of original inspiration.

But why should Skelton have been given so short a deadline, and why should Wolsey have taken the remarkable step of releasing reports on what was, after all, an extremely sensitive subject to a poet who had only months before been lampooning him, seemingly with little regard for Crown sensibilities? Clearly the answer to such questions is to be found in the need, as Wolsey perceived it, to counter swiftly the propaganda claims of Albany, in order to prevent their undermining the national and royal honour, and adversely affecting national morale. That Skelton's commission involved a definite instruction to tackle Albany's rhetoric directly is evident from any careful reading of the text, for the Duke's boasts are a central theme of the invective. And that Wolsey was the source of this instruction is evident from a study of his correspondence from this period, which reveals something of a preoccupation with Albany's rhetoric; significantly referred to throughout as his 'boastes' and brags. In an undated letter of October 1523 the Cardinal had informed Surrey that Albany's claim to be able to expel Henry from England was simply the result of French brags, and that the English preparations would soon force him to 'put water in his wine'.[43] On 23 October he informed the Earl that it was only Albany's brags which kept the Scots from suing for peace, and on 4 December he instructed Sampson and Jermingham

---

[42] Compare, for example, lines 318–19 with *Why Come Ye Nat?*, 784–5; lines 296–7 with *Speke, Parott*, 89; lines 145 and 382 with *Why Come Ye Nat?*, 125–6; and line 164 with *Agaynst the Scottes*, 172.

[43] B.L. Cotton MS Caligula B III fo. 50 (*L.P.*, III (ii) 3447).

to inform the Emperor that, despite the 'greate preparacions bragges and bostes' of Albany, the latter had been forced to 'shamfully and cowardly flee away'.[44] This preoccupation is mirrored in the work which the Cardinal commissioned from Skelton. The first stanza sets the tone for what is to follow.

> This Duke so fell
> Of Albany,
> So cowardly,
> With all his hoost
> Of the Scottyshe coost,
> *For all theyr boost,*
> Fledde lyke a beest. (6–12, my italics)

Always Albany's ambitious claims are contrasted with the total failure of his expedition.

> But ye and your hoost,
> Full of bragge and boost,
> And full of waste wynde,
> Howe ye wyll beres bynde
> And the devill downe dynge,
> Yet ye dare do nothynge
> But lepe away lyke frogges
> And hyde you under logges,
> Lyke pygges and lyke hogges
> And lyke maungy dogges. (206–15)

> For thou can not but brag,
> Like a Scottyshe hag.
> Adue, nowe, Sir Wrig-wrag!
> Adue, Sir Dalyrag! (294–7)

All this is very predictable journeyman invective, reminiscent of passages from all Skelton's earlier vitriolic satires and invectives, and thus might be dismissed as nothing more than simple taunting. Elsewhere, however, it is evident that the poet is concerned to counter and refute with the potent weapons of ridicule and scorn, not simply abstract 'boasting' on Albany's part but the very propaganda claims which had so worried Surrey and Wolsey, and which predicted the fall of Henry VIII and his replacement by Richard de la Pole. So much becomes obvious when Skelton rhetorically asks Albany for the substance of his boasts.

> Harke yet, Sir Duke, a worde
> In ernest or in borde.
> What have ye, villayn, forged,
> And virulently dysgorged
> As though ye wolde parbrake

---

[44] B.L. Cotton MS Caligula B VI fo. 295 (*St. P.*, VI 70).

> Your avauns to make,
> With words enbosed,
> Ungraciously engrosed,
> Howe ye wyll undertake
> Our royall Kyng to make
> His owne realme to forsake?
> Suche lewde langage ye spake. (318–29)

Hereafter the response of the text to such boasts becomes evident, and with it the reason for Skelton's commission, as the poem becomes more and more obviously not a news bulletin concerning the relief of Wark but a prospectus for a stable and contented realm, and an invective against the folly of those who have claimed that it is otherwise.

The sheer length of those passages which laud Henry and proclaim the tranquillity and strength of England is the best indication of their importance to the poem. The overall burden of the text is clearly the message contained in the lines which declare that,

> . . . it is impossible
> · For you to bring about
> Our Kyng for to dryve out
> Of this, his realme royall
> And lande imperiall (390–4)

This same point is made at lines 330–50, but the most oft-repeated theme is the vaunting of Henry's personal honour and Skelton clearly warms to his task as the poem progresses.

> So noble a prince as he
> In all actyvite
> Of hardly merciall actes,
> Fortunate in all his fayctes.
> And now I wyll me dresse
> His valiaunce to expresse,
> Though insufficient am I
> His grace to magnify
> And laud equivalently.
> Howe be it, loyally
> After myne allegyaunce
> My pen I will avaunce
> To extoll his noble grace
> In spyght of thy cowardes face. (395–408)
>
> But nowe will I expounde
> What noblenesse dothe abounde,
> And what honour is founde
> And what vertues be resydent
> In our royall regent,
> Our perelesse president,
> Our Kyng most excellent. (423–9)

Henry is compared to Hercules in 'merciall prowes', to Solomon in 'prudence and wysdom', to Absalom 'in his goodly person', to Hector 'In loyalty and foy', to Scipio Africanus in glory, and to Ptolemy, Joshua and Judas Maccabaeus in 'royal mageste' (lines 430–43). There then follows a list of the qualities of 'all the roiall sorte / Of his nobilyte', namely, magnanimity, animosity, frugality, liberality, affability, humanity, stability, humility, benignity and royal dignity, ending with another jibe at the inadequacies of his enemies.

> What losels then are ye
> Lyke cowardes as ye be
> To rayle on his astate
> With wordes inordinate? (459–62)

At which point the poet then returns to the stability of the realm with a clear retort to Albany's suggestion that an insurrection and invasion would find 'somoche helpe of Englishmen that [it] . . . shuld not be resisted'.[45]

> He [Henry] rules his cominalte
> With all benignite.
> His noble baronage
> He putteth them in corage
> To exployte dedes of armys
> To the domage and harmys
> Of suche as be his foos
> Where ever he rydes or goos.
> His subjectes he dothe supporte,
> Maintayne them with comforte
> Of his most princely porte,
> As all men can reporte. (463–74)

> All his subjectes and he
> Moost lovyngly agre
> With hole hart and true mynde,
> They fynde his grace so kynde;
> Wherewith he dothe them bynde
> At all houres to be redy
> With hym to lyve and dye,
> And to spende their hart blode,
> Their bodyes and their gode,
> With hym in all dystresse,
> Alway in redynesse
> To assyst his noble grace . . . (480–91)

Such passages as these are far from a simple narrative of the siege of Wark. What Skelton is actually providing is a remarkable reassertion of the unity of the realm and the honour of its King at a time when both are under attack

---

[45] B.L. Cotton MS Caligula B VI fo. 313 (*St. P.*, IV 21).

from the slights of their enemies. And once again it seems evident that the poet's commission required just such a reassertion. For Wolsey can be found advancing precisely the same line of argument to Surrey in October 1523. He, reassuring the Earl, insisted that Albany could never invade England successfully, even with the support of de la Pole and 4,000 German mercenaries 'with the frask of the French King to make him king', for Francis was so vexed in Italy by the Emperor and by the Duke of Bourbon's rising at home that he could hardly keep his own crown, let alone win another for de la Pole. Surrey was therefore to put such worries out of his mind, 'for assured may ye be, as ye well know there can not be more integrity, perfect and sure fidelity in lords and subjects to their prince than, thancked be God, the King's highnes hath in this realm'.[46] Again Skelton's text seems to have been designed to reflect remarkably closely the political concerns of its patron.[47]

On a careful reading of the text, then, it becomes evident that the siege of Wark is treated, not as the centre-piece of the poem, but simply as a symbol of the futility of the boasts of the King's enemies. It is both the inevitable consequence and the ideal refutation of Albany's apparent over-confidence. The emptiness of the Duke's rhetoric forms the substance of the remainder of the poem, and the point to which the poet continually returns.

> Are ye not frantyke madde,
> And wretchedly bestadde,
> To rayle agaynst his grace
> That shall bring you full bace (363–6)
>
> Ye muse somwhat to far;
> All out of joynt ye jar.
> God let you never thrive!
> Wene ye, daucockes, to drive
> Our Kyng out of his reme?
> Go heme, ranke Scot, ge heme,
> With fonde Fraunces, French Kyng.
> Our mayster shall you brynge,
> I truste, to lowe estate
> And mate you with chek mate. (377–86)

These passages bring one to the heart of the text and to the most immediate reasons for its creation. Moreover they provide further confirmation of its date of completion. They clearly demonstrate the reasons for the claim that this is not, despite appearances, a victory poem, or as Pollet would have it, a

---

[46] B.L. Cotton MS Caligula B III fo. 50 (*L.P.*, III (ii) 3447).

[47] Those critics who have suggested that Skelton's rapprochement with Wolsey involved no significant alteration in his expressed political views might note that, less than a year previously, he was far less charitable about the 'noble baronage' and their 'exployte dedes of armys', and was dismissing the border magnates as 'a mayny of shepe' who were 'Nat worth a cockly fose', *Why Come Ye Nat?*, lines 287–99.

'triumphal rhapsody',[48] born out of a desire for celebration, but a piece of propaganda, born out of political necessity. From them one immediately perceives that the siege of Wark was not seen at the time by the Crown as a triumphant conclusion to the Scots war of 1523 and as the epitaph for Albany's ambitions, but simply as a small engagement in what was potentially a larger and still unresolved campaign. This is a poem written while that war was still very much in progress, while Albany and his army were still perceived to post a threat, and while de la Pole's invasion could still not entirely be discounted as impossible. Most crucially this is a poem which was conceived and written at a point when the diplomatic duel between Henry and Wolsey and Francis and Albany over the place of Scotland in their respective spheres of influence was far from over.

Critics have certainly observed that this was a propaganda poem and some have even allowed Skelton's assertion that he was offering 'tidinges newe' some interest.[49] But no one has attempted to fit such random and imprecise observations into any sort of logical framework based on the events which the poet was describing. To say that this is a propaganda poem is to make a very specific statement about its nature and origins, but the implications of that statement have not been fully pursued. Propaganda is, of course, commissioned for a purpose and at a time when it is useful to the patron for whom it is written. Its lifespan is usually short and clearly definable. Such a poem as Skelton's would have been of little use to Wolsey once the threat posed by Albany's host had been removed, once the King's honour had been vindicated, once the country had been seen to remain quiet and the Anticipation loyally yielded up. As was suggested above, Wolsey had no interest in 'victory poems'. This text is an immediate response to an immediate threat, not the triumphal retort to a threat already removed. Clearly the poem is written in parts as if it *were* the victorious last word on the subject, as if the victory at Wark *had* destroyed Albany's army and his reputation, but this was just morale-boosting rhetoric on the poet's part: such is the way with propaganda. The remainder of the text betrays its real, unstated, purpose.

The use of the present and future tenses in the passages quoted above indicates the immediate importance of their theme. Henry '*shall* bring [Albany] . . . full bace', (line 366), and the latter is told that he *should*,

> Go heme, ranke Scot, ge heme,
> With fonde Fraunces, French kyng.
> Our mayster *shall* you brynge,
> I trust, to lowe estate
> And mate you with chek mate. (382–6, my italics)

---

[48] Pollet, *Poet of Tudor England*, p. 147.
[49] See, for example, Scattergood's somewhat vague assertion that the text must have been written 'shortly after 2–3 November', p. 18.

Despite the stress placed on Albany's withdrawal from Wark (treated as if it was a rout), a close reading of the text makes clear that, at the time it was written the decisive action of the campaign, and thus the final victory, was still thought to be in the future, something to be hoped for rather than already achieved. The poet even betrays a doubt as to the outcome of such an action through his use of the conditional 'I trust' in the passage. Thus Albany's army must have been intact, and a field battle between it and Surrey's force must have been seen as a possibility, at the time of the poem's completion. Hence Skelton's commission involved his pre-empting that possibility and portraying Wark as a turning point in the campaign, despite official doubts concerning the actual significance of the action, in order to re-inforce English morale, to encourage the taxpayers with the thought that their money was being well spent and had secured a concrete achievement,[50] and to secure a possibly decisive point in the propaganda battle.[51] Such a function also reinforces the assertions concerning the dating of the text, and the conclusion that its main source of inspiration lay in Surrey's despatches. For only during the period between the receipt of the Earl's report of 3 November and that of 5 November did official doubts remain concerning the condition of Albany's army and the possiblity of further attacks.

On 3 November Surrey despatched the report of the encounter which formed the basis of Skelton's account in the poem. In that report the Earl could only inform Wolsey that Albany had 'departed hymself with his hoole company, but as yet I cannot advertise your Grace of trouthe howe far he is goon, but tomorrowe I doubte not I shall knowe the certentie'. This account was not only uninformative for its readers at Court, it was also worded in such a manner as almost certainly to create amongst them precisely that mood of anxious uncertainty which lies beneath Skelton's verse. For Surrey continued his despatch with the cautionary observation,[52]

Sir I doubt moche that if he [Albany] here that I breke this army that he woll retorne with his ordynance unto Wark, which I feare wol not hold long againste hym; for and if I had not made newe fortifications of bulwerks of erthe, it had not be tenable one half daye. I wold it were in the See, for I knowe not howe to get men to remayne in it.

---

[50] Significantly, Suffolk's campaign in France was losing its way at precisely this point and so could not be relied upon to provide any major victories. I owe this point to Dr S. J. Gunn.

[51] That Wolsey was concerned to justify the expense of the campaign to the reluctant tax-payers, and to avoid the impression (played on by Skelton in 1522) that the money raised had been wasted on a 'phoney war', is suggested by his annotations of Surrey's report of 28 October, which raised the possibility that Albany might not cross the border at all. 'This result', the Cardinal angrily noted, 'should have been forseen and the expense of raising the King's main power to no purpose spared'. As it was, it would only lead to 'inconvenience' (*L.P.*, III (ii) 3477 (B.L. Cotton MS Caligula B II fo. 27)):

[52] B.L. Cotton MS Caligula B VI fo. 304.

The earliest that Surrey's report could have reached London was not 'shortly after 2–3 November', as Scattergood loosely suggests, but late on 6 November. For earlier on that day Wolsey was still writing to Sampson and Jermingham in ignorance of the events of 2–3 November, stating that Surrey's army was 'attending nowe hourely the batail, if it be not striken before this, or the Duke of Albany and Scottes fled'.[53] More realistically, working on the estimate of a six- or seven-day journey time, the despatch would have arrived on 9–10 November.

On 4 November Surrey wrote his supplementary account of the battle, and reported the Prioress of Coldstream's assertion that Albany had 'clearly departed'. Yet the Earl was not sufficiently confident of the Prioress's testimony to guarantee it as certain news and could only promise to ascertain the truth on the following day. The inconclusive nature of this account is reflected in Henry VIII's reply to Surrey, which noted[54]

the reaporte of the Priores of Calstreme howe that on Tuesday at nyght last past about mydyn[gh]t the said Duke being then at Eccles, Informed that our armye passed the Ryver after hym, removed from thens, toke his ordenance away, and is clerely departed; *the truthe wherof ye doubted not to be advertised from divers wayes by the next daye.*

It was not until Surrey's despatch of 5 November that he was able to pass on the definite news to 'conferm … the shameful departure of the Duke fro thAbeey of Eccles at mydnyght upon Tuysdaye'.[55] Thus the period of uncertainty concerning the whereabouts and condition of Albany's army matched exactly the period during which Skelton must have written the poem.

A further significant point to note about Henry's reply to Surrey, cited above, is its date: 12 November. This reveals that, by that date, the Earl's reports of 3 and 4 November had reached the King (Henry said as much), but the crucial report of 5 November, which contained the revised information about the siege which Skelton did not know and which reassured Wolsey about Albany's intentions, thus making such propaganda as *The Douty Duke* far less necessary, had not yet arrived. For it is unlikely that Wolsey would have kept such crucial tidings from his master's ear, and equally so that Henry, having heard them, would have failed to remark on them to Surrey. Thus the clear inference to be drawn is that, probably owing to the weather conditions, Surrey's report of 5 November did not reach the Court until, at the earliest, late on 12 November. Thus the dates between which the poem must have been written are re-emphasised and clarified. The first point, late on 6 November, is the very earliest that the poet could have begun

[53] *St. P.,* VI 66.
[54] B.L. Cotton MS Caligula B I fo. 307. My italics.
[55] *St. P.,* IV 28.

to write the substantial portion of the text's narrative;[56] the second point, late on or soon after 12 November, is the very latest that it could have been completed without Surrey's despatch of 5 November having arrived to supersede Skelton's 'tidinges newe'. Only between these two dates did the conditions revealed in the text obtain.

Thus *The Douty Duke*, for all its literary shortcomings, is in fact a very interesting historical document, for it reveals a great deal about a period of marked anxiety within the English administration which otherwise would have remained concealed by a narrative of the bland events of Albany's singularly unimpressive expedition. It also reveals much about how the Scottish war was perceived by that administration. For the threat which, in all probability, concerned Wolsey the most was not the physical one posed by Albany's troops but the political and diplomatic one posed by his propaganda to the internal security of the realm, the efficient collection of its taxes and the honour of its King. Certainly Surrey's disturbing account of the potentially serious consequences for Wark of a second invasion gave the Cardinal genuine cause for concern, but such concern would not merit the sudden, almost hysterical, defence of Henry's honour which he commissioned. The worst possible consequences of a second invasion, as Wolsey had been assured in previous correspondence with Surrey, was the loss of the already badly damaged castle at Wark, as the poor weather and lack of supplies would restrict Albany to a maximum of five days campaigning within England, and the major English fortresses were all sufficiently well-defended not to be reducible in that time.[57] And Wark, given the lateness of the season and the prevailing weather, could not have been held once taken. Why then this remarkable anxiety? What was there to lose which merited Wolsey's concern? Partly there was the threat to internal security and confidence, and the possible effect on the collection of the Subsidy posed by Albany's propaganda, but there was also the possibility of a loss of honour, and the effect on morale and on England's Scottish policy which such a loss might entail.

The whole military campaign of 1523, and the diplomatic activity which preceded it, with their tangible effects on life, lands and limb, were inextricably interwoven in the minds of the leading participants with a personalised, almost metaphysical, confrontation on the field of honour. Underlying the various raids, counter-raids and musters, the diplomatic approaches and their rejection, and the war of rhetoric between England, France and Scotland, was a fierce trial of honour between the national figureheads and their clients: between Francis I, Albany and de la Pole on the one side; and Henry

---

[56] Although it is more realistic to expect the earlier reports to have taken six to seven days, thus extending the starting date for the project to 10–11 November.

[57] B.L. Cotton MSS Caligula B VI fos. 313, 284; *L.P.*, III (ii) 3466.

and Surrey on the other. And this duel, even more than the concrete results of the campaign, seems to have been what engaged the attentions of Henry and Wolsey.[58]

It struck at Henry's honour as much as at national security that Albany should attempt to take Scotland into the French camp and thus scorn his own pretensions towards the overlordship of that kingdom, and it struck deeper still when the Duke presumed to criticise Henry's kingship and question the loyalty of his subjects. Thus the conflict not only concerned the turning back of an invasion and the securing of Albany's expulsion from Scotland – it also involved the refutation of his claims.

For Henry this was largely a personalised quarrel, in which Surrey was simply his representative in the field and the major prize was not land but honour. Nor was this an entirely frivolous concern. In the circumstances of the 1523 campaign it was very likely that, owing to the lateness of the season and the weather conditions, any further Scottish attacks would prove indecisive in terms of the overall strategic position. Even a field battle might prove inconclusive. Consequently what was important was that any such encounter should not appear to be a reverse or sign of military weakness on the part of the English. In the attempt to prevent such an eventuality, the Crown was presented with a godsend by the encounter at Wark. It provided an ideal opportunity to claim a signal victory, despite the fact that both Surrey and Wolsey realised that it was no such thing. Had Albany attacked Wark again and finally reduced it, he might have been able to claim the symbolic victory as his own. Had he simply withdrawn to Edinburgh, it would still have been possible for him to have claimed a successful raid, and the trial of honour would only have been indecisively concluded. To counter such possibilities and to establish the idea of an English triumph, Wolsey hastily commissioned Skelton to broadcast to a popular audience, as only he could, the English 'victory' of Wark, to demonstrate the shameful futility of Albany's boasts and to restore to its untarnished glory Henry's slighted honour. In so doing the poet played his part in both the trial of honour and the strategic struggle.

Thus *The Douty Duke* was a poem written with a number of audiences in mind. Clearly it was commissioned primarily as a means to prevent Albany's propaganda finding a responsive audience in England, and so was aimed at an English and, again, primarily London, popular audience. It was intended to take the sting out of the Duke's allegations of impending insurrection and royal incompetence by subjecting them and him to the basest forms of ridicule. In devising the project Wolsey also paid due regard to both his royal

[58] See, for example, B.L. Cotton MS Caligula B VI fo. 302 (*St. P.*, IV 25); *St. P.*, IV 24 and 26; B.L. Cotton MSS Caligula B VI fo. 311 and II fo. 27 (*L.P.*, III (ii) 3466, 3477); *St. P.*, IV 27, 28 and B.L. Cotton MS Caligula B I fo. 307.

master's personal feelings and the dictates of the Crown's foreign policy. It was evident that, in the long term, the inevitable outcome of the border war of 1523 would be a truce or peace. The only unresolved question concerned upon whose terms that treaty would be drawn up. Albany's desire was to settle the conflict on terms which allowed him to remain in Scotland and recognised his right to retain the guardianship of James V. The English demand was that no peace would be negotiated until the Scots had expelled Albany from the realm and returned James V to his mother and nominal independence.[59]

Hence the propaganda battle between the two camps was as important for the eventual outcome of the conflict as the military encounters. Neither Albany nor Henry could afford to lose face. If Albany was openly discredited, half of the battle to gain his expulsion would have been won. If the Duke could present himself as a national hero and convince the Scots lords that his presence as Regent would not bring down on them another Flodden as the dire consequence of English wrath, half of that battle would have been lost. Hence Skelton's treatment of the two national figureheads in his text, which constantly vaunted Henry and denigrated Albany. Hence also his portrayal of the retreat from Wark as the catastrophic epitaph of all the latter's overweening ambitions, and his declaration that he should 'ge heme [to France] / With fonde Fraunces, French kyng'.

Evidently the poem was also constructed with a Scottish audience in mind, or with a view to its message being disseminated into Scotland by written report or word of mouth. For its English audience it was intended to stiffen morale, prevent disaffection and promote loyalty. For its Scottish audience it was intended to deflate Albany's campaign of self-promotion and to assist English attempts to secure his expulsion or voluntary withdrawal from Scotland. Beyond these there was also an English royal audience, whether Henry read the text or simply heard of its existence, for whom the text was intended as a salve for the wounds inflicted on his sensitive honour by Albany's attacks – and no doubt also to demonstrate that his chief minister was once again working diligently and efficiently to defend his name and to protect the national interest.

Thus, far from being a minor and inconsequential work, *The Douty Duke* may well have been Skelton's most public and most influential performance. Certainly the text is informative to the modern reader for a number of reasons. First it shows that Skelton's rapprochement with Wolsey after the completion of *Why Come Ye Nat?* was not simply a grudging truce, as some commentators have suggested, but rather the start of a short-lived but none the less remarkable close working relationship between poet and patron,

---

[59] These terms were carefully articulated in Wolsey's despatch to Surrey of 23 October. B.L. Cotton MS Caligula B VI fo. 295.

prompted by the Cardinal's realisation that Skelton's particular satiric talents might be utilised in the interests of the state. The result was a unique example of how a government might directly employ the talents of a poet in the furtherance of its policies, not merely as part of a long-prepared for and costly spectacular performance at Court, but in a more direct manner, as a spontaneous response to the dictates of its day-to-day handling of policy. Second, the text penetrates the smooth surface of the narrative accounts of Albany's failed invasion to the more troubled currents below. It reveals that during the first twelve days of November 1523, the English Crown was far from unconcerned about the consequences, both material and diplomatic, of Albany's attack. And finally, it demonstrates just how complex were the links which bound together diplomacy, personal honour and military success in even so 'unimportant' a war as that conducted against Scotland in 1523. It shows how a single event such as the attack on Wark could be open to any number of interpretations by rivals anxious to seize on it, and to establish a monopoly on its interpretation for their own ends. In this case it demonstrates how Wolsey, fearing that the siege might be portrayed by Albany as either an English defeat or, at best, a drawn encounter, strove in his own correspondence and through the more public medium of Skelton's poetry to invest it with a significance of his own devising, as a major and signal English victory.

Perhaps few poets can claim not only to have recorded the events of a war in verse, but actually to have been commissioned to contribute to the successful outcome of that war through their writings. Certainly few can have done so whilst still attracting only the minimal attention afforded to Skelton's 'minor' work.

CONCLUSION

Whilst the text of *Howe The Douty Duke of Albany* vividly illuminates the events in Skelton's life of November 1523, it is unfortunate that its glow reveals no clue to those which followed its composition. For after that work there comes a gap in the poet's biography until the composition of his final extant work, the *Replycacion* of *c*. 1528. What happened to the poet after the period of brief but feverish co-operation with Wolsey in 1523 is unknown. It is possible, but unlikely, that he continued to work under the Cardinal's patronage on the production of other, now lost, political works. Equally possibly he may have been used in some minor administrative role which has now slipped from the records. More plausibly he may have returned to teaching, or into semi-retirement, in the hope of further commissions in the future. Whichever was the case, all that remains to posterity is the text of the *Replycacion*, an aggressive invective against the persons and beliefs of the heretical students Thomas Bilney and Thomas Arthur.[1] This text, coupled with a reference in Strype's *Ecclesiastical Memorials*, which suggests that an individual ('Mag. Skelton') who may well have been the poet was present at the public recantation, at Norwich Inn, Charing Cross, of another heretic, Thomas Bowgas, on 4 May 1528,[2] suggests that Skelton finished his life (he died on 21 June 1529, and was buried in St Margaret's Church, Westminster[3]) once more in the service of the Cardinal, defending the Church against heresy in the same way in which he had defended the realm against the Scots in 1523.[4]

The texts upon which this study has concentrated are, then, critical works in the poet's career in all senses of the word. They are the most extreme and the most dangerous examples of Skelton's genius for satire and invective in action. They are also the most interesting texts in the canon from the point of view of the political historian. And they mark a crucial turning point:

---

[1] See Scattergood, pp. 373–86. I hope to write a separate study of this text in the near future.
[2] Printed in Edwards, p. 303.
[3] St Margaret's churchwarden's accounts, printed in Edwards, p. 304.
[4] The fact that the text was dedicated to Wolsey (see Scattergood, p. 372) indicates that this text at least was commissioned by the Cardinal.

literally a point of crisis, in the poet's life and career. If the arguments here advanced are correct, the satires were written at a time when his career was at its lowest ebb and when his own desire for self-publicity was at its most frustrated. In a dramatic attempt to restore the former glories of his career, the poet launched the satirical assault on Wolsey and, despite initial failure, finally attracted a substantial popular audience to his work, and won some portion of the patronage he sought – albeit from the Cardinal himself, who put him to work in the service of the Crown.

For the historian, or for the reader interested in placing a literary work in its correct social and political context, the satires are thus illuminating in a variety of ways. In part this is a product of their particular nature and purpose. For they are texts firmly tied to their historical context: works which make possible, indeed insist upon, a close correlation between their content and contemporary political events. This is particularly true of *Speke, Parott*, with its individually dated envoys and clear relevance to the political situation of the late summer and autumn of 1521, and *Why Come Ye Nat?*, the satirical attack of which cannot be fully understood until the reader appreciates the precise circumstances of the autumn of 1522, during which the text was written and to which it continually refers.

During this study questions have arisen for which there is no sure or definite answer. Why, for example, did Wolsey act to silence Skelton only after the completion of *Why Come Ye Nat?*? No doubt the answers to this question advanced above may contain much of the truth of the matter. But it is interesting to speculate more generally that the gradual evolution of Skelton's stance from *Speke, Parott* to *Why Come Ye Nat?* is a graphic illustration of how and when a satirist moved from being acceptable to unacceptable in the eyes of the Crown and of the men and institutions which he criticised. An examination of some of the more stinging satires of the period might suggest that the lengths to which satirical writers were permitted to go in condemning their targets without provoking an angry response were quite remarkable, given the emphasis placed on order, degree and deference in the propaganda of Church and state.[5] But such radicalism was socially 'safe'. The conventions and norms of satire and social commentary provided an essentially conservative framework which effectively neutralised dangerous utterances. Apparently radical political statements there were, but they remained simply statements: expressions of positions within a

---

[5] See, for example, the radical utterances of the Ploughman in W. Rastell's, *Gentleness and Nobility*, in R. Axton (ed.), *Three Rastell Plays* (Cambridge, 1979), pp. 97–125. He challenges the Knight's claim to social superiority on the grounds that 'I see not that ye can any thyng do / For the commyn well . . . / But ech man, beyng in auctoryte, / Havyng wit, may do it as well as ye' (lines 333–6), and produces the seemingly revolutionary assertion that 'the law of inherytaunce' is 'a thyng agayns all good reason', 'ordeynyd' by extortioners to keep the goods of 'the labouryng people' in the hands of the former and their heirs (lines 598–613).

framework of debate or dialogue, which were qualified by, and which in turn qualified, other statements to contrary effect. They never achieved the status and were never allowed to attain the semblance of an independent social philosophy. For every radical declaration the text provided a conservative response which qualified its effects, with the net result that the 'philosophy' of the complete work was one of compromise, of the need to maintain the *status quo* for fear of upsetting it, but with a more virtuous and more Christian approach from all elements of society.[6]

In such a form satire, and even invective, could perform an acceptable, even laudable, role in society, as an adjunct to conservative religious thinking analogous to the teaching of the Christian humanists. The satirist could attack abuses in the Church, in the economy, in estate management and in government, as *everyone* was opposed to abuses, and he could attack the abuses of a class, if he was careful, as then each individual member of that class was free to assume that he was the exception rather than the condemned rule and so treat the work with amused tolerance. Only when the fundamental institutions themselves came under unequivocal attack, when the neutralising framework was removed, or when specific individuals came in for abuse, did satire become unassimilable into an individual or institution's world-view.

Did Skelton step outside these mutually recognised and tacitly accepted norms with *Why Come Ye Nat?*, with its vicious invective against a known, powerful, individual and with its unqualified criticism of the Crown's fiscal policy? Moreover did the fact that he advanced such criticism, not within the well-insulated walls of an academic or courtly *coterie*, nor from an idealistic Christian standpoint, but in an extremely public and populist manner – from the standpoint of the ordinary tax-payer – did the element of popularity provoke Wolsey (and the Crown's?) anxiety? It is interesting to note that, according to the account of Sir Thomas More's son-in-law, William Roper, Wolsey was extremely concerned at the prospect of politics becoming popularised during the period, in 1523, when his difficulties with Parliament over the Subsidy arose, and when he commissioned Skelton to write *The Douty Duke* for the Crown. As Roper reports,[7]

At this parliament Cardinall Wolsey found himself much grieved with the Burgesses thereof, for that nothing was so soone done or spoken therein but that it was ymmediately blowen abrode in every Alehouse.

Did *Why Come Ye Nat?* threaten to 'blow abroad' criticism of the forced

[6] See G. W. Bernard, *The Power of the Early Tudor Nobility: A Study of the Fourth and Fifth Earls of Shrewsbury* (Brighton, 1985), p. 192.

[7] E. V. Hitchcock (ed.), *The Lyfe of Sir Thomas Moore Knighte, By William Roper*, E.E.T.S., O.S. 117 (London, 1935), pp. 19–20.

loans in 1522, at another time of financial and political difficulties for the Crown, and did Skelton's strident attack on those loans and his attempt to popularise political debate, take him beyond the bounds of tolerated academic or moral criticism and into the field of active political opposition? The point must remain unresolved for lack of evidence, but Wolsey's move to silence the poet after the completion of that satire is certainly suggestive.

The majority of the historiographical problems concerned with the Skeltonic canon have, however, arisen as the result of previous misreadings of the poet's life and writings, rather than from any insoluble difficulties inherent in the texts themselves. Even if the analysis of Skelton's satires conducted above is only partially correct, the need for a radical reassessment of received views of the poet, his texts and his value as a commentator on Wolsey and the politics of his time is obvious. The unanswered questions and unquestioned answers which have, for most of this century, been the substance of historians' perceptions of Skelton and his motivation need to be addressed if the poet's testimony is to have any place in serious historical scholarship. If it is to be alleged in the future, contrary to the argument of this study, that Skelton *was* a client of the Howards, earls of Surrey and dukes of Norfolk, then more substantial evidence ought to be brought to the support of that assertion than the unconvincing mixture of coincidences, inspired inference and superficial readings of the poet's texts which have hitherto been employed on the task. Furthermore those critics who might wish to advance such a case ought to suggest why the Howards felt the need to sponsor such an attack, when all the evidence suggests that they harboured no grudge against the Cardinal, either in the 1520s or earlier.

Similarly if historians continue to suggest that Wolsey became and remained widely unpopular throughout the 1520s, one ought to insist that they bring forward more convincing evidence of that unpopularity than Skelton's satires, coupled with a handful of isolated incidents of personal criticism. For a clear distinction must be drawn between the unpopularity of certain policies and measures among distinct social or political groups, for which Wolsey acted as the focus of resentment and of which evidence exists, and any wider, more personal unpopularity, for which the evidence is lacking. That the continental ambassadors found Wolsey difficult to manipulate, and that he used a mixture of protocol, ceremony and theatricality to maintain the upper hand in his dealings with them, does not prove that the Cardinal was a feared and hated tyrant in domestic politics. That popular resentment against the financial demands of 1522 was focused on Wolsey, the commissioner for the loans in London, does not suggest a deeper-seated general dislike for him as an individual. Such feelings were unconnected and affected distinct groups at distinct times. Any apparent continuity of unpopularity provided by Skelton's satires is entirely illusory. The poet was not the spokesman for a consistent opposition to Wolsey. In *Speke, Parott*, far from articulating the grievances of a powerful group, he spoke solely for himself and was widely misunderstood. Again, in *Why Come Ye Nat?* he did not speak for an opposition to Wolsey but merely reflected, for opportunist reasons, a temporary protest against a specific imposition.

The satires do not demonstrate that Wolsey was consistently unpopular, or tyrannical, or corrupt. Their general analyses are conditioned far more by literary tradition than by the specific political circumstances of the early 1520s. Because Skelton wished to satirise Wolsey, and because Wolsey was a leading churchman, convention determined many of the charges which the poet was to use against him. Far from indicating profound truths about the Cardinal's personality or conduct of business, they often have little or no relevance to him as an individual at all, but are simply conventional allegations which satire directed at the clerical estate. Indeed often, as was suggested above, because of Wolsey's particular position as both churchman and statesman they lacked even the relevance of the generalised critique of his estate, for his 'worldliness', far from being evidence of his dereliction of his spiritual duties, was evidence of his conscientiousness as a servant of the Crown. In such cases Skelton's analyses are positively unhelpful as source material for a study of Wolsey.

Where Skelton's texts are more useful is on a smaller scale, in illuminating certain events and the public perception of them, from a new perspective, and in confirming or qualifying the accounts of such events provided by other sources.

A close reading of the political passages of *Speke, Parott*, for example, tends to support Professor Scarisbrick's reading of the correspondence between Henry and Wolsey during this period, and suggests that the argument between the two over the merits of permitting the English wine merchants to sail to Bordeaux marked the occasion of a period of considerable tension between King and Cardinal, and that that tension was perceived and appreciated for what it was by the poet, although ultimately he misjudged the extent of the disagreement. Similarly Skelton's mistaken assumption that a desire for Christian unity and a crusade governed Crown foreign policy during 1521 suggests that the stress placed on that theme in public ceremonial and pageantry in the period between 1518 and 1521 did have its effect on the public understanding of policy, despite modern assertions that such graphic demonstrations of an idealistic policy were simply meaningless postures adopted by a government which had no interest at all in the general defence of Christendom.[8] Such an analysis of the reality behind the public face of Crown policy might well be correct, although it is unwise to discount entirely

---

[8] J. J. Scarisbrick, *Henry VIII*, (London, 1968) pp. 67–75; S. Anglo, *Spectacle Pageantry, and Early Tudor Policy* (Oxford, 1969), pp. 124–69.

Henry's personal, theoretical, concern for the defence of Christendom. Certainly Skelton's testimony suggests that such posturing was not seen for what it was by everyone.

Similarly the recurrent theme of poverty in *Why Come Ye Nat?* provides some measure of the concern felt in London at the forced loans of 1522, and stands as further evidence of the hardship which the latter caused in the City. In this way the text both expands upon the treatment of the loans to be found in Edward Hall's *Chronicle* and adds authenticity to the chronicler's account, whilst a careful reading of *The Douty Duke* supports the impression to be gained from a study of the royal correspondence of 1523 that the Crown took the threat posed by Albany and the Scots very seriously indeed, and was extremely anxious not to lose the war of rhetoric conducted against the Duke for fear of the diplomatic consequences of such a defeat.

It is in such areas as these that the greatest value of the texts as historical documents lies, not in their more lurid condemnations of the 'frantycke', rapacious, 'bochers dogge', which have been the poet's most enduring legacy to historical scholarship. Such a portrait was almost entirely a combination of the poet's misreading of the limited evidence available to him and of deliberate literary artifice. Future studies of 'the Great Cardinal' would do well to bear such reservations in mind when considering Skelton's testimony, and to heed Collyn Clout's advice to his readers that only

> Yf ye take well therwith
> It hath in it some pyth. (57–8)

INDEX